Logico-Linguistic Papers

By the same author

INTRODUCTION TO LOGICAL THEORY
INDIVIDUALS
THE BOUNDS OF SENSE

P. F. STRAWSON

Logico-Linguistic Papers

METHUEN & CO LTD

First published in 1971
by Methuen & Co Ltd
11 New Fetter Lane, London EC4
© 1971 P. F. Strawson
Printed in Great Britain by
Richard Clay (The Chaucer Press) Ltd
Bungay, Suffolk

SBN 416 09010 9

Distributed in the USA
by Barnes & Noble Inc

Contents

PREFACE   vii

1. On Referring   1

2. Particular and General   28

3. Singular Terms and Predication   53

4. Identifying Reference and Truth-Values   75

5. The Asymmetry of Subjects and Predicates   96

6. Propositions, Concepts, and Logical Truths   116

7. Grammar and Philosophy   130

8. Intention and Convention in Speech Acts   149

9. Meaning and Truth   170

10. Truth   190

11. A Problem about Truth   214

12. Truth: A Reconsideration of Austin's Views   234

INDEX OF NAMES   251

Preface

The twelve essays which are collected in this volume have all been previously published and are here reprinted with a very few minor alterations. I have grouped them by subject-matter rather than in strict chronological order of publication.

The first five essays are all concerned with the topic of singular reference and predication, a topic treated also in the second part of *Individuals*. Although my understanding of the question has naturally undergone some change during the twenty years which separate the first from the last essay in this group, there is nevertheless a certain unity of view underlying the whole sequence. Some of the material from the second essay, 'Particular and General', has been used in *Individuals*; but I have thought the essay worth reprinting as a whole.

The last three essays in the volume form a still more evident unity. They are all responses, direct or indirect, to Austin's treatment of the topic of truth in 1950. Some exaggerations of the first response are implicitly or explicitly corrected in its successors.

The ninth essay, 'Meaning and Truth', has obvious links with those that follow and with that which immediately precedes it. There are connections, though remoter ones, between the topic of 'Propositions, Concepts, and Logical Truths' and those of both the first and the last group of essays. 'Grammar and Philosophy', highly general and programmatic, stands a little apart from the other essays in the volume; but between its subject and that of the first group of papers there are, I think, connections, no more than hinted at here, which must ultimately be established and understood.

Details of the original publication of the papers are as follows:

1. 'On Referring', in *Mind*, vol. lix, N.S., 1950. Some of the footnotes reproduced here, did not appear in *Mind*, but were added when the paper was reprinted in *Essays in Conceptual Analysis*, edited by Antony Flew (Macmillan, 1956).

2. 'Particular and General', in *Proceedings of the Aristotelian Society*, 1953–4.

3. 'Singular Terms and Predication', in *The Journal of Philosophy*, vol. lviii, 1961.

4. 'Identifying Reference and Truth-Values', in *Theoria*, vol. xxx, 1964.

5. 'The Asymmetry of Subjects and Predicates', in *Language, Belief and Metaphysics* (Volume I of *Contemporary Philosophic Thought*), edited by Howard E. Kiefer and Milton K. Munitz, 1970. Reprinted by permission of the State University of New York Press.

6. 'Propositions, Concepts, and Logical Truths', in *The Philosophical Quarterly*, vol. 7, 1957.

7. 'Grammar and Philosophy', in *Proceedings of the Aristotelian Society*, 1969–70.

8. 'Intention and Convention in Speech Acts', in *The Philosophical Review*, vol. lxxiii, 1964.

9. 'Meaning and Truth', delivered as an Inaugural Lecture at the University of Oxford in November 1969 and subsequently published by the Oxford University Press.

10. 'Truth', in *Proceedings of the Aristotelian Society, Supplementary Volume*, 1950.

11. 'A Problem about Truth – A Reply to Mr. Warnock' in George Pitcher, Ed., *Truth*, © 1964. Reprinted by permission of Prentice-Hall, Inc., Englewood Cliffs, New Jersey.

12. 'Truth: a Reconsideration of Austin's Views', in *The Philosophical Quarterly*, vol. 15, 1965.

I have to thank the editors and publishers in question for permission to reprint these essays.

Oxford
July 1970

P. F. S.

1. *On Referring*

We very commonly use expressions of certain kinds to mention or refer to some individual person or single object or particular event or place or process, in the course of doing what we should normally describe as making a statement about that person, object, place, event, or process. I shall call this way of using expressions the 'uniquely referring use'. The classes of expressions which are most commonly used in this way are: singular demonstrative pronouns ('this' and 'that'); proper names (e.g. 'Venice', 'Napoleon', 'John'); singular personal and impersonal pronouns ('he', 'she', 'I', 'you', 'it'); and phrases beginning with the definite article followed by a noun, qualified or unqualified, in the singular (e.g. 'the table', 'the old man', 'the king of France'). Any expression of any of these classes can occur as the subject of what would traditionally be regarded as a singular subject-predicate sentence; and would, so occurring, exemplify the use I wish to discuss.

I do not want to say that expressions belonging to these classes never have any other use than the one I want to discuss. On the contrary, it is obvious that they do. It is obvious that anyone who uttered the sentence, 'The whale is a mammal', would be using the expression 'the whale' in a way quite different from the way it would be used by anyone who had occasion seriously to utter the sentence, 'The whale struck the ship'. In the first sentence one is obviously *not* mentioning, and in the second sentence one obviously *is* mentioning, a particular whale. Again if I said, 'Napoleon was the greatest French soldier', I should be using the word 'Napoleon' to mention a certain individual, but I should not be using the phrase, 'the greatest French soldier', to mention an individual, but to say something about an individual I had already mentioned. It would be natural to say that in using this sentence I was talking *about* Napoleon and that what I was *saying* about him was that he was the greatest French soldier. But of course I *could* use the expression, 'the greatest French soldier', to mention an individual; for example, by saying: 'The greatest French soldier died in exile'. So it is obvious that at least some expressions belonging to the classes I mentioned *can* have uses other than the use I am anxious to discuss. Another thing I do not want to say is that in any given sentence there is never more than one expression used in the way I propose to discuss. On the contrary, it is obvious that there may be more than one. For example, it would be natural to say that, in seriously using the sentence, 'The whale struck the ship', I was saying something about both a certain whale and a certain ship, that I was using each of the expressions 'the whale' and 'the ship' to mention a particular object; or, in other words, that I was using each of these expressions in the uniquely referring way. In general, however, I shall confine my attention to cases where an expression used in this way occurs as the grammatical subject of a sentence.

I think it is true to say that Russell's Theory of Descriptions, which is concerned with the last of the four classes of expressions I mentioned above (i.e. with expressions of the form 'the so-and-so'), is still widely accepted among logicians as giving a correct account of the use of such expressions in ordinary language. I want to show in the first place, that this theory, so regarded, embodies some fundamental mistakes.

What question or questions about phrases of the form 'the so-and-so' was the Theory of Descriptions designed to answer? I think that at least one of the questions may be illustrated as follows. Suppose someone were now to utter the sentence, 'The king of France is wise'. No one would say that the sentence which had been uttered was meaningless. Everyone would agree that it was significant. But everyone knows that there is not at present a king of France. One of the questions the Theory of Descriptions was designed to answer was the question: How can such a sentence as 'The king of France is wise' be significant even when there is nothing which answers to the description it contains, i.e. in this case, nothing which answers to the description 'The king of France'? And one of the reasons why Russell thought it important to give a correct answer to this question was that he thought it important to show that another answer which might be given was wrong. The answer that he thought was wrong, and to which he was anxious to supply an alternative, might be exhibited as the conclusion of either of the following two fallacious arguments.

Let us call the sentence 'The king of France is wise' the sentence S. Then the first argument is as follows:

(1) The phrase, 'the king of France', is the subject of the sentence S.

Therefore (2) if S is a significant sentence, S is a sentence *about* the king of France.

But (3) if there in no sense exists a king of France, the sentence is not about anything, and hence not about the king of France.

Therefore (4) since S is significant, there must in some sense (in some world) exist (or subsist) the king of France.

And the second argument is as follows:

(1) If S is significant, it is either true or false.

(2) S is true if the king of France is wise and false if the king of France is not wise.

(3) But the statement that the king of France is wise and the statement that the king of France is not wise are alike true only if there is (in some sense, in some world) something which is the king of France.

Hence (4) since S is significant, there follows the same conclusion as before.

These are fairly obviously bad arguments, and, as we should expect, Russell rejects them. The postulation of a world of strange entities, to which the king of France belongs, offends, he says, against 'that feeling for reality which ought to be preserved even in the most abstract studies'. The fact that Russell rejects these arguments is, however, less interesting than the extent to which, in rejecting their conclusion, he concedes the more important of their principles. Let me refer to the phrase, 'the king of France', as the phrase D. Then I think Russell's reasons for rejecting these two arguments can be summarized as follows. The mistake arises, he says, from thinking that D, which is certainly the *grammatical* subject of S, is also the *logical* subject of S. But D is not the logical subject of S. In fact S, although grammatically it has a singular subject and a predicate, is not logically a subject-predicate sentence at all. The proposition it expresses is a complex kind of *existential* proposition, part of which might be described as a 'uniquely existential' proposition. To exhibit the logical form of the proposition, we should rewrite the sentence in a logically appropriate grammatical form; in such a way that the deceptive similarity of S to a sentence expressing a subject-predicate proposition would disappear, and we should be safeguarded against arguments such as the bad ones I outlined above. Before recalling the details of Russell's analysis of S, let us notice what his answer, as I have so far given it, seems to imply. His answer seems to imply that in the case of a sentence which is similar to S in that (1) it is grammatically of the subject-predicate form and (2) its grammatical subject does not refer to anything, then the only alternative to its being meaningless is that it should not really (i.e. logically) be of the subject-predicate form at all, but of some quite different form. And this in its turn seems to imply that if there are any sentences which are genuinely of the subject-predicate form, then the very fact of their being significant, having a meaning, guarantees that there *is* something referred to by the logical (and grammatical) subject. Moreover, Russell's answer seems to imply that there are such sentences. For if it is true that one may be misled by the grammatical similarity of S to other sentences into thinking that it is logically of the subject-predicate form, then surely there must be other sentences grammatically similar to S, which *are* of the subject-predicate form. To show not only that Russell's answer seems to imply these conclusions, but that he accepted at least the first two of them, it is enough to consider what he says about a class of expressions which he calls 'logically proper names' and contrasts with expressions, like D, which he calls 'definite descriptions'. Of logically proper names Russell says or implies the following things:

(1) That they and they alone can occur as subjects of sentences which are genuinely of the subject-predicate form.

(2) That an expression intended to be a logically proper name is *meaningless* unless there is some single object for which it stands: for the *meaning* of such an expression just is the individual object which the expression designates. To be a name at all, therefore, it *must* designate something.

It is easy to see that if anyone believes these two propositions, then the only way for him to save the significance of the sentence S is to deny that it is a logically subject-predicate sentence.

Generally, we may say that Russell recognizes only two ways in which sentences which seem, from their grammatical structure, to be about some particular person or individual object or event, can be significant:

(1) The first is that their grammatical form should be misleading as to their logical form, and that they should be analysable, like S, as a special kind of existential sentence.

(2) The second is that their grammatical subject should be a logically proper name, of which the meaning is the individual thing it designates.

I think that Russell is unquestionably wrong in this, and that sentences which are significant, and which begin with an expression used in the uniquely referring way, fall into neither of these two classes. Expressions used in the uniquely referring way are never either logically proper names or descriptions, if what is meant by calling them 'descriptions' is that they are to be analysed in accordance with the model provided by Russell's Theory of Descriptions.

There are no logically proper names and there are no descriptions (in this sense).

Let us now consider the details of Russell's analysis. According to Russell, anyone who asserted S would be asserting that:

(1) There is a king of France.
(2) There is not more than one king of France.
(3) There is nothing which is king of France and is not wise.

It is easy to see both how Russell arrived at this analysis, and how it enables him to answer the question with which we began, viz. the question: How can the sentence S be significant when there is no king of France? The way in which he arrived at the analysis was clearly by asking himself what would be the circumstances in which we would say that anyone who uttered the sentence S had made a true assertion. And it does seem pretty clear, and I have no wish to dispute, that the sentences (1)–(3) above do describe circumstances which are at least *necessary* conditions of anyone making a true assertion by uttering the sentence S. But, as I hope to show, to say this is not at all the same thing as to say that Russell has given a correct account of the use of the sentence S or even that he has given an account which, though incomplete, is correct as far as it goes; and is certainly not at all the same thing as to say that the model translation provided is a correct model for all (or for any) singular sentences beginning with a phrase of the form 'the so-and-so'.

It is also easy to see how this analysis enables Russell to answer the question of how the sentence S can be significant, even when there is no king of France. For, if this analysis is correct, anyone who utters the sentence S today would be jointly asserting three propositions, one of which (viz. that there is a king of France) would be false; and since the conjunction of three propositions, of which one is false, is itself false, the assertion as a whole would be significant, but false. So neither of the bad arguments for subsistent entities would apply to such an assertion.

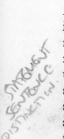

II

As a step towards showing that Russell's solution of his problem is mistaken, and towards providing the correct solution, I want now to draw certain distinctions. For this purpose I shall, for the remainder of this section, refer to an expression which has a uniquely referring use as 'an expression' for short; and to a sentence beginning with such an expression as 'a sentence' for short. The distinctions I shall draw are rather rough and ready, and, no doubt, difficult cases could be produced which would call for their refinement. But I think they will serve my purpose. The distinctions are between:

(A1) a sentence,
(A2) a use of a sentence,
(A3) an utterance of a sentence,

and, correspondingly, between:

(B1) an expression,
(B2) a use of an expression,
(B3) an utterance of an expression.

Consider again the sentence, 'The king of France is wise'. It is easy to imagine that this sentence was uttered at various times from, say, the beginning of the seventeenth century onwards, during the reigns of each successive French monarch; and easy to imagine that it was also uttered during the subsequent periods in which France was not a monarchy. Notice that it was natural for me to speak of 'the sentence' or 'this sentence' being uttered at various times during this period; or, in other words, that it would be natural and correct to speak of *one and the same* sentence being uttered on all these various occasions. It is in the sense in which it would be correct to speak of one and the same sentence being uttered on all these various occasions that I want to use the expression (A1) 'a sentence'. There are, however, obvious differences between different *occasions of the use* of this sentence. For instance, if one man uttered it in the reign of Louis XIV and another man uttered it in the reign of Louis XV, it would be natural to say (to assume) that they were respectively talking about different people; and it might be held that the first man, in using the sentence, made a true assertion, while the second man, in using the same sentence, made a false assertion. If on the other hand two different men simultaneously uttered the sentence (e.g. if one wrote it and the other spoke it) during the reign of Louis XIV, it would be natural to say (assume) that they were both talking about the same person, and, in that case, in using the sentence, they *must* either both have made a true assertion or both have made a false assertion. And this illustrates what I mean by *a use* of a sentence. The two men who uttered the sentence, one in the reign of Louis XV and one in the reign of Louis XIV, each made a different use of the same sentence; whereas the two men who uttered the sentence simultaneously in the reign of Louis XIV, made the same use[1] of the same sentence. Obviously in the case of this sentence, and equally obviously in the case of many others, we cannot talk of *the sentence* being true or false, but only of its being used to make a true or false assertion, or (if this is preferred) to express a true or a false proposition. And equally obviously we cannot talk of *the sentence* being *about* a particular person, for the same sentence may be used at different times to talk about quite different particular persons, but only of *a use* of the sentence to talk about a particular person. Finally it will make sufficiently clear what I mean by an utterance of a sentence if I say that the two men who simultaneously uttered the sentence in the

---

[1] This usage of 'use' is, of course, different from (*a*) the current usage in which 'use' (of a particular word, phrase, sentence) = (roughly) 'rules for using' = (roughly) 'meaning'; and from (*b*) my own usage in the phrase 'uniquely referring use of expressions' in which 'use' = (roughly) 'way of using'.

reign of Louis XIV made two different utterances of the same sentence, though they made the same *use* of the sentence.

If we now consider not the whole sentence, 'The king of France is wise', but that part of it which is the expression, 'the king of France', it is obvious that we can make analogous, though not identical distinctions between (1) the expression, (2) a use of the expression, and (3) an utterance of the expression. The distinctions will not be identical; we obviously cannot correctly talk of the expression 'the king of France' being used to express a true or false proposition, since in general only sentences can be used truly or falsely; and similarly it is only by using a sentence and not by using an expression alone, that you can talk about a particular person. Instead, we shall say in this case that you *use* the expression to *mention* or *refer to* a particular person in the course of using the sentence to talk about him. But obviously in this case, and a great many others, the *expression* (B1) cannot be said to mention, or refer to, anything, any more than the *sentence* can be said to be true or false. The same expression can have different mentioning-uses, as the same sentence can be used to make statements with different truth-values. 'Mentioning', or 'referring', is not something an expression does; it is something that someone can use an expression to do. Mentioning, or referring to, something is a characteristic of *a use* of an expression, just as 'being about' something, and truth-or-falsity, are characteristics of *a use* of a sentence.

A very different example may help to make these distinctions clearer. Consider another case of an expression which has a uniquely referring use, viz. the expression 'I'; and consider the sentence, 'I am hot'. Countless people may use this same sentence; but it is logically impossible for two different people to make *the same use* of this sentence: or, if this is preferred, to use it to express the same proposition. The expression 'I' may correctly be used by (and only by) any one of innumerable people to refer to himself. To say this is to say something about the expression 'I': it is, in a sense, to give its meaning. This is the sort of thing that can be said about *expressions*. But it makes no sense to say of the *expression* 'I' that it refers to a particular person. This is the sort of thing that can be said only of a particular use of the expression.

Let me use 'type' as an abbreviation for 'sentence or expression'. Then I am not saying that there are sentences and ex-

NOT DISTINGUISHING THESE AS SEPARATE THINGS, BUT THAT WE CANNOT TALK OF THEM IN THE SAME WAY.

pressions (types), *and* uses of them, *and* utterances of them, as there are ships *and* shoes *and* sealing-wax. I am saying that we cannot say *the same things* about types, uses of types, and utterances of types. And the fact is that we do talk about types; and that confusion is apt to result from the failure to notice the differences between what we can say about these and what we can say only about the *uses* of types. We are apt to fancy we are talking about sentences and expressions when we are talking about the uses of sentences and expressions.

Russell's mistake

This is what Russell does. Generally, as against Russell, I shall say this. Meaning (in at least one important sense) is a function of the sentence or expression; mentioning and referring and truth or falsity, are functions of the use of the sentence or expression. To give the meaning of an expression (in the sense in which I am using the word) is to give *general directions* for its use to refer to or mention particular objects or persons; to give the meaning of a sentence is to give *general directions* for its use in making true or false assertions. It is not to talk about any particular occasion of the use of the sentence or expression. The meaning of an expression cannot be identified with the object it is used, on a particular occasion, to refer to. The meaning of a sentence cannot be identified with the assertion it is used, on a particular occasion, to make. For to talk about the meaning of an expression or sentence is not to talk about its use on a particular occasion, but about the rules, habits, conventions governing its correct use, on all occasions, to refer or to assert. So the question of whether a sentence or expression *is significant or not* has nothing whatever to do with the question of whether the sentence, *uttered on a particular occasion*, is, on that occasion, being used to make a true-or-false assertion or not, or of whether the expression is, on that occasion, being used to refer to, or mention, anything at all.

The source of Russell's mistake was that he thought that referring or mentioning, if it occurred at all, must be meaning. He did not distinguish B1 from B2; he confused expressions with their use in a particular context; and so confused meaning with mentioning, with referring. If I talk about my handkerchief, I can, perhaps, produce the object I am referring to out of my pocket. I cannot produce the meaning of the expression, 'my handkerchief', out of my pocket. Because Russell confused meaning with mentioning, he thought that if there were any expressions having

B

a uniquely referring use, which were what they seemed (i.e. logical subjects) and not something else in disguise, their meaning must *be* the particular object which they were used to refer to. Hence the troublesome mythology of the logically proper name. But if someone asks me the meaning of the expression 'this' – once Russell's favourite candidate for this status – I do not hand him the object I have just used the expression to refer to, adding at the same time that the meaning of the word changes every time it is used. Nor do I hand him all the objects it ever has been, or might be, used to refer to. I explain and illustrate the conventions governing the use of the expression. This *is* giving the meaning of the expression. It is quite different from giving (in any sense of giving) the object to which it refers; for the expression itself does not refer to anything; though it can be used on different occasion, to refer to innumerable things. Now as a matter of fact there is, in English, a sense of the word 'mean' in which this word does approximate to 'indicate, mention or refer to'; e.g. when somebody (unpleasantly) says, 'I mean you'; or when I point and say, 'That's the one I mean'. But *the one I meant* is quite different from *the meaning of the expression* I used to talk of it. In this special sense of 'mean', it is people who mean, not expressions. People use expressions to refer to particular things. But the meaning of an expression is not the set of things or the single thing it may correctly be used to refer to: the meaning is the set of rules, habits, conventions for its use in referring.

It is the same with sentences: even more obviously so. Everyone knows that the sentence, 'The table is covered with books', is significant, and everyone knows what it means. But if I ask, 'What object is that sentence about?' I am asking an absurd question – a question which cannot be asked about the sentence, but only about some use of the sentence: and in this case the sentence has not been used to talk about something, it has only been taken as an example. In knowing what it means, you are knowing how it could correctly be used to talk about things: so knowing the meaning has nothing to do with knowing about any particular use of the sentence to talk about anything. Similarly, if I ask: 'Is the sentence true or false?' I am asking an absurd question, which becomes no less absurd if I add, 'It must be one or the other since it is significant'. The question is absurd, because the *sentence* is neither true nor false any more than it is *about* some object. Of course the fact that it is significant is the same as the fact that it *can* correctly be used to talk about something and that, in so using it, someone will be making a true or false assertion. And I will add that it will be used to make a true or false assertion *only* if the person using it *is* talking about something. If, when he utters it, he is not talking about anything, then his use is not a genuine one, but a spurious or pseudo-use: he is not making either a true or a false assertion, though he may think he is. And this points the way to the correct answer to the puzzle to which the Theory of Descriptions gives a fatally incorrect answer. The important point is that the question of whether the sentence is significant or not is quite independent of the question that can be raised about a particular use of it, viz. the question whether it is a genuine or a spurious use, whether it is being used to talk about something, or in make-believe, or as an example in philosophy. The question whether the sentence is significant or not is the question whether there exist such language habits, conventions or rules that the sentence logically could be used to talk about something; and is hence quite independent of the question whether it is being so used on a particular occasion.

III

Consider again the sentence, 'The king of France is wise', and the true and false things Russell says about it.

There are at least two true things which Russell would say about the sentence:

(1) The first is that it is significant; that if anyone were now to utter it, he would be uttering a significant sentence.

(2) The second is that anyone now uttering the sentence would be making a true assertion only if there in fact at present existed one and only one king of France, and if he were wise.

What are the false things which Russell would say about the sentence? They are:

(1) That anyone now uttering it would be making a true assertion or a false assertion.

(2) That part of what he would be asserting would be that there at present existed one and only one king of France.

I have already given some reasons for thinking that these two statements are incorrect. Now suppose someone were in fact to say to you with a perfectly serious air: 'The king of France is wise'. Would you say, 'That's untrue'? I think it is quite certain that you would not. But suppose he went on to *ask* you whether you thought that what he had just said was true, or was false; whether you agreed or disagreed with what he had just said. I think you would be inclined, with some hesitation, to say that you did not do either; that the question of whether his statement was true or false simply *did not arise*, because there was no such person as the king of France. You might, if he were obviously serious (had a dazed astray-in-the-centuries look), say something like: 'I'm afraid you must be under a misapprehension. France is not a monarchy. There is no king of France.' And this brings out the point that if a man seriously uttered the sentence, his uttering it would in some sense be *evidence* that he *believed* that there was a king of France. It would not be evidence for his believing this simply in the way in which a man's reaching for his raincoat is evidence for his believing that it is raining. But nor would it be evidence for his believing this in the way in which a man's saying, 'It's raining', is evidence for his believing that it is raining. We might put it as follows. To say 'The king of France is wise' is, in some sense of 'imply', to *imply* that there is a king of France. But this is a very special and odd sense of 'imply'. 'Implies' in this sense is certainly not equivalent to 'entails' (or 'logically implies'). And this comes out from the fact that when, in response to his statement, we say (as we should) 'There is no king of France', we should certainly *not* say we were *contradicting* the statement that the king of France is wise. We are certainly not saying that it is false. We are, rather, giving a reason for saying that the question of whether it is true or false simply does not arise.

And this is where the distinction I drew earlier can help us. The sentence, 'The king of France is wise', is certainly significant; but this does not mean that any particular use of it is true or false. We use it truly or falsely when we use it to talk about someone; when, in using the expression, 'The king of France', we are in fact mentioning someone. The fact that the sentence and the expression, respectively, are significant just is the fact that the sentence *could* be used, in certain circumstances, to say something true or false, that the expression *could* be used, in certain circumstances, to mention a particular person; and to know their meaning is to know what sort of circumstances these are. So when we utter the sentence without in fact mentioning anybody by the use of the phrase, 'The king of France', the sentence does not cease to be significant: we simply *fail* to say anything true or false because we simply fail to mention anybody by this particular use of that perfectly significant phrase. It is, if you like, a spurious use of the sentence, and a spurious use of the expression; though we may (or may not) mistakenly think it a genuine use.

And such spurious uses[1] are very familiar. Sophisticated romancing, sophisticated fiction,[2] depend upon them. If I began, 'The king of France is wise', and went on, 'and he lives in a golden castle and has a hundred wives', and so on, a hearer would understand me perfectly well, without supposing *either* that I was talking about a particular person, *or* that I was making a false statement to the effect that there existed such a person as my words described. (It is worth adding that where the use of sentences and expressions is overtly fictional, the sense of the word 'about' may change. As Moore said, it is perfectly natural and correct to say that some of the statements in *Pickwick Papers* are *about* Mr Pickwick. But where the use of sentences and expressions is not overtly fictional, this use of 'about' seems less correct, i.e. it would not *in general* be correct to say that a statement was about Mr X or the so-and-so, unless there were such a person or thing. So it is where the romancing is in danger of being taken seriously that we might answer the question, 'Who is he talking about?' with 'He's not talking about anybody'; but, in saying this, we are not saying that what he is saying is either false or nonsense.)

Overtly fictional uses apart, however, I said just now that to use such an expression as 'The king of France' at the beginning of a sentence was, in some sense of 'imply', to imply that there was a king of France. When a man uses such an expression, he does not *assert*, nor does what he says *entail*, a uniquely existential proposition. But one of the conventional functions of the definite article is to act as a *signal* that a unique reference is being made – a signal, not a disguised assertion. When we begin a sentence with 'the

[1] The choice of the word 'spurious' now seems to me unfortunate, at least for some non-standard uses. I should now prefer to call some of these 'secondary' uses.

[2] The unsophisticated kind begins: 'Once upon time there was . . .'

such-and-such' the use of 'the' shows, but does not state, that we are, or intend to be, referring to one particular individual of the species 'such-and-such'. *Which* particular individual is a matter to be determined from context, time, place, and any other features of the situation of utterance. Now, whenever a man uses any expression, the presumption is that he thinks he is using it correctly: so when he uses the expression, 'the such-and-such', in a uniquely referring way, the presumption is that he thinks both that there is *some* individual of that species, and that the context of use will sufficiently determine which one he has in mind. To use the word 'the' in this way is then to imply (in the relevant sense of 'imply') that the existential conditions described by Russell are fulfilled. But to use 'the' in this way is not to *state* that those conditions are fulfilled. If I begin a sentence with an expression of the form, 'the so-and-so', and then am prevented from saying more, I have made no statement of any kind; but I may have succeeded in mentioning someone or something.

The uniquely existential assertion supposed by Russell to be part of any assertion in which a uniquely referring use is made of an expression of the form 'the so-and-so' is, he observes, a compound of two assertions. To say that there is a ϕ is to say something compatible with there being several ϕs; to say there is not more than one ϕ is to say something compatible with there being none. To say there is one ϕ and one only is to compound these two assertions. I have so far been concerned mostly with the alleged assertion of existence and less with the alleged assertion of uniqueness. An example which throws the emphasis on to the latter will serve to bring out more clearly the sense of 'implied' in which a uniquely existential assertion is implied, but not entailed, by the use of expressions in the uniquely referring way. Consider the sentence, 'The table is covered with books'. It is quite certain that in any normal use of this sentence, the expression 'the table' would be used to make a unique reference, i.e. to refer to some one table. It is a quite strict use of the definite article, in the sense in which Russell talks, on p. 30 of *Principia Mathematica*, of using the article '*strictly*, so as to imply uniqueness'. On the same page Russell says that a phrase of the form 'the so-and-so', used strictly, 'will only have an application in the event of there being one so-and-so and no more'. Now it is obviously quite false that the phrase 'the table' in the sentence 'the table is covered with books', used normally, will 'only have an application in the event of there being one table and no more'. It is indeed tautologically true that, in such a use, the phrase will have an application only in the event of there being one table and no more *which is being referred to*, and that it will be understood to have an application only in the event of there being one table and no more which it is understood as being used to refer to. To use the sentence is not to assert, but it is (in the special sense discussed) to imply, that there is only one thing which is *both* of the kind specified (i.e. a table) *and is being referred to* by the speaker. It is obviously not to assert this. To refer is not to say you are referring. To say there is *some table or other* to which you are referring is not the same as referring to a particular table. We should have no use for such phrases as 'the individual I referred to' unless there were something which counted as referring. (It would make no sense to say you had pointed if there were nothing which counted as pointing.) So once more I draw the conclusion that referring to or mentioning a particular thing cannot be dissolved into any kind of assertion. To refer is not to assert, though you refer in order to go on to assert.

Let me now take an example of the uniquely referring use of an expression not of the form, 'the so-and-so'. Suppose I advance my hands, cautiously cupped, towards someone, saying, as I do so, 'This is a fine red one'. He, looking into my hands and seeing nothing there, may say: 'What is? What are you talking about?' Or perhaps, 'But there's nothing in your hands'. Of course it would be absurd to say that, in saying 'But you've got nothing in your hands', he was *denying* or *contradicting* what I said. So 'this' is not a disguised description in Russell's sense. Nor is it a logically proper name. For one must know what the sentence means in order to react in that way to the utterance of it. It is precisely because the significance of the word 'this' is independent of any particular reference it may be used to make, though not independent of the way it may be used to refer, that I can, as in this example, use it to *pretend* to be referring to something.

The general moral of all this is that communication is much less a matter of explicit or disguised assertion than logicians used to suppose. The particular application of this general moral in which I am interested is its application to the case of making a unique reference. It is a part of the significance of expressions of the kind I am discussing that they can be used, in an immense variety of contexts, to make unique references. It is no part of their significance to assert that they are being so used or that the conditions of their being so used are fulfilled. So the wholly important distinction we are required to draw is between

(1) using an expression to make a unique reference; and
(2) asserting that there is one and only one individual which has certain characteristics (e.g. is of a certain kind, or stands in a certain relation to the speaker, or both).

This is, in other words, the distinction between

(1) sentences containing an expression used to indicate or mention or refer to a particular person or thing; and
(2) uniquely existential sentences.

What Russell does is progressively to assimilate more and more sentences of class (1) to sentences of class (2), and consequently to involve himself in insuperable difficulties about logical subjects, and about values for individual variables generally: difficulties which have led him finally to the logically disastrous theory of names developed in the *Enquiry into Meaning and Truth* and in *Human Knowledge*. That view of the meaning of logical-subject-expressions which provides the whole incentive to the Theory of Descriptions at the same time precludes the possibility of Russell's ever finding any satisfactory substitutes for those expressions which, beginning with substantival phrases, he progressively degrades from the status of logical subjects.[1] It is not simply, as is sometimes said, the fascination of the relation between a name and its bearer, that is the root of the trouble. Not even names come up to the impossible standard set. It is rather the combination of two more radical misconceptions: first, the failure to grasp the importance of the distinction (section II above) between what may be said of an expression and what may be said of a particular use of it; second, a failure to recognize the uniquely referring use of expressions for the harmless, necessary thing it is, distinct from, but complementary to, the predicative or ascriptive use of expressions. The expressions which can in fact occur as singular logical subjects are expressions of the class I listed at the outset (demonstratives, substantival phrases, proper names, pronouns): to

[1] And this in spite of the danger-signal of that phrase, '*misleading* grammatical form'.

say this is to say that these expressions, together with context (in the widest sense), are what one uses to make unique references. The point of the conventions governing the uses of such expressions is, along with the situation of utterance, to secure uniqueness of reference. But to do this, enough is enough. We do not, and we cannot, while referring, attain the point of complete explicitness at which the referring function is no longer performed. The actual unique reference made, if any, is a matter of the particular use in the particular context; the significance of the expression used is the set of rules or conventions which permit such references to be made. Hence we can, using significant expressions, pretend to refer, in make-believe or in fiction, or mistakenly think we are referring when we are not referring to anything.[1]

This shows the need for distinguishing two kinds (among many others) of linguistic conventions or rules: rules for referring, and rules for attributing and ascribing; and for an investigation of the former. If we recognize this distinction of use for what it is, we are on the way to solving a number of ancient logical and metaphysical puzzles.

My last two sections are concerned, but only in the barest outline, with these questions.

IV

One of the main purposes for which we use language is the purpose of stating facts about things and persons and events. If we want to fulfil this purpose, we must have some way of forestalling the question, 'What (who, which one) are you talking about?' as well as the question, 'What are you saying about it (him, her)?' The task of forestalling the first question is the referring (or identifying) task. The task of forestalling the second is the attributive (or descriptive or classificatory or ascriptive) task. In the conventional English sentence which is used to state, or to claim to state, a fact about an individual thing or person or event, the performance of these two tasks can be roughly and approximately

[1] This sentence now seems to me objectionable in a number of ways' notably because of an unexplicitly restrictive use of the word 'refer'. It could be more exactly phrased as follows: 'Hence we can, using significant expressions, refer in secondary ways, as in make-believe or in fiction, or mistakenly think we are referring to something in the primary way when we are not, in that way, referring to anything.'

assigned to separable expressions.[1] And in such a sentence, this assigning of expressions to their separate roles corresponds to the conventional grammatical classification of subject and predicate. There is nothing sacrosanct about the employment of separable expressions for these two tasks. Other methods could, and are, employed. There is, for instance, the method of uttering a single word or attributive phrase in the conspicuous presence of the object referred to; or that analogous method exemplified by, for example, the painting of the words 'unsafe for lorries' on a bridge, or the tying of a label reading 'first prize' on a vegetable marrow. Or one can imagine an elaborate game in which one never used an expression in the uniquely referring way at all, but uttered only uniquely existential sentences, trying to enable the hearer to identify what was being talked of by means of an accumulation of relative clauses. (This description of the purposes of the game shows in what sense it would be a game: this is not the normal use we make of existential sentences.) Two points require emphasis. The first is that the necessity of performing these two tasks in order to state particular facts requires no transcendental explanation: to call attention to it is partly to elucidate the meaning of the phrase, 'stating a fact'. The second is that even this elucidation is made in terms derivative from the grammar of the conventional singular sentence; that even the overtly functional, linguistic distinction between the identifying and attributive roles that words may play in language is prompted by the fact that ordinary speech offers us separable expressions to which the different functions may be plausibly and approximately assigned. And this functional distinction has cast long philosophical shadows. The distinctions between particular and universal, between substance and quality, are such pseudo-material shadows, cast by the grammar of the conventional sentence in which separable expressions play distinguishable roles.[2]

To use a separate expression to perform the first of these tasks is to use an expression in the uniquely referring way. I want now to say something in general about the conventions of use for expressions used in this way, and to contrast them with conven-

---

[1] I neglect relational sentences; for these require, not a modification in the principle of what I say, but a complication of the detail.

[2] What is said or implied in the last two sentences of this paragraph no longer seems to me true, unless considerably qualified.

tions of ascriptive use. I then proceed to the brief illustration of these general remarks and to some further applications of them.

What in general is required for making a unique reference is, obviously, some device, or devices, for showing both *that* a unique reference is intended and *what* unique reference it is; some device requiring and enabling the hearer or reader to identify what is being talked about. In securing this result, the context of utterance is of an importance which it is almost impossible to exaggerate; and by 'context' I mean, at least, the time, the place, the situation, the identity of the speaker, the subjects which form the immediate focus of interest, and the personal histories of both the speaker and those he is addressing. Besides context, there is, of course, convention; – linguistic convention. But, except in the case of genuine proper names, of which I shall have more to say later, the fulfilment of more or less precisely stateable contextual conditions is *conventionally* (or, in a wide sense of the word, *logically*) required for the correct referring use of expressions in a sense in which this is not true of correct ascriptive uses. The requirement for the correct application of an expression in its ascriptive use to a certain thing is simply that the thing should be of a certain kind, have certain characteristics. The requirement for the correct application of an expression in its referring use to a certain thing is something over and above any requirement derived from such ascriptive meaning as the expression may have; it is, namely, the requirement that the thing should be in a certain relation to the speaker and to the context of utterance. Let me call this the contextual requirement. Thus, for example, in the limiting case of the word 'I' the contextual requirement is that the thing should be identical with the speaker; but in the case of most expressions which have a referring use this requirement cannot be so precisely specified. A further, and perfectly general, difference between conventions for referring and conventions for describing is one we have already encountered, viz. that the fulfilment of the conditions for a correct ascriptive use of an expression is a part of what is stated by such a use; but the fulfilment of the conditions for a correct referring use of an expression is never part of what is stated, though it is (in the relevant sense of 'implied') implied by such a use.

Conventions for referring have been neglected or misinterpreted by logicians. The reasons for this neglect are not hard to see, though they are hard to state briefly. Two of them are, roughly: (1) the preoccupation of most logicians with definitions; (2) the preoccupation of some logicians with formal systems. (1) A definition, in the most familiar sense, is a specification of the conditions of the correct ascriptive or classificatory use of an expression. Definitions take no account of contextual requirements. So that in so far as the search for the meaning or the search for the analysis of an expression is conceived as the search for a definition, the neglect or misinterpretation of conventions other than ascriptive is inevitable. Perhaps it would be better to say (for I do not wish to legislate about 'meaning' or 'analysis') that logicians have failed to notice that problems of use are wider than problems of analysis and meaning. (2) The influence of the preoccupation with mathematics and formal logic is most clearly seen (to take no more recent examples) in the cases of Leibniz and Russell. The constructor of calculuses, not concerned or required to make factual statements, approaches applied logic with a prejudice. It is natural that he should assume that the types of convention with whose adequacy in one field he is familiar should be really adequate, if only one could see how, in a quite different field – that of statements of fact. Thus we have Leibniz striving desperately to make the uniqueness of unique references a matter of logic in the narrow sense, and Russell striving desperately to do the same thing, in a different way, both for the implication of uniqueness and for that of existence.

It should be clear that the distinction I am trying to draw is primarily one between different roles or parts that expressions may play in language, and not primarily one between different groups of expressions; for some expressions may appear in either role. Some of the kinds of words I shall speak of have predominantly, if not exclusively, a referring role. This is most obviously true of pronouns and ordinary proper names. Some can occur as wholes or parts of expressions which have a predominantly referring use, and as wholes or parts of expressions which have a predominantly ascriptive or classificatory use. The obvious cases are common nouns; or common nouns preceded by adjectives, including participial adjectives; or, less obviously, adjectives or participial adjectives alone. Expressions capable of having a referring use also differ from one another in at least the three following, not mutually independent, ways:

(1) They differ in the extent to which the reference they are used to make is dependent on the context of their utterance. Words like 'I' and 'it' stand at one end of this scale – the end of maximum dependence – and phrases like 'the author of *Waverley*' and 'the eighteenth king of France' at the other.

(2) They differ in the degree of 'descriptive meaning' they possess: by 'descriptive meaning' I intend 'conventional limitation, in application, to things of a certain general kind, or possessing certain general characteristics'. At one end of this scale stand the proper names we most commonly use in ordinary discourse; men, dogs, and motor-bicycles may be called 'Horace'. The pure name has no descriptive meaning (except such as it may acquire *as a result of* some one of its uses as a name). A word like 'he' has minimal descriptive meaning, but has some. Substantival phrases like 'the round table' have the maximum descriptive meaning. An interesting intermediate position is occupied by 'impure' proper names like 'The Round Table' – substantival phrases which have grown capital letters.

(3) Finally, they may be divided into the following two classes: (i) those of which the correct referring use is regulated by some *general* referring-cum-ascriptive conventions; (ii) those of which the correct referring use is regulated by no general conventions, either of the contextual or the ascriptive kind, but by conventions which are *ad hoc* for each particular use (though not for each particular utterance). To the first class belong both pronouns (which have the least descriptive meaning) and substantival phrases (which have the most). To the second class belong, roughly speaking, the most familiar kind of proper names. Ignorance of a man's name is not ignorance of the language. This is why we do not speak of the meaning of proper names. (But it won't do to say they are meaningless.) Again an intermediate position is occupied by such phrases as 'The Old Pretender'. Only an old pretender may be so referred to; but to know which old pretender is not to know a general, but an *ad hoc*, convention.

In the case of phrases of the form 'the so-and-so' used referringly, the use of 'the' together with the position of the phrase in the sentence (i.e. at the beginning, or following a transitive verb or preposition) acts as a signal *that* a unique reference is being made; and the following noun, or noun and adjective, together with the context of utterance, shows *what* unique reference is being made. In general the functional difference between common nouns and adjectives is that the former are naturally and commonly used referringly, while the latter are not commonly, or so naturally, used in this way, except as qualifying nouns; though they can be, and are, so used alone. And of course this functional difference is not independent of the descriptive force peculiar to each word. In general we should expect the descriptive force of nouns to be such that they are more efficient tools for the job of showing what unique reference is intended when such a reference is signalized; and we should also expect the descriptive force of the words we naturally and commonly use to make unique references to mirror our interest in the salient, relatively permanent and behavioural characteristics of things. These two expectations are not independent of one another; and, if we look at the differences between the commoner sort of common nouns and the commoner sort of adjectives, we find them both fulfilled. These are differences of the kind that Locke quaintly reports, when he speaks of our ideas of substances being *collections* of simple ideas; when he says that 'powers make up a great part of our ideas of substances'; and when he goes on to contrast the identity of real and nominal essence in the case of simple ideas with their lack of identity and the shiftingness of the nominal essence in the case of substances. 'Substance' itself is the troublesome tribute Locke pays to his dim awareness of the difference in predominant linguistic function that lingered even when the noun had been expanded into a more or less indefinite string of adjectives. Russell repeats Locke's mistake with a difference when, admitting the inference from syntax to reality to the extent of feeling that he can get rid of this metaphysical unknown only if he can purify language of the referring function altogether, he draws up his programme for 'abolishing particulars'; a programme, in fact, for abolishing the distinction of logical use which I am here at pains to emphasize.

The contextual requirement for the referring use of pronouns may be stated with the greatest precision in some cases (e.g. 'I' and 'you') and only with the greatest vagueness in others ('it' and 'this'). I propose to say nothing further about pronouns, except to point to an additional symptom of the failure to recognize the uniquely referring use for what it is; the fact, namely, that certain logicians have actually sought to elucidate the nature of a variable by offering such *sentences* as 'he is sick', 'it is green', as examples of something in ordinary speech like a *sentential function*. Now of course it is true that the word 'he' may be used on different occasions to refer to different people or different animals: so may the word 'John' and the phrase 'the cat'. What deters such logicians from treating these two expressions as quasi-variables is, in the first case, the lingering superstition that a name is logically tied to a single individual, and, in the second case, the descriptive meaning of the word 'cat'. But 'he', which has a wide range of applications and minimal descriptive force, only acquires a use as a referring word. It is this fact, together with the failure to accord to expressions, used referringly, the place in logic which belongs to them (the place held open for the mythical logically proper name), that accounts for the misleading attempt to elucidate the nature of the variable by reference to such words as 'he', 'she', 'it'.

Of ordinary proper names it is sometimes said that they are essentially words each of which is used to refer to just one individual. This is obviously false. Many ordinary personal names – names *par excellence* – are correctly used to refer to numbers of people. An ordinary personal name is, roughly, a word, used referringly, of which the use is *not* dictated by any descriptive meaning the word may have, and is *not* prescribed by any such general rule for use as a referring expression (or a part of a referring expression) as we find in the case of such words as 'I', 'this', and 'the', but is governed by *ad hoc* conventions for each particular set of applications of the word to a given person. The important point is that the correctness of such applications does not follow from any *general* rule or convention for the use of the word as such. (The limit of absurdity and obvious circularity is reached in the attempt to treat names as disguised description in Russell's sense; for what is in the special sense implied, but not entailed, by my now referring to someone by name is simply the existence of someone, *now being referred to*, who is *conventionally referred to* by that name.) Even this feature of names, however, is only a symptom of the purpose for which they are employed. At present our choice of names is partly arbitrary, partly dependent on legal and social observances. It would be perfectly possible to have a thoroughgoing *system* of names, based for example on dates of birth, or on a minute classification of physiological and anatomical differences.

But the success of any such system would depend entirely on the convenience of the resulting name-allotments for the purpose of making unique references; and this would depend on the multiplicity of the classifications used and the degree to which they cut haphazard across normal social groupings. Given a sufficient degree of both, the selectivity supplied by context would do the rest; just as is the case with our present naming habits. Had we such a system, we could use name-words descriptively (as we do at present, to a limited extent and in a different way, with some famous names) as well as referringly. But it is by criteria derived from consideration of the requirements of the referring task that we should assess the adequacy of any system of naming. From the naming point of view, no kind of classification would be better or worse than any other simply because of the kind of classification – natal or anatomical – that it was.

I have already mentioned the class of quasi-names, of substantival phrases which grow capital letters, and of which such phrases as 'the Glorious Revolution', 'the Great War', 'the Annunciation', 'the Round Table' are examples. While the descriptive meaning of the words which follow the definite article is still relevant to their referring role, the capital letters are a sign of that extra-logical selectivity in their referring use, which is characteristic of pure names. Such phrases are found in print or in writing when one member of some class of events or things is of quite outstanding interest in a certain society. These phrases are embryonic names. A phrase may, for obvious reasons, pass into, and out of, this class (e.g. 'the Great War').

V

I want to conclude by considering, all too briefly, three further problems about referring uses.

(a) *Indefinite references*. Not all referring uses of singular expressions forestall the question 'What (who, which one) are you talking about?' There are some which either invite this question, or disclaim the intention or ability to answer it. Examples are such sentence-beginnings as 'A man told me that . . .', 'Someone told me that . . .'. The orthodox (Russellian) doctrine is that such sentences are existential, but not uniquely existential. This seems wrong in several ways. It is ludicrous to suggest that part of what is asserted is that the class of men or persons is not empty. Certainly this is *implied* in the by now familiar sense of implication; but the implication is also as much an implication of the *uniqueness* of the particular object of reference as when I begin a sentence with such a phrase as 'the table'. The difference between the use of the definite and indefinite articles is, very roughly, as follows. We use 'the' either when a previous reference has been made, and when 'the' signalizes that the same reference is being made; or when, in the absence of a previous indefinite reference, the context (including the hearer's assumed knowledge) is expected to enable the hearer to tell *what* reference is being made. We use 'a' either when these conditions are not fulfilled, or when, although a definite reference *could* be made, we wish to keep dark the identity of the individual to whom, or to which, we are referring. This is the *arch* use of such a phrase as 'a certain person' or 'someone'; where it could be expanded, not into 'someone, but you wouldn't (or I don't) know who' but into 'someone, but I'm not telling you who'.

(*b*) *Identification statements*. By this label I intend statements like the following:

(i*a*) That is the man who swam the channel twice on one day.
(ii*a*) Napoleon was the man who ordered the execution of the Duc d'Enghien.

The puzzle about these statements is that their grammatical predicates do not seem to be used in a straightforwardly ascriptive way as are the grammatical predicates of the statements:

(i*b*) That man swam the channel twice in one day.
(ii*b*) Napoleon ordered the execution of the Duc d'Enghien.

But if, in order to avoid blurring the difference between (i*a*) and (i*b*) and (ii*a*) and (ii*b*), one says that the phrases which form the grammatical complements of (i*a*) and (ii*a*) are being used referringly, one becomes puzzled about what is being said in these sentences. We seem then to be referring to the same person twice over and either saying nothing about him and thus making no statement, or identifying him with himself and thus producing a trivial identity.

The bogy of triviality can be dismissed. This only arises for

C

those who think of the object referred to by the use of an expression as its meaning, and thus think of the subject and complement of these sentences as meaning the same because they could be used to refer to the same person.

I think the differences between sentences in the (*a*) group and sentences in the (*b*) group can best be understood by considering the differences between the circumstances in which you would say (i*a*) and the circumstances in which you would say (i*b*). You would say (i*a*) instead of (i*b*) if you knew or believed that your hearer knew or believed that *someone* had swum the channel twice in one day. You say (i*a*) when you take your hearer to be in the position of one who can ask: 'Who swam the channel twice in one day?' (And in asking this, he is not saying that anyone did, though his asking it implies – in the relevant sense – that someone did.) Such sentences are like answers to such questions. They are better called 'identification-statements' than 'identities'. Sentence (i*a*) does not assert more or less than sentence (i*b*). It is just that you say (i*a*) to a man whom you take to know certain things that you take to be unknown to the man to whom you say (i*b*).

This is, in the barest essentials, the solution to Russell's puzzle about 'denoting phrases' joined by 'is'; one of the puzzles which he claims for the Theory of Descriptions the merit of solving.

(*c*) *The logic of subjects and predicates.* Much of what I have said of the uniquely referring use of expressions can be extended, with suitable modifications, to the non-uniquely referring use of expressions, i.e. to some uses of expressions consisting of 'the', 'all the', 'all', 'some', 'some of the', etc. followed by a noun, qualified or unqualified, in the *plural*; to some uses of 'they', 'them', 'those', 'these'; and to conjunctions of names. Expressions of the first kind have a special interest. Roughly speaking, orthodox modern criticism, inspired by mathematical logic, of such traditional doctrines as that of the Square of Opposition and of some of the forms of the syllogism traditionally recognized as valid, rests on the familiar failure to recognize the special sense in which existential assertions may be implied by the referring use of expressions. The universal propositions of the fourfold schedule, it is said, must *either* be given a negatively existential interpretation (e.g. for A, 'there are no Xs which are not Ys') *or* they must be interpreted as conjunctions of negatively and positively existential statements of, for example, the form (for A) 'there are no Xs which are not Ys, and there are Xs'. The I and O forms are normally given a positively existential interpretation. It is then seen that, whichever of the above alternatives is selected, some of the traditional laws have to be abandoned. The dilemma, however, is a bogus one. If we interpret the propositions of the schedule as neither positively, nor negatively, nor positively *and* negatively, existential, but as sentences such that *the question of whether they are being used to make true or false assertions does not arise except when the existential condition is fulfilled for the subject term*, then all the traditional laws hold good together. And this interpretation is far closer to the most common uses of expressions beginning with 'all' and 'some' than is any Russellian alternative. For these expressions are most commonly used in the referring way. A literal-minded and childless man asked whether all his children are asleep will certainly not answer 'Yes' on the ground that he has none; but nor will he answer 'No' on this ground. Since he has no children, the question does not arise. To say this is not to say that I may not use the sentence, 'All my children are asleep', with the intention of letting someone know that I have children, or of deceiving him into thinking that I have. Nor is it any weakening of my thesis to concede that singular phrases of the form 'the so-and-so' may sometimes be used with a similar purpose. Neither Aristotelian nor Russellian rules give the exact logic of any expression of ordinary language; for ordinary language has no exact logic.

2. *Particular and General*

There is a cetain philosophical question which, if antiquity confers respectability, is as respectable as any. It was not long ago discussed by Ramsey in the form 'What is the difference between a particular and a universal?'[1], and more recently by Ayer in the form 'What is the difference between properties and individuals?'[2] Ramsey decided that there was no ultimate difference; but perhaps he set the standard for an ultimate difference higher than we should wish to, or drew it from a theory we no longer wish to hold. Ayer, after some interesting suggestions, changed the subject, and discussed instead two other questions, viz. what is the difference in function between indicator words and predicates, and could we in principle say what we want to say without using the former?[3] It may be that the original question is made easier to start on, and more difficult to settle, by an initial failure to make even fairly clear what types or classes of things are to be included in the two general categories between which a satisfying difference is sought. The words of the questions I quoted are not very helpful. Universals are said to include qualities and relations. But if, for example, we take the words 'quality', 'relation', and 'property' in their current uses, much that we should no doubt wish to include on the side of the general, as opposed to the particular, would be left out; and if we do not take them in their current uses, it is not clear how we are to take them. Thus snow,

[1] Ramsey, *Foundations of Mathematics*, pp. 112–34.

[2] Ayer, 'Individuals', *Mind*, 1952.

[3] To the second question Ayer's answer was affirmative; and, things being as they are, this is no doubt correct as a matter of what is theoretically practicable. Ayer also acknowledges (*a*) that in actual practice we could scarcely dispense with indicator words, and (*b*) that the attempt to do so would always involve a theoretical failure to individuate, since no elaboration of predicates rules out the theoretical possibility of reduplication. But I doubt if the original question can be answered unless we take these two facts more seriously than he does.

gold, and clothing are not properties; nor is man, nor any other species; nor is chess nor furniture; nor is the Union Jack – by which I mean, not the tattered specimen the porter keeps in a drawer, but the flag designed in the nineteenth century, examples of which are taken from drawers by porters and hung from windows. But all these are things which we might well wish to classify with properties correctly so called, like inflammability, or with qualities correctly so called, like prudence, when we contrast these latter with individuals or particulars. For there are individual flakes or drifts or falls of snow, pieces of gold, articles of clothing or furniture, games of chess,[1] members of species; and there are hundreds of Union Jacks. These are all (are they not?) particular instances of the general things named in *their* names. Sometimes the unlikeness of these general things to properties or qualities correctly so called is masked by the introduction of expressions like 'being (a piece of) gold', 'being snow', 'being a man', 'being a Union Jack', 'being a chair', 'being a game of chess' – phrases like these being said to name properties. Now such expressions no doubt have a participial use; and some (e.g. 'being a man') may have a use as noun-phrases, as singular terms. But it is dubious whether many of them have a use as singular terms; and it is dubious whether any of them can be regarded as names of properties. And however we resolve these doubts in different cases, the following dilemma arises in each. Either these verbal nouns (where they are nouns) have the same use as the general names they incorporate – and in that case they may as well be discarded in favour of those general names, which are more familiar, and about the use of which we are consequently less liable to be misled; or they have a different use from those general names – and in this case we still have on our hands, to be differentiated, like properties correctly so called, from particulars, the general things designated by those familiar general names.

II

This initial unclarity about the limits of the two great categories of general and particular shows itself also in that arbitrary narrowing of the field which must be presumed to occur whenever certain answers to our question seem plausible. I shall con-

---

[1] But a game of chess *may* be something which itself has instances.

sider again some of these answers, which were dismissed by Ayer
or Ramsey or both, not so much on the ground that they thought
them false as on the ground that they did not think them fundamental. There is, for example, the suggestion that general, unlike
particular, things cannot be perceived by means of the senses; and
this seems most plausible if one is thinking of the things designated
by certain abstract nouns. It is not with the eyes that one is said to
see hope. But one can quite literally smell blood or bacon, watch
cricket, hear music or thunder; and there are, on the other hand,
certain particulars which it makes dubious sense to say one per-
ceives. Then there is the suggestion that general, unlike particular,
things, can be in several places at once. There can be influenza in
London as well as in Birmingham, and gold in Australia as well as
in Africa. But then so can many particulars be scattered over the
surface of the table or the globe. Moreover, it makes dubious
sense to say of some general things (e.g. solubility) that they are
in any place, let alone in many; and equally dubious sense to say
of some particular things (a sudden thought, a mental image, the
constitution of France) that they have a particular spatial location.
It may be said that I have missed the point of both these theories;
that, first, when we say we perceive general things, what we really
perceive is individual instances of them, not the general things
themselves; and, second, to say that general things can be in
several places at once is to say that they may have different
instances, differently located; whereas it makes no sense to speak
of different instances of individuals. But so to explain these
theories is to give them up. It is to fall back on saying that general
things may have instances, and individual instances of general
things may not. This is, perhaps, an unexceptionable statement of
the general distinction between the two categories, but scarcely
seems to count as an explanation of it.

A third suggestion is that individual things, unlike general
things, have dates or histories. But similar objections apply to
this. We may speak of the history of dress or engineering, the
origins of civilization, the invention of golf, and the evolution of
man. This theory, like the others (when taken at their face value),
may draw a logically interesting distinction; but, like them, does
not draw one that coincides with the categorial line between
particular and general.

A doctrine which might appear more promising, because more

general, than these, is that individuals can function in propositions only as subjects, never as predicates; whereas general things can function as both. But it is not clear what this doctrine amounts to. Suppose, first, it is a grammatical point. Then if it says that the names of individuals never have adjectival or verbal forms, whereas names of general things do, it is false. If it says that individual names never form parts of grammatical predicates, or alternatively, never stand by themselves after the word 'is' in a grammatical predicate, it is equally false. In any case, a grammatical point could scarcely be fundamental, since it is easy to imagine the elimination of those distinctions upon which such points must rely, in favour of the device of merely coupling names of appropriate types, in any order, in a singular sentence. We should not, by so doing, eliminate the category-distinction. For we might imagine changing the language once more, requiring that our names should stand on one side or the other of the phrase 'is an instance of', and then simply distinguishing the individual names as those that could never stand on the right of this phrase.[1] So I think we must conclude that the point misleadingly made in the languages of grammar is simply once more the point that individuals, unlike general things, cannot have instances. To say that general things, unlike individuals, can be predicated of other things, is simply to paraphrase this; and neither expression seems more perspicuous than the other.

III

But will the word 'instance' itself really bear the weight of this distinction? Of course, as a philosopher's word, understood in terms of that distinction, it cannot fail to bear it; but then it ceases to explain the distinction for us. If we ask what expressions we actually use to refer to or describe an individual thing as an instance of a general thing, we find that they are many; and that perhaps none of them is appropriate in every case. They include: 'a case of', 'an example of', 'a specimen of', 'a member of', 'a piece of', 'a quantity of', 'a copy of', 'a performance of', 'a game of', 'an

---

[1] Ramsey seems to suggest that this would simply be to manufacture an empty verbal distinction. (Cf. *Foundations of Mathematics*, pp. 132–3). But it would not. For it would not be an arbitrary matter to decide which names to put on which side of the coupling phrase.

article of', and so on. Though each can be followed by the name of a general thing, many can also be followed by expressions we should hesitate to regard as the names of general things. This is true of the phrase 'an instance of' itself. We may speak of a signal instance of generosity; but we may also speak of a signal instance of Smith's generosity. Similarly we may speak not only of a piece of gold and an article of clothing, but of a piece of Smith's gold and an article of Smith's clothing. So if we seek to draw our distinction in terms of the words actually used to play the part of the philosopher's word 'instance' – including the word 'instance' itself – then it will not be enough to say that general things may have instances. For so may non-general things.

The point here may be put roughly as follows. We are tempted to explain the distinction between two types of things, T_1 and T_2, by means of a certain relation R; by saying, that is, that only things belonging to T_2 can appear as the second term of this relation, whereas both things belonging to T_2 and things belonging to T_1 can appear as its first term. R is something like, but more general than, *is characterized by* or *is a member of* or the converse of *is predicated of*. But then it appears that we really have no notion of R except one which is useless for explanatory purposes since it is itself to be explained in terms of the difference between T_1 and T_2; this is what I called the philosopher's notion of 'an instance of'. What we have instead is a lot of notions which are either too restricted to serve our purpose (e.g. 'has the property of'), or fail to be restricted in precisely the way in which we want them to be, or both. As a member of this set of notions, pre-eminent for its abstract character, we may take the logician's idea of class-membership. The difficulty is, roughly, that we can form closed classes on what principle we please; we could count almost any particular we are likely to mention as such a class, and hence as the second term of our relation. (These remarks are very rough and schematic; but they serve, I hope, to make the point in a general form.) Consequently, we shall have to give up the idea of explaining the difference between the particular and the general in terms of such a relation. This will not lead us, as it perhaps led Ramsey, to despise the philosopher's notion of an instance, and to think that there is nothing in it; for it is easy enough to teach anyone the application of it, without precise explanations. But it will lead us to look further for such explanations.

IV

To begin with, I want to draw a rough distinction between three classes of nouns, all of which would traditionally be regarded either as themselves the names of universals (general things) or – in the case of the nouns of group (2) – as closely linked to such names. The distinctions are indicated only by examples; and the three classes are by no means exhaustive of the field. But this does not matter for my purpose.

(1) Examples of the first class are such partitive nouns as 'gold', 'snow', 'water', 'jam', 'music'. These I shall call *material-names*, and what they name, *materials*.[1]

(2) Examples of the second are certain articulative nouns such as '(a) man', '(an) apple', '(a) cat'. These I shall call *substance-names*, and what they apply to, *substances*.

(3) Examples of the third are such abstract nouns as 'redness' (or 'red'), 'roundness', 'anger', 'wisdom'. These I shall call *quality*- or *property-names*, and what they name, *qualities* or *properties*.[1] These three classes of nouns may be compared and contrasted with one another in a number of ways. But the contrast on which I wish to lay most emphasis is

(i) The contrast between the nouns of group (3) and those of groups (1) and (2). The nouns of group (3) are the most sophisticated and the most dispensable. They are derived from adjectives and the general things they name usually enter our talk by way of the adjectives from which their names are derived. When we consider the things which philosophers are prepared to count as individual instances of these general things, we find a considerable latitude in the categories of the things to which these instances may belong. Thus an instance of wisdom may be a man, a remark, or an action. An instance of the colour red may be a material thing like a pillar-box, an event like a sunset, or a mental thing like an image. A word, a gesture, an expression, a man may all be instances of anger. In contrast, unsystematic ambiguities aside, there is no latitude at all about what category of thing can be an individual instance of a cat or an apple. There is some latitude, but one would often hesitate to call it a category-latitude, about what can be an individual instance of the general things named by the

[1] The terminology, evidently, is not to be taken too seriously. Music is hardly a material. Anger is a state, not a property or quality.

nouns of group (1). An instance of gold may be a vein, a piece, or a quantity of gold; an instance of snow may be a drift, an expanse, a piece, and even a fall, of snow.

(ii) Next I want to emphasize a respect in which the nouns of group (2) differ from those of groups (1) and (3). Philosophers may speak of 'an individual (particular) instance (example, specimen) of ϕ', where 'ϕ' is replaced by a noun from any of these three groups. Suppose the noun is drawn from group (2). Then we have such phrases as 'an instance of a horse' or 'an instance of an apple'. It is to be noticed that what follows the expression 'an instance of' is a phrase which can and does *by itself* function as an indefinite designation of an individual instance. (An instance of a horse is the same as a horse.) This is not the case if the nouns are drawn from groups (1) or (3). (Gold is not the same as a piece of gold.) It seems as if, when we say that x is an instance of y, then when y is such that there is no choice about the sort of thing we can count as an instance of it, we feel no need of a true general-thing name for y, i.e. of a name differing from an indefinite designation of an individual instance of y. (It is true that we have the expressions '*the* horse', '*the* apple', etc., names of species or kinds, obvious collectors of homogeneous individuals; but these follow less naturally after the expression 'an instance of' than does the phrase containing the indefinite article.) Philosophers have felt this difference, and tried to blur it with the invention of such expressions as 'horseness' (cf. 'being a horse'). But it should rather be treated as a clue until proved an anomaly.

(iii) Finally, I want to note the existence of a special class of individual instances of general things whose names belong to group (3). The simplest, though not the only recipe, for forming the names of members of this class is as follows: in the formula 'the . . . of . . .', fill the first gap with the property-name in question and the second gap with the definite designation of a suitable individual. Thus we may speak of *the wisdom of Socrates* as an instance of wisdom; of *the redness of Smith's face* as an instance of redness; and we may also speak of *Jones's present mental state* as an instance of anger. This class of individual instances of properties, or property-like things, will include the 'particular qualities' which Stout defended. And an analogy may be found between referring to a horse as 'an instance of a horse' and referring to Jones's present state of anger as 'an instance of anger'.

V

Next, I want to make some general, and still propaedeutic, remarks about the notion of an individual or particular.

(1) The idea of an individual is the idea of an individual instance *of* something general. There is no such thing as a pure particular. (This truth is too old to need the support of elaboration.)

(2) The idea of an individual instance of ϕ is the idea of something which we are able in principle

(*a*) to distinguish from other instances of ϕ; and
(*b*) to recognize as the same instance at different times (where this notion is applicable).

So, to have the idea of a particular instance of ϕ, we need (in general)

(*a*) criteria of distinctness,
(*b*) criteria of identity

for a particular instance of ϕ. On the need for these criteria the following comments must be made:

(i) It might be supposed that the distinction between the two kinds of criteria is a mistake; that there is no such distinction. For identity and difference are two sides of the same coin. It is possible, however, at least in some cases, to consider separately the criteria by which we distinguish and enumerate objects of the same sort, in a situation in which the question of identifying any one of them as, or distinguishing it from, the one which had such-and-such a history, does not arise or is not considered. It is to criteria of this kind that I give the name 'criteria of distinctness'. They might also be called 'criteria of enumeration'.[1]

(ii) What the criteria of distinctness and identity for instances of ϕ may be is obviously closely connected with what ϕ is; but is not wholly determined by it in every case. That it is not so determined is obvious in the case of properties, qualities, states, etc.; we have already seen how wide a range of categories their

[1] It might be true, if intelligible, that *if* we had so time-indifferent a perspective of things as to see them as four-dimensional objects in space-time, then there would be no point in giving separate consideration to criteria of distinctness. But we do not have such a perspective.

instances may be drawn from (4(i)). It is less obvious, but still true, in the case of general things named by material-names. The *general* question of the criteria of distinctness and identity of individual instances of snow or gold cannot be raised or, if raised, be satisfactorily answered. We have to wait until we know whether we are talking of *veins*, *pieces*, or *quantities* of gold, or of *falls*, *drifts*, or *expanses* of snow. There are cases, however, where this indeterminateness regarding the criteria of identity and distinctness does not seem to exist, where it seems that once ϕ is given, the criteria are given, too. And among these cases are those where 'ϕ' is a substance-name (4(ii)). It should once more be noted that these are the cases where we do not find a true name of a general thing following the phrase 'an instance of', but instead an expression which can by itself function as an indefinite designation of an individual instance (e.g. 'a horse').

(3) When it has been said that a particular must be an instance of something general, and that there must be criteria of distinctness and (where applicable) of identity for individual instances of a general thing, something of central importance still remains unsaid. In giving the relevant criteria – or sets of criteria – for individual instances of a certain general thing, we do not indicate how such particulars are brought into our discourse. Nor do we bring a particular into our discourse by mentioning these criteria. (To mention them is still to talk *in general*.) We bring a particular into our discourse only when we determine, select, *a point of application* for such criteria, only when we mention, refer to, something to which these criteria are to be applied; and no theory of particulars can be adequate which does not take account of the means by which we determine such a point of application *as* a point of application for these criteria.

VI

In the rest of this paper I shall try to do two things. First, I shall try to show how, in the case of *certain kinds* of particulars (particular instances of *certain kinds* of general things), the notion of a particular may be seen as something logically complex in relation to other notions (a kind of compound of these notions). That is, I shall try to produce a partial explanation (analysis) of the notion of an individual instance, for certain cases; and then I shall try to show how this notion, as explained for these cases, may be used in the explanation of the notion of individual instances of *other* sorts of general things, and in the explanation of the notions of those other types of general things themselves. So in this part of the paper (sections VI–IX), no general account is offered of the distinction we are concerned with. The procedure is essentially one of indicating, step by step, how certain types of notion can be seen as depending upon others; and it makes no claim at all to completeness. Second (section XII), this procedure is found to suggest a possible general account of the distinction we are concerned with; though the acceptability or otherwise of this general account seems to be independent of that of the step-by-step schema of explanation.

Now it might seem that the difficulty of finding an explanation of the notion of an individual instance arises from the fact that the category distinction between general and individual is so fundamental that there is nothing logically simpler, or more fundamental, in terms of which this notion could be explained. But I think this view can be challenged for a certain range of important cases, which can then perhaps serve as the basis for the explanation of others. To challenge it successfully, we have to envisage the possibility of making statements which (*a*) do not make use of the notion of individual instances, and (*b*) do not presuppose the existence of statements which do make use of this notion. The second condition may be held to rule out general statements; for though many general statements make no direct mention of individuals, they have often and plausibly been held in some sense to presuppose the existence of statements which do. So what we have to consider is the possibility of singular statements which make no mention of (i.e. contain no names for, or other expressions definitely or indefinitely referring to) individual instances of general things. Now there certainly does exist, in ordinary use, a range of empirical singular statements answering to this description. I suggest, as examples, the following:

> It is (has been) raining
> Music can be heard in the distance
> Snow is falling
> There is gold here
> There is water here.

All these sentences contain either the material-name of a general thing ('music', 'snow') or a corresponding verb; but none contains any expression which can be construed as serving to make a definite or indefinite mention of individual instances of those general things (i.e. falls or drops of rain, pieces of gold, pools of water, and so on). Of course, when these sentences are used, the combination of the circumstances of their use with the tense of the verb and the demonstrative adverbs, if any, which they contain, provides an indication of the incidence of the general thing in question. Such an indication must be provided somehow, if empirical singular statements are to be made at all. But it is important that it can be provided by means of utterance-centred indications which do not include noun-expressions referring definitely or indefinitely to individual instances. *Such sentences as these do not bring particulars into our discourse.*

Languages imagined on the model of such sentences are sometimes called 'property-location' languages. But I think the word 'property' is objectionable here because (*a*) the general things which figure in my examples are not properties, and (*b*) the idea of a property belongs, with the idea of an individual instance itself, to a level of logical complexity we are trying to get below. So I propose to substitute the less philosophically committed word 'feature'; and to speak of feature-placing sentences.

Though feature-placing sentences do not introduce particulars into our discourse, they provide the materials for this introduction. Suppose we compare a feature-placing *sentence* ('There is snow here') with a *phrase* ('This (patch of) snow') in the use of which an individual instance of the feature is mentioned. It seems possible, in this case, to regard the notion of the individual instance as something logically complex in relation to the two simpler notions of the feature and of placing. The logical complexity may be brought out in the following way. In making the feature-placing statement, we utter a completed sentence without mentioning individuals. If we *merely* mention the individual without going on to say anything about it, we fail to utter a completed sentence; yet what the feature-placing sentence does explicitly is, in a sense, implicit in this mere mention. So, as the basic step in an explanatory schema, we may regard the notion of a particular instance of *certain sorts* of general things as a kind of logical compound of the simpler notions of a feature and of placing.

But what about the criteria of distinctness and identity which were said in general to be necessary to the notion of an individual instance of a general thing? The *basis* for the criteria of distinctness can already be introduced at the feature-placing level, without yet introducing particulars. For where we can say 'There is snow here' or 'There is gold here', we can also, perhaps, more exactly, though not more correctly, say 'There is snow (gold) *here* – and *here* – and *here*'. And when we can say 'It snowed today', we can also, perhaps, more exactly, but not more correctly, say 'It snowed twice today'. The considerations which determine multiplicity of placing become, when we introduce particulars, the criteria for distinguishing this *patch of* snow from that, or the first *fall of* snow from the second. Of criteria of identity I shall say more in general later.

It might be objected that it is absurd to speak of an imagined transition from feature-placing sentences to substantival expressions definitely designating particular instances of features as the *introduction* of particulars; that it is absurd to represent this imagined transition as part of a possible analysis of the notion of a particular instance, even for these simple cases of material-names which seem the most favourable; and that at most what is achieved is the indication of a possible way of looking at certain *designations* of certain particulars. For are not the particulars as much a relevant part of the situation in which a feature-placing sentence is employed as they are of a situation in which a substantival particular-designation is employed? To this I would reply by asking what philosophical question there would be about particulars if we did not designate them, could not make lists of them, did not predicate qualities of them, and so on. What we have to explain is a certain mode of speech.

VII

When we turn from material-names to substance-names, the attempt to provide an analogous explanation of the notion of an individual instance seems much harder. But though it is harder, it is perhaps worth making; for if it succeeds, we may find we have then an adequate basis for the explanation of the notion of an individual instance in other cases, and for the explanation of further kinds of general things. In order for the attempt to succeed, we must be able to envisage a situation in which, instead of operating with the notion of an individual instance of a cat or an apple, we operate with the notions of a corresponding feature and of placing. Ordinary language does not seem to provide us, in these cases, with feature-placing sentences. And it might be argued that the idea of such sentences was, in these cases, absurd. For (1) it might be pointed out that an all-important difference between such things as snow and such things as cats lay in the fact that different instances of snow are, in a sense, indefinitely additive, can be counted together as one instance of snow; while this is not true in the case of instances of cats; and it might be suggested that herein lay a reason for the possibility of feature-placing sentences in the case of snow and for their impossibility in the case of cats. And (2) it might be added that we have no name for a general thing which could count as the required feature in the case of cats. It is true that we speak of *the cat* in general; but 'the cat' ranks as a species-name, and the notion of a species as surely presupposes the notion of individual members as the notion of a property involves that of individual things to which the property belongs or might belong. It is also true that we may speak of an instance (specimen) of *a* cat, as we may speak of an instance of gold; but here what follows the phrase 'an instance of' is not, as 'gold' is, a general-thing name which could figure in a merely feature-placing sentence, but an expression which also serves as an indefinite designation of an individual. Does not all this strongly suggest that there *could* be no concept of the 'cat-feature' such as would be required for the analysis to work, that any general idea of cat must be the idea of *a* cat, i.e. must involve criteria of identity and distinctness for cats as individuals and hence the notion of an individual instance?

These objections have great force and importance; but I do not think them decisive. For they do not show that it is logically absurd to suppose that we might recognize the presence of cat or signs of the past or future presence of cat, without ever having occasion to distinguish one cat from another as the cat on the left, or identify a cat as ours or as Felix.[1] The second argument merely reminds us that the resources of our language are such that on any actual occasion of this kind we in fact use, not a partitive noun,

[1] Cf. Price, *Thinking and Experience*, pp. 40-1, on identity of individuals and of characteristics.

but the indefinite forms ('cats' or 'a cat') of the articulative noun. But this fact can be explained in a way consistent with the advocated analysis (see section X). Nevertheless, these arguments show something. The point about the species-name, for example, is sound; the notion of a species, like that of a property, belongs to a level of logical complexity we are trying to get below. Second, and more immediately important, the first argument shows that if there is to be a general concept of the cat-feature, corresponding in the required way to the notion of an individual instance, it must already include in itself the *basis* for the criteria of *distinctness* which we apply to individual cats. (Roughly, the idea of cat, unlike that of snow, would include the idea of a characteristic shape.) But to concede this is not to concede the impossibility of the analysis. It is worth adding that sometimes we do find verbal indications of our use of feature-concepts such as those we are trying to envisage; as, for example, when we speak of 'smelling cat' or 'hunting lion', using the noun in the singular without the article.

There might seem to exist a more general objection to this whole procedure. For it seems that it would always be possible in practice to paraphrase a given feature-placing sentence in use, by means of a sentence incorporating *indefinite* designations of particular instances; e.g. 'There is gold here' by 'There is *a quantity of* gold here'; 'Snow has fallen twice' by 'There have been *two falls of* snow'; 'There is snow here – and here' by 'There are *patches (expanses) of* snow here and here'; and so on. And if sentences incorporating definite *or* indefinite designations of particular instances bring particulars into our discourse; and if statements made by the use of feature-placing sentences are *equivalent* to statements made by the use of sentences incorporating indefinite designations of particular instances; then do not feature-placing sentences themselves bring particulars into our discourse? But this argument can be turned in favour of the explanation it is directed against. Suppose there is a statement S made by means of a feature-placing sentence; and an equivalent statement S' made by means of a sentence incorporating an indefinite particular-designation; and a statement T made by means of a sentence incorporating a definite designation of the particular indefinitely designated in S'. *Now only if a language admits of statements like T can it admit of statements correctly described as I have described S'.* (There are no *indefinite*

D

designations of particulars where there are no *definite* designations of particulars.) But a language might admit of statements like S without admitting of statements like T. So the existence of statements like S′, in a language which admits of both statements like S and statements like T, is not destructive of the analysis, but is a proof of its correctness.

VIII

If the argument so far is acceptable, then at least in the case of some materials and some substances, we can regard the notion of an individual instance as partially explained in terms of the logical composition of the two notions of a feature and of placing. When we turn to properties and qualities, we may make use of a different kind of explanation which is also, in a sense, the completion of the first kind. I shall not, that is to say, try to explain the notion of individual instances of anger or wisdom or red in terms of the logical composition of a feature, such as *anger* or *red*, and placing. But nor shall I maintain that it would be wrong or impossible to do so. We *might* think of such general things as anger (or red) *not* primarily as qualities, properties, states, or conditions of persons or things, but primarily as instantiated in, say, situations (or patches) which acquired their status as individuals from just such a logical composition. But though this is how we might think, it is not, for the most part, how we do think. It is natural, rather, to regard those general things which are properly called qualities, conditions, etc., as belonging at least to the same level of logical complexity as the idea of individual instances of the kinds we have so far been concerned with; to regard them, that is, as feature-*like* things, the incidence of which, however, is primarily indicated, not by placing, but by their *ascription* to individual instances of material or substantial features the incidence of which *is* primarily indicated by placing.[1] We have seen that the notion of an individual instance of some materials and substances can be regarded as a logical compound of the notions of a feature and of placing. We have now to see the ascription of a quality (etc.) to such an individual as an operation *analogous* to the placing of a feature. Indeed, we may find in the possibility of this operation the

[1] These remarks, of course, apply only to some of the things correctly called properties, states, qualities, etc.

point – or one important point – of that logical composition which yields us the particular. The individual instance of the simply placeable feature emerges as a possible location-point for general things other than the feature of which it is primarily an instance, and hence as also an individual instance of *these* general things, its properties or qualities or states. One might exaggeratedly say: the *point* of having the idea of individual instances of material or substantial features is that they may be represented as individual instances of property-like features. The individuals are distinguished as individuals in order to be contrasted and compared.

Other notions call for other treatment. I consider two more.

(*a*) I mentioned, at IV (iii), a rather special class of individual instances of properties or property-like things. We form the notion of such an instance when, for example, we speak not of a man or an action as an instance of wisdom or anger, but of the wisdom of Socrates as an individual (a case of wisdom) or of Jones's present mental state as an individual instance of anger. Here the notion of the individual instance can be seen as a new kind of logical compound, viz. a compound which includes as elements both the notion of the general thing (property) in question and that of the material or substantial individual which is an instance of it; it may sometimes include a further element of temporal placing (cf. 'his *present* state of anger').

(*b*) Instances of events, processes, and changes I have so far scarcely mentioned. Most of our most familiar words for happenings strike us essentially as names for the actions and undergoings of individual instances of material or substantial features. But there is a difference between these happening words and quality or state-words. A wise man is an instance of wisdom, but a dead or dying man is not an instance of death. Only a death is that. As regards such happening-words as these, then, we have to see the idea of an individual instance as reached by a kind of logical composition analogous to that considered in the paragraph immediately above: an individual instance of a material or substantial feature is an element in the compound. But these, though perhaps the most important, are not the only kinds of happening-words.

IX

The general form of these explanations may be roughly indicated as follows. The notion of placing a feature is taken as basic, as consisting of the logically simplest elements with which we are to operate. It is pointed out that neither of these elements involves the notion of an individual instance, nor therefore the notions of certain types of general things, such as properties and species; and it is shown that the idea of operating solely with these simplest elements can be made intelligible for certain cases. (Features in fact of course belong to the class of general things; but so long as we remain at the feature-placing level, they cannot be assigned to it; for there is nothing to contrast the general with.) From this basis we proceed by composition and analogy. The designations of individual instances of (some) material and substantial features are first introduced, as expressions, not themselves complete sentences, which include placing-indications; and, complementarily, certain types of general things (e.g. properties and types of happening) are introduced as items the designations of which do not include placing-indications and which are ascribed to material or substantial individuals. The ascription of such a thing as a property to a substantial individual is represented simply as an operation analogous to the placing of a feature; so no circularity attends the word 'ascription'. Individuals of certain other types (e.g. events happening to substances, states of substances, and 'particularized' qualities) are then introduced as the designata of expressions which include the designations of individuals of earlier types, and hence indirectly include the notion of placing.

There are many types of individual and of general thing besides these here considered. Some may admit of analogous treatment; and it might be possible to introduce others, on the basis already provided, by other methods of construction and explanation. But every introduction of a particular, in terms of such a schema, will either directly contain the notion of placing or will preserve, by way of individuals already introduced, the original link with this notion. Of course the value of this suggestion, as it stands, is small. For the notion of an individual instance extends itself indefinitely, by way of far more complicated connections than I have so far indicated; and the limits of plausibility for the kinds of construction-procedure I have used would, no doubt, soon be reached, if they are not already overpassed. Nevertheless, I think this sketch of a procedure has certain merits:

(1) Some of the difficulties which attend any attempt to elucidate the category-distinction between the particular and the general arise from the fact that these two classes include so many different category-distinctions within themselves. This fact creates a dilemma for the theorist of the distinction. On the one hand, he is tempted, in a way illustrated at the beginning of this paper, into drawing distinctions which indeed separate one or more sub-categories of one class from one or more sub-categories of the other, but which fail to yield the desired result if applied over the whole field. Or, on the other hand, in the effort to escape from this domination by irrelevant category differences, he is tempted by the prospect of a purely formal distinction, drawing for this purpose on the terms and concepts of grammar or of formal logic. But distinctions so drawn can only seem to succeed by forfeiting their formal character and silently incorporating the problematic category-distinction. The present procedure offers at least a hope of escape from this difficulty. For it fully allows for the differences between types of general thing and of individual; and instead of producing one single explanation, the same for every case, it offers a serial method of explaining later types of general or particular things on the basis of earlier ones, while preserving a continuous general differentiation between the two major categories in the course of the explanation. Too much must not be claimed for the suggested procedure, however; in particular, it must not be thought that it has been so described as to provide a *criterion* for the distinction we are concerned with.

(2) Another characteristic of the schema of explanation is that it accords a central place to the notion of an individual instance of certain kinds of general things, viz. of material and substantial features. This (see section VIII) is not an essential characteristic; it could be modified. But there is reason to think that it corresponds to our actual way of thinking; that these individuals *are* the 'basic particulars'. Why this should be so, and whether it might not be otherwise, are questions which I shall not now consider.

(3) Finally, while not itself providing a criterion of general and particular, the schema points the way to a possible general distinction which might be defensible even if the procedure which

suggests it should prove unsatisfactory. This general distinction I shall outline in section XII. Before I do so, some further points remain to be considered.

X

Something further must first be said on the subject of criteria of identity for individual instances of a general thing. We saw (V (2)) how in many cases the question of the criteria of distinctness and identity of an individual instance of a general thing was incompletely determined when the general thing was named. This was particularly evident in the case of some properties and was evident also in the case of materials. Where substance-names were concerned, however, this indeterminateness seemed not to exist; when the name was given, the criteria were fixed. And this was connected with the fact that in these cases there seemed to exist no true general-thing name, apart from expressions which ranked as species-names and obviously presupposed certain definite criteria of identity for individual members. As far as criteria of distinctness are concerned, this raises no particular difficulty. We saw, for example, how the idea of a simply placeable feature might include – might indeed *be* – the idea of a characteristic shape, and in this way provide a basis for criteria of distinctness for individual instances of the feature. But it is not so easy to account for the apparent determinateness of criteria of identity. The explanatory schema advanced required that we should theoretically be able to form concepts of some substance-features which were logically prior to, and independent of, the corresponding concepts of an individual instance of such features; and this requirement seems to clash with the apparent determinateness of the criteria of identity for such individuals. A parallel answer to that given in the case of criteria of distinctness is theoretically available, but is unattractively unplausible. If we reject this answer, and cannot find an alternative, then we must at least radically revise, though in a not unfamiliar direction, the basis of the explanatory schema. (The difficulty is essentially a more specific form of that encountered already in section VII.)

I think, however, that an acceptable alternative can be found. For in all cases where a feature-concept can be assumed to be possible, the criteria of identity (and of distinctness) for an instance of the general thing in question – or the sets of such criteria, where there is more than one set – can be seen as determined by a *combination* of factors, viz. the nature of the feature itself, the ways in which the feature empirically manifests itself in the world, and – to adopt a possibly misleading mode of expression – the kind of incentives[1] that exist for having a notion of an individual instance of the feature in question. The relevance of this third factor even, perhaps, gives us the right to say that there is something arbitrary about the criteria we adopt, something which, given the other two factors, is – in at any rate a stretched sense – a matter of choice. In extreme cases this is obvious. Even those who had witnessed the whole of the affair under discussion might, for example, give varying answers to such a question as: Is this the same quarrel going on now as was going on when I left? The answer we choose may depend on just what distinctions we are interested in; and one can imagine many situations for this example, and many different things which might influence us. There may, on the other hand, be very many cases of features where the adoption of a certain particular set of criteria of identity (and distinctness) for their instances is so utterly natural that it would seem to be stretching the phrase 'matter of choice' intolerably to apply it to them. But, even in these cases, the naturalness may still be seen as depending on the combination of factors I mentioned; and, if we bear this in mind, we can sometimes imagine the possibility of alternatives. (Here is a question which might with advantage be explored for many different types of case.)

It seems reasonable to view substantial features as cases of this kind. If this view is acceptable, we can find in it an explanation of that difference between substance-names and certain other true general-thing names to which I have several times referred. Given a true general-thing name, like 'gold' or 'wisdom', the question of the criteria of identity of its instances cannot be answered until the kind of instance is specified, by such a phrase as 'a *piece* of gold' or 'a wise *action*'. But where one set of criteria of identity is peculiarly dominant, its adoption peculiarly compelling, we find

---

[1] What I mean by 'incentives' here may be illustrated from the convenience of the institution of property. Suppose there is a general feature, ϕ, which human beings wish to make use of. Even if there is enough ϕ for all, friction may be avoided if criteria are used for distinguishing my ϕ from yours. ('Mine' is indeed one of the earliest individuating words used by children.)

no such non-committal general name in current, adult, unsophisticated use. All that we might wish to do with it, we can equally
well do without it, by the use of the indefinite singular or plural
forms of the ordinary substance-name (e.g. 'a horse' or 'horses').

XI

It is, perhaps, necessary to guard briefly against a misunderstanding. Of course, I am not denying that we can very well use
individual-designations as such without being, or ever having
been, in a position to make a relevant placing of some feature
which, in terms of the explanatory schema I have defended, is
immediately or ultimately relevant to the explanation of the type
of instance concerned. To deny this would be absurd. It would be
to deny, for example, that when we talk about remoter historical
characters, we are really talking about individuals. But the view
I am defending does not require such a denial. For this view seeks
merely to explain the notion of an individual instance of a general
thing in terms, ultimately, of feature-placing. It does not at all
imply that we cannot make use of this notion in situations other
than those in terms of which it is explained. In fact, of course, the
expansiveness of our talk about individuals is in marked contrast
with the restrictedness of our contacts with them. Both the possibility of, and the incentives to, this expansiveness have an empirical ground; in the variousness of individuals, the non-
repetitiveness of situations. But this fact may nevertheless mislead
us, may make the theoretical problem of individuation look more
difficult than it is by distracting our attention from an essential
element in the notion of an individual instance. The problem
would scarcely seem difficult for the case of an imagined universe
in which all that happened was the repetition of a single note,
varying, perhaps, in volume. Individual instances could then be
described only as, say, 'the third before now' or 'the next one to
come'. But in such a universe the incentives to forming the notion
of an individual instance would be small. We might say that, in
general, what is essential to the notion of an individual instance is
not what is interesting about individuals.

XII

To conclude. I remarked earlier that the explanatory schema I have
sketched points the way to a possible general distinction between

the two major categories we are concerned with. To recall, first, some vague, figurative and unsatisfactory terms I have already used: the schema suggests that the notion of a particular individual always includes, directly or indirectly, that of placing, whereas the notion of a general thing does not. Now placing is characteristically effected by the use of expressions the *reference* of which is in part determined by the context of their use and not by their *meaning*, if any, alone. And this suggests the possibility of formulating a general distinction in a more satisfactory way. We may say: *it is a necessary condition for a thing's being a general thing that it can be referred to by a singular substantival expression, a unique reference for which is determined solely by the meaning of the words making up that expression; and it is a necessary condition of a thing's being a particular thing that it cannot be referred to by a singular substantival expression, a unique reference for which is determined solely by the meaning of the words making up that expression.* This specification of mutually exclusive necessary conditions could be made to yield definitions by stipulating that the conditions were not only necessary, but also sufficient. But there is point in refraining from doing so. For as we consider substantival expressions increasingly remote from the simplest cases, there may be increasing reluctance to apply the distinction at all. Nor is this reluctance quite irrational; for the simplest cases are those which form the basis of the general distinction. (Hence, roughly, the association of particularity with concreteness.) We may admit that the traditional distinction was vague as well as unclear, and respect its well-founded vagueness in this way.

To elucidate this quasi-definition of particular and general, I add some miscellaneous comments of varying degrees of importance.

(1) It might be objected to the conditions given that expressions like 'The third tallest man who ever lived or lives or will live' answer to the specifications for a general-thing designation. If they did, it would perhaps not be difficult to legislate them out, by suitable amendments of those specifications. But in fact they do not. For their meaning does not suffice to determine for them a unique object of reference. It is, if true, contingently true that there is a single thing answering to such a description. This case, however, does raise a problem about how the words 'expression a unique reference for which is determined solely by the meaning'

are to be construed. If we construe them as 'expression the *existence* of just one object of reference for which is *guaranteed* by the meaning', we may find ourselves in (possibly circumventable) trouble over, for example, 'phlogiston' and 'the unicorn'. Yet this is the construction at first suggested by the present case. It will be better, therefore, to construe them as follows: 'expression the (or a) meaning of which is such that it is both logically impossible for it to refer to more than one thing (in that meaning)[1] and logically impossible for the expression to fail to have reference because of the existence of competing candidates for the title'. And the sense of 'competing candidates' can be explained as follows: x, y, and z are competing candidates (and the only competing candidates) for the title Dif, if any two of them had not existed, D would apply to the third.

(2) It may seem, perhaps, a more troublesome fact that the names we commonly employ for certain *types*, like Beethoven's Fifth Symphony, do not answer to the specifications given for a general-thing designation, although we may be more than half inclined to count such types as general things; for these names include, as a part of themselves or of their explanation, proper names like 'Beethoven'. We have, however, an easy remedy here. We can regard the pattern of sounds in question as a general thing for which there might (perhaps does) exist a general description the meaning of which uniquely determines its reference; and then it will appear as the contingent truth it is that Beethoven stands to the general thing so designated in a certain special relation. This does not commit us to saying that it is a contingent truth tha Beethoven's Fifth Symphony was composed by Beethoven; but the necessity here is simply a consequence of the fact that we ordinarily and naturally refer to the general thing in question by means of an expression which incorporates a reference to a particular individual who stands in a special relation to it. Analogous considerations apply to many other types. Of course, the alternative is always open to us of declining to apply the criterion in such cases.

(3) It is clear that numbers, if we apply our criterion to them,

[1] This qualification allows for the possible case where there is no convenient unambiguous designation of the general thing in question; but is not strictly necessary since an unambiguous designation could always be framed.

will emerge as general things. But this is a result which will disturb few, and will certainly disturb no one who continues to feel the charm of the class-of-classes analysis.

(4) If we choose to apply the test to facts, we get the not wholly unappealing result that, for example, the facts that $2 + 2 = 4$, that all crows are black and that crows exist (in one use of 'exist') are general things, while the facts that Brutus killed Caesar and that all the people in this room are philosophers are particular things. For propositions, of course, the result is similar. The distinction will correspond roughly to the old distinction between those propositions (or facts) which are 'truly universal' and those which are not. In the case of facts and propositions, however, we may well feel a *very* strong reluctance to classify in this way at all; and, if we do, there is no reason why we should struggle to overcome it.[1]

Some points of more general significance remain.

(5) As historical evidence for the general correctness of this doctrine, we may note that Russell who, for so large a part of his philosophical life, showed an anxiety to equate meaning and reference in the case of *names*, finally inclined to the conclusion that the only true names are those of universals.[2] We do not, of course, need to adopt his idiosyncratic use of the word 'name', in acknowledging the correctness of his implied view of universals.

(6) It will be clear that the quasi-definition I am suggesting has points of contact with some of those more familiar ways of marking the distinction which turn out to be more or less unsatisfactory. For instance, it will not do to say that general things do not have spatio-temporal positions and limits, whereas particular things do. Some general things, those of appropriate categories, like gold, do have spatial distribution; and some may have temporal limits. It is rather that when we refer to general things, we abstract from their actual distribution and limits, if they have any, as we cannot do when we refer to particulars. Hence, with general things, meaning suffices to determine reference. And with

[1] What I have said here of facts and propositions must not lead us to suppose that we should obtain a similar result for *sentences*. These, and expression-*types* generally, will emerge as general things (e.g. in virtue of the conventions for the use of inverted commas, the expression 'the word "and" ' may be said to determine, by meaning alone, a unique object of reference).

[2] See *Enquiry into Meaning and Truth* and *Human Knowledge: Its Scope and Limits*.

this is connected the tendency, on the whole dominant, to ascribe superior reality to particular things. Meaning is not enough, in their case, to determine the reference of their designations; the extra, contextual element is essential. They are, in a quite precise sense, less abstract; and we are, on the whole, so constituted as to count the less abstract as the more real.

(7) Finally, we may, if we choose, revert to the original philosophical way of marking the distinction in terms of the concept of an instance, and give it a sense in terms of the final definition. Instantiability, in the philosopher's sense, ends precisely at the point at which contextual dependence of referring expressions begins, or where referring expressions, as being proper names of individuals, have meaning only in a sense in which it is altogether divorced from reference. So general things may have instances, while particular things may not.

3. Singular Terms and Predication

The ideas of *singular term* and of *general term in predicative position* play a central part in Quine's theory of canonical notation. I examine two attempts to explain these ideas, and I argue that they rest upon certain other notions whose role as foundations is not clearly acknowledged in Quine's explanations.

I

In his new book[1] Quine distinguishes once more between singular terms and general terms. He also speaks of different 'positions' which terms may occupy in sentences, notably of referential and of predicative position. 'Referential', or 'purely referential', position is more narrowly understood by Quine than 'position for a singular term'; and if, later on in what follows, I appear to ignore this fact, my reasons are: (1) that I may do so without risk of confusion since I shall not be concerned with, or introduce, any of those referentially opaque contexts which yield positions for singular terms other than purely referential positions; and (2) that 'referential position' is a more convenient expression than 'position for a singular term'.

The relations between these notions of terms and positions are not altogether simple; but fortunately it appears from Quine's exposition that there is one quite fundamental distinction a grasp of which will serve as the basis for everything else. This is the distinction between a *singular term* on the one hand and a *general term in predicative position* on the other. A union of the two is necessary and sufficient for a fundamental kind, though not perhaps the most primitive kind, of sentence of ordinary language; and in canonical notation, where the only singular terms are variables, a union of the two is necessary and sufficient to yield

---

[1] *Word and Object*, published by the Technology Press of the Massachusetts Institute of Technology, Cambridge, Mass., 1960. Page references are given in parentheses. Italics are mine, except where otherwise indicated.

an atomic open sentence such as all true or false sentences are
obtained from by quantification and other devices of sentence
composition.

The fundamental distinction can, in fact, be yet more narrowly
specified. Quine distinguishes between definite and indefinite
singular terms. (Examples of definite singular terms are 'Leo',
'that lion', 'the lion', and, sometimes, 'he' and 'it'; examples of
indefinite singular terms are 'everything', 'something', 'every
lion', 'some lion', and, sometimes, 'a lion'.)[1] This is not merely a
distinction of kind, of species within a genus. It is more like a
distinction of senses of the phrase 'singular term'. Definite singular terms are singular terms in the primary sense; indefinite
singular terms are singular only in a secondary or derivative sense.
Part of the evidence for this comes from Quine's own incidental
remarks in which, for example, he contrasts indefinite singular
terms, as being *'dummy* singular terms', with *'ordinary* or definite
ones' (pp. 112–14). But more decisive than these passing remarks is
the character of Quine's explanations. The explanation of the
fundamental distinction in role between *singular term* and *general
term in predicative position* is an explanation which has to be understood as applying only to *definite* singular terms. The *position* which
definite singular terms occupy, when they play a certain characteristic role in predication, may also be occupied by other terms
which do not play this characteristic role, but are allowed the *title*
of singular terms just because they can occupy this position; and
these are the dummy or indefinite singular terms.

The basic distinction we have to consider, then, is between
definite singular terms on the one hand and *general terms in predicative
position* on the other. Before we look at Quine's explanation of it
let us note a negative remark he makes about the distinction between singular and general terms at large. He points out that this
distinction does not consist in each singular term's having application to just one object while each general term has application to

[1] Only sometimes 'he' and 'it', for these may function like bound variables
of quantification and then are to be distinguished from *definite* singular terms;
only sometimes 'a lion', for nouns preceded by an indefinite article often
appear in purely predicative position and then are not singular terms at all.
Indeed, these qualifications are still insufficient; for not only 'he' and 'it', but
'the lion' and 'that lion', too, may function like bound variables of quantification, as in such a sentence as 'If you tweak a lion's tail, the (that) lion will
resent it'.

more than one. That the difference does not consist in this is, he says, evident from the fact that some singular terms such as 'Pegasus', may apply to nothing at all, while some general terms such as 'natural satellite of the earth' may each apply to just one thing. There is another reason, which Quine does not mention, for rejecting this account of the difference. 'The captain is angry' is a sentence containing the singular term 'the captain' and the general term 'angry' in predicative position. If we consider at large the two terms 'the captain' and 'angry', it is obvious that both of them *have application* to, may be correctly applied to, *many* things; and may be so applied by the use, among others, of this very sentence. If, on the other hand, we think of this sentence as used to make a particular assertion on a particular occasion, it is evident that *both* the singular and the general term, on that particular occasion, are equally *being applied* to *just one* (and the same) thing. Neither way of taking the expressions brings out a difference which we can express in terms of the difference between applying (or being applied) to just one thing and applying (or being applied) to more than one thing.

Quine mentions another way, which he also thinks unsatisfactory, of trying to bring out the difference between definite singular terms and general terms in predicative position. One adopts this way in saying that the singular term *purports* to refer to just one object while the general term does not: even if the general term, like 'natural satellite of the earth' in fact has singularity of reference, this singularity of reference is not something *purported* in the term. Of this way of explaining the difference Quine says: 'Such talk of purport is only a picturesque way of alluding to the distinctive grammatical roles that singular and general terms play in sentences. It is by grammatical role that singular and general terms are properly to be distinguished' (p. 96). Elsewhere, discussing the notion of referential position (i.e. the position occupied by a definite singular term when it plays its characteristic, distinctive role in predication), he speaks of the 'intuitive' idea behind this notion as the idea that the term occupying this position 'is used purely to specify its object for the rest of the sentence to say something about' (p. 177). Quine is right in thinking that these descriptions which he calls 'picturesque' or 'intuitive' are unsatisfactory. They are unsatisfactory not because they are intuitive or picturesque, but because they are inaccurate or unclear or both.

Nevertheless we shall see that they may be inaccurate and unclear attempts to express an idea which is essential to full understanding of Quine's own explanation of the 'distinctive roles' of general and singular terms and yet is an idea to which he himself scarcely succeeds in giving a clear expression.

I turn now to Quine's explanation. It runs: 'The basic combination in which general and singular terms find their contrasting roles is that of *predication*.[1] . . . Predication joins a general term and a singular term to form a sentence that is true or false according as the general term is true or false of the object, if any, to which the singular term refers' (p. 96). This is supposed to be a description of a contrast of grammatical *roles*; the dichotomy of terms that Quine is concerned with is supposed to be 'clarified' by this description of roles (p. 97). Distinctions of grammatical *form* are associated with this contrast of roles: e.g. grammar requires that the predicative role be signalized by the form of the verb; if the general term does not already possess this form, it must, to be fitted for predicative position, be prefixed with the copula 'is' or 'is a (n)' (pp. 96–7). But it is the distinction of role thus signalized, and not the form of signalling, that is important for logical theory.

But what is this distinction? The passage I quoted seems to envisage a situation in which there is, on the one hand, a sentence formed by joining two terms and in which there may or may not be, on the other hand, an object to which both terms are correctly applied. The difference in role of the two terms might be held to be shown by the implied differences between the ways in which there might fail to be such an object. Thus the failure might, so to speak, be justly laid at the door of the general term; but only if (1) there indeed was a certain object to which the singular term was correctly applied, and (2) the general term failed to apply to *that* object, i.e. *the* object to which the singular term was correctly applied. It is implied that in this case of failure the sentence (statement) is false. Or again the failure might be justly laid at the door of the singular term; but this would be quite a different kind of failure. It would not be a failure of the singular term to apply to *the object which* . . . – where this 'which' clause could be filled out by mentioning the general term. The failure of application of the singular term would not, like that of its partner, depend on its

[1] Quine's italics.

partner's success. It would be a quite independent failure. And it appears to be here implied, and it is elsewhere stated, that the result of this failure would be not that the sentence was to be assessed as false, but that it was not to be assessed for truth-value at all. Whether the sentence is true or false depends on the success or failure of the general term; but the failure of the singular term appears to deprive the general term of the chance of either success or failure.

If this is a correct reading of Quine's sentence, then it is clear that the description he gives of the crucial distinction is designed to fit at most (on the side of singular terms) only *definite* singular terms; for it contains no attempt to mention any contrast there may be *in role or function* between indefinite singular terms and general terms in predicative position. Quine's complementary account of such a sentence as '*A comet* was *observed by astronomers tonight*', containing one indefinite singular term and one composite general term in predicative position, would be that it is true if there is an object, any object, to which both terms apply; otherwise false. In respect of *role* the two terms are not distinguished at all. If we ask why one of the two terms is nevertheless to be called a singular term and the other not, we may indeed appeal to grammar; but it will now be an appeal to what Quine contrasts with grammatical *role*, viz. to grammatical *form*. The term 'a comet' is formally like a (definite) singular term in that it is a substantive occupying the position of grammatical subject to the predicative copula (a special case of the verb of predication in general). It is formally unlike a general term in predicative position in that it has no predicative copula prefixed to it and does not itself possess the form of a verb. In no other way mentioned by Quine does it differ from the general term. As for 'everything' and 'something', the description leaves us to presume that they are entitled to classification as singular terms in so far as they too may occupy this position, may share these formal characteristics.

If my reading of Quine's sentence is correct, there is a much more important point to be made. It is that the distinction drawn remains inadequately explained. The explanation raises, rather than answers, questions. 'Predication joins a general term and a singular term to form a sentence . . .' – a sentence in which the two kinds of term exhibit the obscure differences I have set out. But what is it that *accounts* for these differences? Unless we can

E

answer this question, we shall certainly not fully understand the distinction; indeed we shall scarcely know what predication is. We cannot give up the question and be content with talk of verbs and substantives, of grammatical subjects and predicates. Quine is no more one of Ramsey's schoolchildren doing English grammar than Ramsey himself was. But neither can we be satisfied with the distinction as I have interpreted it. Singular terms are what yield truth-value gaps when they fail in their role. General terms are what yield truth or falsity, when singular terms succeed in their role, by themselves applying, or failing to apply, to what the singular terms apply to. This is more or less what we have. It scarcely seems enough. We want to ask 'Why?'

It might be objected at this point that my interpretation of Quine's sentence was perverse, that the cumbrousness and obscurity of the reading were quite unnecessary. In Quine's sentence there occur the two contrasting expressions, 'is true of', associated with the general term, and 'refers to', associated with the singular term; and this contrast I have deliberately ignored, contenting myself with the single expression 'applies to'. May not this difference of expression, which I ignored, be intended to reflect a difference in the ways in which singular and general terms respectively apply or are applied to objects? And may not the explanation we are still seeking be found in this difference of mode of application?

This seems a reasonable suggestion. But there are several reasons why we cannot be content simply to *repeat* these expressions, to say 'In the successful predication, the singular term *refers* to its object, while the general term is *true of* it'. For one thing, Quine himself does not adhere consistently to this usage. On p. 95 he writes: ' "Pegasus" counts as a singular term though *true of* nothing'; and on pp. 108–9 he repeatedly uses the idioms of *being true of* and *referring (having reference) to* interchangeably in connection with general terms. This point is not very important. Even if Quine had been perfectly consistent in his usage, it would still be the case that the difference in force between the expressions 'is true of' and 'refers to' calls as loudly for explanation as the expressions 'general term' and 'singular term' themselves. Neither pair, unaided, serves to explain the other. This is why I ignored the difference of expression and used instead the undifferentiated idiom of *application*. The deliberate non-differentiation of expression diminishes the risk of our seeming to understand a distinction when we do not.

This is the point at which we have to return to ideas of the kind that Quine dismissed as vague and picturesque. Let us consider those predications in which singular and general term alike may fairly be said to be applied to a single concrete and spatiotemporally continuous object (e.g. 'Mama is kind', 'That picture is valuable', 'The doctor is coming to dinner'). What is the characteristic difference in the mode in which they are applied? Let us recall that, in such a predication, neither of the terms employed need be such that it *applies* to only one object, though both are currently *being applied to* just one object, and, if all goes well, both do in fact *apply to* that object. Now what is the characteristic difference between the relations of the two terms to the object? The characteristic difference, I suggest, is that the singular term is used for the purpose of *identifying* the object, of bringing it about that the hearer (or, generally, the audience) knows *which* or *what* object is in question; while the general term is not. It is enough if the general term in fact applies to the object; it does not also have to identify it.

But what exactly is this task of identifying an object for a hearer? Well, let us consider that in any communication situation a hearer (an audience) is antecedently equipped with a certain amount of knowledge, with certain presumptions, with a certain range of possible current perception. There are within the scope of his knowledge or present perception objects which he is able *in one way or another* to distinguish for himself. The identificatory task of *one* of the terms, in predications of the kind we are now concerned with, is to bring it about that the hearer knows *which* object it is, of all the objects within the hearer's scope of knowledge or presumption, that the *other* term is being applied to. This identificatory task is characteristically the task of the definite singular term. That term achieves its identificatory purpose by drawing upon what in the widest sense might be called the conditions of its utterance, *including* what the hearer is presumed to know or to presume already or to be in a position there and then to perceive for himself. This is not something incidental to the use of singular terms in predications of the kind we are now concerned with. It is quite central to this use. The possibility of identification in the relevant sense exists only for an audience antecedently equipped with knowledge or presumptions, or placed in a position of possible perception, which can be drawn on in this way.[1]

Perhaps the phrase about purporting singularity of application that Quine found unsatisfactory should be construed as a shot at describing the identificatory function of singular terms. If so, Quine was right to think it unsatisfactory. Not only is the phrase far from clear. But at least one fairly natural sense that it might bear is foreign to the purpose. Thus an expression might be said to 'purport singularity of application' if it contained phrases making express uniqueness claims, phrases such as 'the only', 'unique in', 'alone', 'just one'. But terms used for the identificatory purpose will rarely contain such phrases. Such phrases will more naturally occur where the purpose on hand is a different one: e.g. to inform a hearer, with regard to some independently identified object, that it is unique in a certain respect, or to inform him that *there is* something unique in a certain respect. But then the expressions containing such phrases do not have the characteristic role of definite singular terms. They can, as Quine would say, readily be parsed as general terms in predicative position.

Slightly better, but still unsatisfactory, is Quine's alternative description of 'the intuitive idea behind *purely referential position*', viz. 'that the term is used purely to specify its object for the rest of the sentence to say something about'. Still unsatisfactory, since 'specify' by itself remains vague. To remove the vagueness we need the concept of 'identifying for an audience' which I have just

[1] A full account of the matter would call for much more detail and many qualifications. I cannot claim to be doing more than drawing attention to a *characteristic* difference of function between definite singular terms and general terms in predicative position, in cases where both terms alike may fairly be said to be applied to a single concrete object. Thus it would not be true to say that the use of a definite singular term for a particular is *always* designed to draw upon resources of identifying knowledge or presumption antecedently in possession of the audience. For *sometimes* the operations of supplying such resources and of drawing on them may be conflated in the use of a singular term. Nor would it be true to say the general term is *never* used, whereas the singular term is *always* used, for the purpose of indicating to the audience which object it is that the other term is being applied to. For it is easy to think of cases in which, as one would be inclined to say, the roles are reversed. But counter-examples to a universal thesis about differences of function are not necessarily counter-examples to a thesis about characteristic difference of function. We must *weigh* our examples, and not treat them *simply* as counters.

introduced. Fully to elucidate *this* idea a great deal more should be said about the conditions and means of such identification. But we have enough for our immediate purposes: enough to see that a real difference of function is reflected by the difference between the expressions 'refers to' and 'is true of', and that these expressions, used as Quine uses them, are not inappropriate; and enough to understand why Quine should impute the differences that he seems by implication to impute to the nature and consequences of application failure on the part of singular and general terms, respectively.

It is easy enough to see why the distinction of function should lead philosophers to this further distinction. It happens something like this. Let us suppose that the identificatory function has been successfully performed. The successful performance of this function does not, of course, settle the question of the truth or falsity of the predication as a whole. What settles that question would seem to be whether or not the general term applies to the object, whether, as Quine would say, it is true or false *of* the object. But now suppose a radical failure of identificatory function. By a radical failure I mean, not simply the use of an incorrect instead of a correct designation; nor simply the use of a designation which, correct or incorrect, fails to invoke appropriate knowledge in the possession of the hearer and hence leaves him in the dark as to which object is being referred to, or causes him to mistake the identity of that object. I mean the case (rare enough) when there is no appropriate *knowledge*, in anyone's possession, to be invoked; where all such supposed knowledge is not knowledge, but mistake; where there just is no such object as the singular term is supposed to identify. This situation is indeed different from the situation in which the general term simply does not in fact apply to the successfully identified object. We think of the predication as a whole as true in the case where the general term does apply to the object that the singular term is supposed to identify. We think of the predication as a whole as false in the case where the general term does *not* apply to that object, the case where the general term can be truthfully *denied* of that object. But the case where there is no such object is neither a case where the general term can be truly affirmed of it nor a case where the general term can be truly denied of it. Hence there is a strong inclination to say that the predication as a whole is neither true nor false in this case (even that there is no predication at all in this case). Some philosophers have resisted this inclination, and have argued in favour of classifying this case together with the case in which the general term fails to apply to the successfully identified object, under the common appellation, 'false'. There has been debate over this, and it has sometimes seemed that the debate over the use of the word 'false' was the really substantial question, on the answer to which hung all the other debated issues in this area. But this is not so; for many reasons. The claim that the radical failure of a definite singular term results in a truth-value gap is in some cases more intuitively satisfactory, in others less intuitively satisfactory, than the claim that it results in falsity. This is not a mere oddity or 'quirk' of intuition (or usage). It is something that can be explained; though not here and now.

But, however *that* is explained, it remains important that the identificatory function of singular terms should be acknowledged, seen for what it is, and clearly distinguished from the operation of asserting that there is just one thing answering to certain specifications. This distinction is implicitly denied by Russell, at least as far as some classes of singular terms are concerned. It is, on the other hand, implicitly acknowledged by Quine; and to that extent I am with Quine. My present reproach against him is contained in the word 'implicitly'. For when we read that key sentence of his, designed to elucidate the functional distinction between singular and general terms, we are constrained to read it as an obscure statement of a debated consequence of that distinction rather than as a description of the distinction itself; while those more hopeful phrases that might seem to point, however waveringly, in the right direction, are dismissed as vague, intuitive, or pictureque instead of being used as stepping-stones towards the definite, the explicit, and the literal. What makes this the more surprising is that, in the course of some remarks devoted to the discussion of different types of singular terms, Quine shows himself well enough aware of the identifying function of singular terms in general. I content myself with two quotations: 'In "I saw the lion" the singular term "the lion" is presumed to refer to some one lion, *distinguished from its fellows* for speaker and hearer by previous sentences or attendant circumstances' (p. 112). 'In ordinary discourse the idiom of . . . singular description is normally used only where *the intended object* is believed to be *singled out uniquely* by the matter appended to the singular "the" together perhaps with supplementary information . . .' (p. 183). These idioms of 'singling out' or 'distinguishing' the 'intended' object are all in the right spirit. And on p. 103 there even occurs, just once, the key word 'identification'.

There are, of course, as Quine's discussion shows, many different types of situation in which the identificatory function is performed and many different types of resource upon which a speaker may draw or rely in performing it. He may draw upon what the speaker can be presumed to be in a position then and there to see or otherwise perceive for himself. He may rely upon information imparted by earlier sentences in the same conversation. He may rely upon information in the hearer's possession which is not derived from either of these sources, or upon past experience and recognitional capacities of the hearer's which the latter could scarcely articulate into a description. He may draw or rely upon any combination of these. But he *must* draw upon something in this area if the identificatory function is to be performed at all. That function is successfully performed if and only if the singular term used establishes for the hearer an identity, and the right identity, between the thought of *what-is-being-spoken-of-by-the-speaker* and the thought of some object *already within the reach of the hearer's own knowledge, experience, or perception*, some object, that is, which the hearer could, in one way or another, pick out or identify for himself, from his own resources. To succeed in its task, the singular term, together with the circumstances of its utterance, must draw on the appropriate stretch of those resources.

Is there anything in what I have so far said that Quine would wish or need to dispute? I think the answer is a qualified negative. Had I asked this question about Russell, it seems that the answer should be an unqualified affirmative. For Russell appears to claim for the Theory of Descriptions that it gives an exact account of the working of one class of definite singular terms, viz. singular descriptions. And I am bound to deny this. For in the analysis of singular descriptions given in the Theory of Descriptions the identificatory function of singular terms is suppressed altogether. Its place is taken by an explicit assertion to the effect that there exists just one thing with a certain property. But to say this is to do something quite different from identifying that thing for a hearer in the sense I have been concerned with. One who says that there exists just one thing with a certain property typically intends to inform his hearer of this fact. Thereby he does indeed supply the hearer with resources of knowledge which constitute, so to speak, a minimal basis for a subsequent identifying reference to draw on. But the act of supplying new resources is not the same act as the act of drawing on independently established resources.

The non-identity of these acts, on the other hand, constitutes no prima facie objection to Quine's proposal for the elimination of definite singular terms from 'canonical notation'. For Quine does not claim that the sentences which replace those containing definite singular terms have the same meaning as the latter (p. 182). Nor, presumably, would he claim that they would normally serve exactly the same purpose; for this, if I am right, would be to claim too much. He would claim that in some weaker sense the sentences containing singular terms could be replaced by the sentences in canonical notation. What this weaker kind of substitutability is we need not here inquire too closely, if we suppose merely that it is not such as to conflict with the account I have sketched of the characteristic identificatory function of definite singular terms. There remains a point of more immediate significance concerning our understanding of the apparatus of theoretical notions within the framework of which the idea of canonical notation is introduced. The relevant part of Quine's programme of paraphrase can most simply be summed up as follows. All *terms* other than the variables of quantification will be found, in canonical notation, to be general terms in predicative position. The *position* of singular terms is reserved for the quantifiers and the variables of quantification; and since quantifiers themselves do not count as *terms*, the only singular terms left are the variables of quantification. But, merely formal distinctions of grammar apart, how was the distinction between *singular terms* and *general terms in predicative position* explained? It was explained in terms of the contrasting roles in predication of the *definite* singular term and the general term in predicative position. This contrast of roles is our fundamental clue to all the theoretical notions employed. So our theoretical grasp of the nature of canonical notation rests upon our theoretical grasp of the identificatory function of singular terms. And this is why Quine should have elucidated more fully than he did those notions which he was content to dismiss as vague and picturesque.

II

It may be retorted at this point that it is not necessary for Quine to present his distinction of terms and positions as resting on the contrasting roles in predication of the definite singular term and the general term in predicative position. There is, it may be said, a way of presenting the distinction which is independent of any appeal to the function of the definite singular term; and it is a way which Quine sometimes makes use of. The position of a singular term in general can be directly explained as position accessible to quantifiers and variables of quantification or to those expressions of ordinary language to which quantifiers and variables corre- spond. Predicative position, on the other hand, is inaccessible to quantifiers. It is occupied by general terms which complement quantifiers (or other occupants of singular-term position) to yield sentences. All we need now assume is that we can understand the role of quantifiers or of those idioms of ordinary language which the quantifiers 'encapsulate'. If we can assume this much under- standing, we have materials for explaining the concepts of singular term and of predicative position; and the general programme can proceed without the intelligibility of its whole apparatus of theoretical notions appearing to rest on our grasp of the functioning of definite singular terms.

This way out proves delusive; and in observing just how it proves delusive, we shall see how the account I gave in Part I of this paper itself needs to be deepened and strengthened. Predica- tive position is supposed to be inaccessible to quantifiers. But is it? Betty is a better date than Sally. Betty is willing and pretty and Sally too is willing and pretty. But Betty is also witty and Sally is not witty. Surely, it seems, 'willing', 'pretty', and 'witty' are here in predicative position. But is their position inaccessible to quanti- fiers? As a date, Betty is everything that Sally is (i.e. willing and pretty) and something that Sally isn't (i.e. witty). Or, if you like, there is nothing that Sally is that Betty isn't and something that Sally isn't that Betty is.

What are we to do? Are we to stick by the test without qualifica- tion and say that the example shows that 'witty' and 'pretty' are singular terms, and 'Sally' and 'Betty' are in predicative position? This will attract no one, and anyway would obliterate the distinc- tion altogether, since the test could be differently, and more obviously, applied to yield the conclusion that 'Sally' and 'Betty' were singular terms, and 'witty' and 'pretty' were in predicative position.

Are we to try to save the situation by saying that the test for being a singular term includes not only occupancy of a position accessible to quantifiers but also the possession of the grammatical form of the substantive? But this *by itself* would be the wrong kind of appeal to grammar, the kind that Quine would rightly repudiate. Can we buttress this additional requirement with a supposed rationale for it, saying that what it really amounts to is the requirement that the term displaced by the quantifier, if a definite term, should designate an *object*, and that 'Betty' satisfies this requirement while 'pretty' does not? But other objections apart, how shall we then deal with the 'offenders', as Quine calls them (p. 240), who stoutly affirm that 'witty' and 'pretty' in 'Sally is pretty' and 'Betty is witty' *do* designate objects, viz. attributes? Quine's general method of dealing with such offenders is not available here. For to one who says (roughly) that the use of any term commits its user to a corresponding object Quine is wont to reply (roughly) that this is so only where the term occupies a position that it can yield to a quantifier. But the trouble with the terms in question here is that they do occupy positions that they can yield to quantifiers. So we are back where we started.

Let us think again about our example, and in a spirit as sympathetic to Quine as possible. Suppose we redescribe the situation as follows. Prettiness is a quality desirable in a date and Betty has prettiness and Sally has prettiness. Similarly with willingness. Wit is a quality desirable in a date and Betty has wit and Sally has not. Everything which Sally has and which is a quality desirable in a date is something which Betty has; but there is something which is a quality desirable in a date and which Betty has, which Sally does not have. I think that Quine would say that this form of description of the situation is a better, a more logically candid, form than the first. But how does it differ from the first? Well, it differs in that the terms that yield their positions to quantifiers have the grammatical form of substantives and not of adjectives. But we are agreed not to regard this as a vital difference. A more significant difference is this. There is something explicit in the second account of the situation that was only implicit in the first; and it is made explicit by the use of the expression 'quality desirable in a date'.[1] Let us try to follow this clue. It gives us the following result. 'Prettiness' occupies singular-term, or referential, position because it is joined with such an expression as 'desirable in a date', which, relative to it, occupies predicative position. Generally, whenever, explicitly or implicitly, two terms are joined of which the first stands to the second in that characteristic relation in which 'prettiness' (*or* 'pretty') stands to 'desirable in a date', then, relatively to each other, the first is a candidate for referential and the second for predicative position. Thus, even in our first description of the situation, 'pretty' had implicitly referential position. It did not have implicitly referential position considered simply in relation to 'Sally' (or 'Betty'). Rather it was a candidate for predicative position relative to 'Sally'. For it does not stand to 'Sally' as it stands to 'desirable in a date' but rather as 'desirable in a date' stands to it. But it still had implicitly referential position; for it was *implied* that being pretty was desirable in a date. And it was because it had implicitly *referential* position that it could comfortably yield its position to quantification.

But now let us ponder this. A new criterion seems to have emerged for the relative concept of referential and predicative positions. I shall call it the type-criterion. (Elsewhere I have called it – or, rather, its basis – the category-criterion.[2]) 'Pretty' has predicative significance relative to 'Betty', referential significance relative to 'desirable in a date'. We have a series consisting of (1) 'Betty', (2) 'pretty' or 'prettiness', (3) 'desirable in a date', such that any earlier term in the series is a candidate for referential position relative to the immediately succeeding term, and any later term is a candidate for predicative position relative to the immediately preceding term.[3] But what is the general nature of such a series, what is it about its terms and their relations that confers upon them these further relations, these claims to relative referential and predicative position? Well, it will scarcely be

[1] Cf. Quine, p. 119: 'The move that ushers in abstract singular terms has to be one that simultaneously ushers in abstract general ones.'

[2] See *Individuals*, Ch. 5 et. seq.

[3] The variation in form from 'pretty' to 'prettiness' supplies the substantive which is grammatically typical for referential position; the insertion of 'has' before 'prettiness' yields a phrase which as a whole is grammatically suitable for predicative position, while containing a part, 'prettiness', grammatically suitable for referential position.

denied that 'Betty' is typically used to designate a spatiotemporally continuous particular. And it will scarcely be denied that the meaning of 'pretty' is such that it may be said to *group* such particulars in accordance with a certain kind of principle. The term may be said to group all those particulars whose designations may be coupled with it to yield true statements. Now in a certain sense 'Betty' may be said to group particulars too: a particular arm, leg, face, even a particular action, might all be truthfully ascribed to Betty. But obviously the principle on which 'Betty' groups particulars like arms and legs is quite a different sort of principle from the principle on which 'pretty' groups particulars like Betty and Sally. Now consider such a term as (3) 'desirable in a date'. This term has a grouping function too. It does not directly group particulars; it groups *ways*, such as term (2)'s way *of grouping particulars*. But there are analogies and connections between term (3)'s way of grouping ways of grouping particulars and term (2)' way of grouping particulars. The principle that term (3) supplies, of grouping ways of grouping, is like the principle that term (2) supplies, of grouping particulars, in a way in which both are quite unlike the principle of grouping particulars that term (1) supplies. These likenesses and unlikenesses are registered in the terminology of philosophy: in the series that starts with *particular*, and goes on with *property or kind of particular, property or kind of property or kind of particular*, etc.; in the philosophical usage which permits us to say that Betty is a case or instance of prettiness, and prettiness a case or instance of a quality desirable in a date, but forbids us to say that Betty's left arm or anything else is a case or instance of Betty.[1]

---

[1] Not all particulars are spatio temporally *continuous* as Betty is. But the contrast between principles of grouping is not in general dependent on such continuity, though it is seen most easily in cases characterized by continuity. The expression 'The Plough' (used as the name of a constellation) designates a spatio temporal particular, though not a continuous one; whereas even if it should come to pass that all the gold in the universe formed one continuous mass, this would not turn 'gold' into the designation of a spatio-temporal particular. What makes it correct to count a star as a bit of the Plough or an arm as a bit of Betty has at least to do with their spatio-temporal relation to other bits of the Plough or of Betty in a way in which what makes it correct to count something as an instance of gold has nothing to do with its spatio-temporal relations to other instances of gold. The distinction between *being a particular part of* (or *element in*, etc.) and *being a particular instance of* remains bright enough here, even though spatial continuity is gone. Of course this is only the beginning of a long and complex story which perhaps has no very

The result, then, of our reflections on our example is this. Two terms coupled in a true sentence stand in referential and predicative position, respectively, if what the first term designates or signifies is a case or instance of what the second term signifies. Items thus related (or the terms that designate or signify them) may be said respectively to be of lower and of higher type; and this is why I called the new criterion one of type.[1] Part of the explanation of the kind of grouping which terms of higher type than the lowest can do was that it is a kind of grouping which designations of spatio-temporal particulars *cannot* do. So implicit in this criterion of relative position is the consequence that a term designating a particular can never occupy predicative position. A term signifying a kind or property, however, may occupy referential or predicative position, depending upon whether it is, or is not, coupled with a term of still higher type.

Now it might be maintained that we do not need this criterion in addition to the identificatory criterion suggested in Part I of this paper. It was there suggested that the primary occupant of referential position was the term which served to identify the object both terms applied to, the object the sentence was about. Does not this criterion work as well for 'Prettiness is a quality desirable in a date' as it does for 'Betty is pretty'? Just as 'Betty' identifies, and 'pretty' does not, the object the second sentence is about, so 'prettiness' identifies, and 'quality desirable in a date' does not, the attribute the first sentence is about. But before we acquiesce too readily in this suggestion, let us consider more carefully the way in which, both here and originally, we *applied* the identificatory criterion. When we do so, we see that the *type-criterion was already implicit in our application of the identificatory criterion*. We said that 'Betty' identifies, and 'pretty' does not, the object the sentence is about; what the sentence tells us about Betty

---

clear and definite end; for as we bring more sophisticated characters into our story, the clarity and the simplicity of the contrast between principles of grouping tend to diminish. But we are investigating foundations; and it is enough if the beginnings are clear and distinct.

[1] But, of course, by adopting this terminology I by no means intend to suggest that the only differences that can properly be described as differences of type or category are the very broad differences I am concerned with. One may have occasion, for example, to distinguish many different types or categories *within* the very broad category of particulars.

is that she is *pretty*. But in saying this we have already shown a tacit preference for the particular, the item of lower (lowest) type, as the object the sentence is about. There is nothing in the word 'about' or in the concept of identification in general to compel this *exclusive* choice. We could equally well say (and in some contexts it would be correct to say) that the sentence was about prettiness; and that what it says about prettiness is that *Betty* is pretty. The term 'pretty' identifies the attribute the sentence is about; the words 'Betty is' inform us where the attribute is to be found. But though there was nothing in the word 'about' or in the concept of identification in general that compelled this exclusive preference, nevertheless there was something that compelled it: this was the conjunction of the two facts: first, that we were seeking to elucidate the distinction between referential and predicative position, and, second, that the type-criterion is essential to this distinction. This does not mean that we should abandon the identificatory criterion. It only means that we should acknowledge that the exclusive way in which it is applied reflects our acceptance of the type-criterion.

We fuse the two, to obtain the following account of the distinction between referential and predicative position, an account which, if I am right, underlies all that Quine says about this distinction. Referential position is the position primarily and fundamentally occupied by a term definitely identifying a spatio-temporal particular in a sentence coupling that term to another signifying a property-like or kind-like principle of grouping particulars. The particular-identifying term is the primary case of a definite singular term. The other term occupies predicative position. Second, referential position may be occupied by a term signifying a property-like or kind-like principle of grouping particulars provided that this term is itself coupled to another term which signifies a higher principle of grouping such principles of grouping. The first of these terms is then a secondary case of a definite singular term. The other term again occupies predicative position. Finally, the position occupied by a definite singular term of any kind may be coherently yielded to a kind of term which does not characteristically have the identifying function of a definite singular term, and which is called an indefinite singular term.

The above sentences of mine by no means constitute a complete account of the distinction between referential and predicative position, between singular term and general term in predicative position. But they provide, perhaps, the necessary basis on which, by further extension, analogy, and qualification, any complete account must be built.

But now what has happened to quantification? We set out with the suggestion that accessibility to quantifiers might provide a test for referential position independent of the explanations of Part I. We end by returning to the explanations of Part I, with the addition of an explicit awareness of the type-criterion they implicitly involved. Quantification seems to have disappeared from view altogether. Yet quantifiers were supposed to hold the key to referential position. How are we to explain this?

We can understand the situation better if we remember that quantification is also supposed by Quine to hold the key to something else, viz. the ontological commitments of our talk. Quantifiers hold the key to ontic commitment because the objects are 'what count as cases when, quantifying, we say that everything or something is thus-and-so' (p. 240). They hold the key to referential position because they encapsulate certain 'specially selected, unequivocally referential idioms of ordinary language', viz. 'there is an object x such that' and 'every object x is such that' (p. 242). Here the notions of *object*, *reference*, and *quantification* seem to stand in firm connection without any dependence on the ideas of type and of identification that I have invoked. But let us look a little more closely: at the tell-tale word 'cases' in the first quotation and at the way in which 'something' and 'thus-and-so' are balanced about the 'is'; at the word 'object' itself in the second quotation. Does the word 'object' itself already contain, concealed, the type-criterion, the preference for particulars? After all, we readily say that spatiotemporally continuous particulars are *objects* and less readily say this of attributes and the rest. Suppose we leave it out, to guard against prejudice. Then why should we prefer 'There is something *that is thus-and-so*' to 'There is something *that such-and-such is*' as the general form of what we say when we use an existential quantifier? The reason is clear; but it leads us straight back to the type-criterion. In a two-term sentence in which one term identifies an item of lower type to which the other term non-identifyingly applies, it is the identifying term for this item that is the grammatical subject of the predicative 'is' and characteristically precedes it. What characteristically follows the 'is' (as grammatical complement) is the term that applies to, but does not identify, the item of lower type; it is the term that signifies (identifies) an item of higher type, that which the item of lower type is being said to be *a case of*.[1] So it is the type-relation, the type-order, that dictates Quine's choice of phrasing, and thereby seems to vindicate the alleged link between quantification and referential position.

This is not to say that the quantification test is a bad test for referential position. On the contrary, it is, on the whole, a good test.[2] But the explanation of its being a good test leads us once more back to the type-criterion. It is a good test because there is never any point in introducing a quantifier into a place that could be occupied by a term signifying an item of a higher type *unless* this is done in coupling with a term signifying an item of a still higher type.[3] Hence quantifiers always occupy relatively lower-type positions. We saw this, in a not very clear way, in the example about the qualities desirable in a date. In 'There is something that Betty is and Sally is not' we appeared to be quantifying in a higher-type region without any coupling to a term of still higher type. But we had to acknowledge that this was mere appearance, that we were operating implicitly with the still higher-type notion of 'quality desirable in a date'. If we were not implicitly operating with a higher-type notion, the sentence would not be worth affirming. The point becomes clearer if we consider a simpler case. Suppose the term 'Socrates' identifies the philosopher. Then 'There is something that Socrates is' is bound to be true, and 'Socrates is everything' (or 'There is nothing Socrates isn't') is bound to be false. There is no point in either sentence if 'Socrates' functions as a singular term identifying the philosopher; just as there is no point in *any* sentence whatever which declares, with regard to any identified item of any type whatever, that it has

---

[1] The point can indeed be put, though less clearly, without reference to identification. Something a thing *is* is of a higher type than anything which *is* it; a thing which *is* something is of a lower type than anything it *is*. The italicized 'is' here corresponds to 'is a case of', though it differs from the latter phrase, of course, in permitting a grammatically adjectival termination.

[2] The words 'on the whole' signify the need for certain reservations, or at least for further reflection, about some adverbial expressions like 'here', 'there', 'now', 'then'. Quine says these can be 'parsed' as general terms. But no amount of parsing would seem to defend their position from occupation by 'somewhere', 'somewhen', etc.

[3] The point is explained in *Individuals*. See especially p. 327.

some property or that it has every property. In general it will never be to the purpose to quantify over items of a higher type unless some still higher-type principle of collection is being implicitly used.

Thus, in practice, the quantification test for referential position is quite a good test. But it is so only because the notions of referential and predicative position (or, if you like, of singular-logical-subject position and logical-predicate position) have to be understood in the way I have outlined. And if I am right in saying that they have to be understood in this way, then I think it must also be admitted that the whole apparatus of distinctions in terms of which the theory of canonical notation is explained rests upon notions whose role is hardly sufficiently acknowledged. The two essential notions are: first, that of an order of types, based upon the quite fundamental distinction between spatiotemporal particulars on the one hand and property-like or kind-like principles of grouping such particulars on the other; and, second, that of the identificatory function characteristically performed by definite singular terms referring to particulars.

The purpose of this paper was to indicate the fundamental place of these two notions in Quine's own thinking about referential and predicative position. That they have this place there is not, as far as I can see, something he would necessarily wish to dispute. But there is, I think, a further and connected consequence, concerning Quine's views on ontology, which is also worth mentioning; and perhaps he would not wish to dispute this either.

The objects to the existence of which our discourse commits us are, according to Quine, the objects, of whatever sort, which 'the singular terms, in their several ways, name, refer to, take as values. They are what count as cases when, quantifying, we say that everything, or something, is thus-and-so' (p. 240). Now we have sufficiently seen what the primary objects answering to this description are. They are spatiotemporal particulars. And we have seen that this is not something which just happens to be the case. It is a guaranteed consequence of the nature of the fundamental distinction between singular term in referential, and general term in predicative, position. Hence such particulars do not merely happen, for extraneous reasons, to count as objects in Quine's sense. They are the very pattern of objects in this sense. They are

F

not, indeed, the only things that answer to Quine's description. But to say of things of other types that they also answer to this description is simply to say that we have occasion to bring such things under higher principles of grouping, principles which serve to group them in ways analogous to the ways in which expressions signifying properties (or kinds) of particulars serve to group particulars. In so far, then, as things other than spatiotemporal particulars qualify as objects, they do so simply because our thought, our talk, confers upon them the limited and purely logical analogy with spatiotemporal particulars which I have just described. And now, surely, we are in a position to understand the nominalist prejudice, and to discount it – without flattering the fantasies of Platonism. If by accepting as entities, on this logical test, things other than spatiotemporal particulars, we were claiming for them any other, any further, likeness to such particulars than the logical analogy itself contains, we should indeed be running into danger of committing the characteristic category-confusions of Platonist mythology. One who believes that such acceptance inevitably carries such a claim must seem to himself to have every rational motive for the strenuous efforts of paraphrase demanded by a limited and, as nearly as possible, nominalist ontology. But this belief is itself a symptom of confusion. Of course, even when the belief is seen to be illusion, motives of a reasonable kind, elucidatory, aesthetic, for these efforts of paraphrase may still remain. But the motive of metaphysical respectability is gone.

4. *Identifying Reference and Truth-Values*

The materials for this paper are: one familiar and fundamental speech-function; one controversy in philosophical logic; and two or three platitudes.

We are to be concerned with statements in which, at least ostensibly, some particular historical fact or event or state of affairs, past or present, notable or trivial, is reported: as that the emperor has lost a battle or the baby has lost its rattle or the emperor is dying or the baby is crying. More exactly, we are to be concerned with an important subclass of such statements, viz. those in which the task of specifying just the historical state of affairs which is being reported includes, as an essential part, the sub-task of designating some particular historical item or items which the state of affairs involves. Not all performances of the reporting task include the performance of this sub-task – the task, I shall call it, of identifying reference to a particular item. Thus, the report that it is raining now, or the report that it was raining here an hour ago, do not. But the statement that Caesar is dying, besides specifying the historical fact or situation which it is the function of the statement as a whole to report, has, as a part of this function, the sub-function of designating a particular historical item, viz. Caesar, which that situation essentially involves. And this part of the function of the whole statement is the whole of the function of part of the statement, viz. of the name 'Caesar'.

The speech-function we are to be concerned with, then, is the function of *identifying reference* to a particular historical item, when such reference occurs as a sub-function of statement. We are to be concerned with it in relation to a particular point of philosophical controversy, viz. the question whether a radical failure in the performance of this function results in a special case of falsity in statement or, rather, in what Quine calls a truth-value gap. The hope is not to show that one party to this dispute is quite right and the other quite wrong. The hope is to exhibit speech-function, controversy and one or two platitudes in a mutually illuminating way.

I introduce now my first pair, a complementary pair, of platitudes. One, perhaps the primary, but not of course the only, purpose of assertive discourse is to give information to an audience of some kind, viz. one's listener or listeners or reader or readers. Since there is no point in, or perhaps one should say, no possibility of, informing somebody of something of which he is already apprised, the making of an assertive utterance or statement – where such an utterance has in view this primary purpose of assertion – implies a presumption (on the part of the speaker) of ignorance (on the part of the audience) of some point to be imparted in the utterance. This platitude might be called the Principle of the Presumption of Ignorance. It is honoured to excess in some philosophical proposals for analysis or reconstruction of ordinary language, proposals which might appear to be based on the different and mistaken Principle of the Presumption of Total Ignorance. To guard against such excess, we need to emphasize a platitude complementary to the first. It might be called the Principle of the Presumption of Knowledge. The substance of this complementary platitude, loosely expressed, is that when an empirically assertive utterance is made with an informative intention, there is usually or at least often a presumption (on the part of the speaker) of knowledge (in the possession of the audience) of empirical facts relevant to the particular point to be imparted in the utterance. This is *too* loosely expressed. The connection between the presumption of knowledge and the intention to impart just such-and-such a particular point of information may be closer than that of customary association; the connection between the *identity* of the particular point it is intended to impart and the kind of knowledge presumed may be closer than that of relevance. Just as we might say that it could not be true of a speaker that he intended to *inform* an audience of some particular point unless he presumed their ignorance of that point, so we might often say that it could not be true of a speaker that he intended to inform the audience of just *that* particular point unless he presumed in his audience certain empirical knowledge. So the second principle, in which I am mainly interested, is truly complementary to the first.

Now this may sound a little mysterious. But at least there will be no difficulty felt in conceding the general and vague point that we do constantly presume knowledge as well as ignorance on the part of those who are the audiences of our assertive utterances, and that the first kind of presumption, as well as the second, bears importantly on our choice of what we say. The particular application that I want to make of this general point is to the case of identifying reference. To make it, I must introduce the not very abstruse notion of identifying knowledge of particulars.

Everyone has knowledge of the existence of various particular things each of which he is able, in one sense or another, though not necessarily in every sense, to distinguish from all other things. Thus a person may be able to pick a thing out in his current field of perception. Or he may know there is a thing (not in his current field of perception) to which a certain description applies which applies to no other thing: such a description I shall call an *identifying description*. Or he may know the name of a thing and be able to recognize it when he encounters it, even if he can normally give no identifying description of it other than one which incorporates its own name. If a man satisfies any one of these conditions in respect of a certain particular, I shall say he has identifying knowledge of that particular. One is bound to define such a notion in terms of its outlying cases, cases, here, of minimal and relatively isolated identifying knowledge. So it is worth emphasizing that, in contrast with cases of minimal and relatively isolated identifying knowledge, there are hosts of cases of very rich and full identifying knowledge, and that, in general, our identifying knowledge of particulars forms an immensely complex web of connections and relations – the web, one might say, of our historical and geographical knowledge in general, granted that these adjectives are not to be construed as qualifying academic subjects alone, but also knowledge of the most unpretentious kind about the particular things and people which enter into our minute-to-minute or day-to-day transactions with the world.

The notion of identifying reference is to be understood in close relation to the notion of identifying knowledge. When people talk to each other they commonly and rightly assume a large community of identifying knowledge of particular items. Very often a speaker knows or assumes that a thing of which he has such knowledge is also a thing of which his audience has such knowledge.

Knowing or assuming this, he may wish to state some particular fact regarding such a thing, for example, that it is thus-and-so; and he will then normally include in this utterance an expression which he regards as adequate, in the circumstances of utterance, to indicate to the audience *which* thing it is, of all the things in the scope of the audience's identifying knowledge, that he is declaring to be thus-and-so. The language contains expressions of several celebrated kinds which are peculiarly well adapted, in different ways, for use with this purpose. These kinds include proper names, definite and possessive and demonstrative descriptions, demonstrative and personal pronouns. I do not say that *all* expressions of these kinds are well adapted for use with this purpose; nor do I say, of those that are, that they are not regularly used in other ways, with other purposes.

When an expression of one of these classes *is* used in this way, I shall say that it is used to *invoke* identifying knowledge known or presumed to be in possession of an audience. It would now be easy to define identifying reference so that only when an expression is used to invoke identifying knowledge is it used to perform the function of identifying reference. But though it would simplify exposition thus to restrict attention to what we shall in any case count as the central cases of identifying reference, it would not be wholly desirable. For there are cases which cannot exactly be described as cases of invoking identifying knowledge, but which are nevertheless sufficiently like cases which *can* be so described to be worth classifying with them as cases of identifying reference. For instance, there may be within a man's current field of possible perception something which he has not noticed and cannot be said actually to have discriminated there, but to which his attention may be intentionally drawn simply by the use, on the part of a speaker, of an expression of one of the kinds I mentioned, as part of a statement of some fact regarding the particular item in question. In so far as the speaker's intention, in using the expression in question, is not so much to *inform* the audience of the existence of some particular item unique in a certain respect as to bring it about that the audience *sees for itself* that there is such an item, we may think this case worth classifying with the central cases of identifying reference. Again, there are cases in which an audience cannot exactly be credited with *knowledge* of the existence of a certain item unique in a certain respect, but can be credited with a strong *presumption* to this effect, can be credited, we might say, with *identifying presumption* rather than identifying knowledge. Such presumed presumption can be invoked in the same style as such knowledge can be invoked.

So we may allow the notion of identifying reference to a particular item to extend beyond the cases of invoking identifying knowledge. We must then face the unsurprising consequence that if, as we do, we wish to contrast cases in which a speaker uses an expression to perform the function of identifying reference with cases in which the intention and effect of a speaker's use of an expression is to inform the audience of the existence of a particular item unique in a certain respect, then we shall encounter some cases which do not *clearly* belong to either of these contrasting classes, which seem more or less dubious candidates for both. But this is not a situation which should cause us embarrassment, in philosophy; and, having made the point, I shall for simplicity's sake speak in what follows as if all cases of identifying reference were, at least in intention, cases of invoking identifying knowledge.

What I have said so far, in describing the function of identifying reference, is I think, uncontroversial in the sense that the description has proceeded without my having to take up a position on any well-worn point of controversy. It has a consequence, just alluded to, which should be equally uncontroversial, and which I shall labour a little now, partly in order to distinguish it from any *prise de position* on a matter which is undoubtedly one of controversy.

I have explained identifying reference – or the central case of identifying reference – as essentially involving a presumption, on the speaker's part, of the possession by the audience of identifying knowledge of a particular item. Identifying knowledge is knowledge of the existence of a particular item distinguished, in one or another sense, by the audience from any other. The appropriate stretch of identifying knowledge is to be invoked by the use of an expression deemed adequate by the speaker, in the total circumstances of utterance, to indicate to the audience which, of all the items within the scope of the audience's identifying knowledge, is being declared, in the utterance as a whole, to be thus-and-so. Depending upon the nature of the item and the situation of utterance, the expression used may be a name or a pronoun or a definite or demonstrative description; and it is of course not necessary that either name or description should in general be *uniquely* applicable to the item in question, so long as its choice, in the total circumstances of utterance, is deemed adequate to indicate to the audience which, of all the particular items within the scope of his identifying knowledge, is being declared, in the utterance as a whole, to be thus-and-so.

Now one thing that is absolutely clear is that it can be no part of the speaker's intention in the case of such utterances to *inform* the audience of the *existence* of a particular item bearing the name or answering to the description and distinguished by that fact, or by that fact plus something else known to the audience, from any other. On the contrary, the very task of identifying reference, as described, can be undertaken only by a speaker who knows or presumes his audience to be already in possession of such knowledge of existence and uniqueness as this. The task of identifying reference is *defined* in terms of a type of speaker-intention which *rules out* ascription to the speaker of the intention to impart the existence-and-uniqueness information in question. All this can be put, perfectly naturally, in other ways. Thus, that there exists a particular item to which the name or description is applicable and which, if not unique in this respect, satisfies some uniqueness-condition known to the hearer (*and* satisfies some uniqueness-condition known to the speaker) is no part of what the speaker *asserts* in an utterance in which the name or description is used to perform the function of identifying reference; it is, rather, a *presupposition* of his asserting what he asserts.

This way of putting it is still uncontroversial. For it is a natural way of putting what is itself uncontroversial. But it introduces a contrast, between the *asserted* and the *presupposed*, in words which are associated with an issue of controversy.

We can come at this issue by considering some of the ways in which an attempt to perform the function of identifying reference can either fail altogether or at least fall short of complete success and satisfactoriness. There are several ways in which such an attempt can fail or be flawed. For instance, it may be that, though the speaker possesses, the audience does not possess, identifying knowledge of the particular historical item to which the speaker intends to make an identifying reference; that the speaker credits the audience with identifying knowledge the audience does not possess. It may be that though the audience possesses identifying knowledge of the particular item in question, the expression chosen by the speaker fails to invoke the appropriate stretch of identifying knowledge and leaves the audience uncertain, or even misleads the audience, as to who or what is meant. Failures of this kind may be, though they need not be, due to flaws of another kind. For it may be that the speaker's choice of expression reflects mistakes of fact or language on his part; and such mistake-reflecting choices are still flaws, even where they do not mislead, as, for example, references to Great Britain as 'England' or to President Kennedy as 'the U.S. Premier' are not likely to mislead.

Though these are all cases of flawed or failed reference, they are not cases of the most radical possible kind of failure. For my descriptions of these cases imply that at least one fundamental condition of success is fulfilled, even if others are not fulfilled. They imply at least that there *is* a particular historical item within the scope of the speaker's identifying knowledge – even if not all his beliefs about it are true – such that he intends, by suitable choice of expression, to invoke identifying knowledge, presumed by him to be in possession of the audience, of that item. But this condition might fail too; and that in various ways. It might be that there just is no such particular item at all as the speaker takes himself to be referring to, that what he, and perhaps the audience too, take to be identifying knowledge of a particular item is not knowledge at all, but completely false belief. This is but one case of what might uncontroversially be called radical failure of the existence presupposition of identifying reference. It involves no moral turpitude on the part of the speaker. Different would be the case in which the speaker uses an expression, by way of apparently intended identifying reference, to invoke what he knows or thinks the audience thinks to be identifying knowledge, though he, the speaker, knows it to be false belief. The speaker in this case can have no intention actually to refer to a particular historical item, and so cannot strictly fail to carry out *that* intention. He can have the intention to be *taken* to have the former intention; and in *this* intention he may succeed. A full treatment of the subject would call for careful consideration of such differences. For simplicity's sake, I shall ignore the case of pretence, and concentrate on that case of radical reference-failure in which the failure is not a moral one.

Our point of controversy concerns the following question: given an utterance which suffers from radical reference-failure, are we to say that what we have here is just one special case of false statement or are we to say that our statement suffers from a deficiency so radical as to deprive it of the chance of being either true or false? Of philosophers who have discussed this question in recent years some have plumped uncompromisingly for the first answer, some uncompromisingly for the second; some have been eclectic about it, choosing the first answer for some cases and the second for others; and some have simply contented themselves with sniping at any doctrine that offered, while wisely refraining from exposing any target themselves. In virtue of his Theory of Descriptions and his views on ordinary proper names as being condensed descriptions, Russell might be said to be the patron of the first party – the 'special case of false statement' party. One recent explicit adherent of that party is Mr Dummett in his interesting article on *Truth* (P.A.S. 58–9). The second party – the 'neither true nor false' party – might be said, with some reservations, to have included Quine, Austin, and myself. Quine invented the excellent phrase 'truth-value gap' to characterize what we have in these cases (see *Word and Object*). Austin (see *Performative Utterances* and *How to Do Things with Words*) contrasts this sort of deficiency or, as he calls it, 'infelicity' in statement with straightforward falsity and prefers to say that a statement suffering from this sort of deficiency is void – 'void for lack of reference'.

Let us ignore the eclectics and the snipers and confine our attention, at least for the moment, to the two uncompromising parties. I do not think there is any question of demonstrating that one party is quite right and the other quite wrong. What we have here is the familiar philosophical situation of one party being attracted by one simplified, theoretical – or 'straightened out' – concept of truth and falsity, and the other by another. It might be asked: How does ordinary usage speak on the point? And this, as always, is a question which it is instructive to ask. But ordinary usage does not deliver a clear verdict for one party or the other. Why should it? The interests which ordinary usage reflects are too complicated and various for it to provide overwhelming support for either way of *simplifying* the picture. The fact that ordinary usage does not deliver a clear verdict does not mean, of course, that there can be no other way of demonstrating, at least, that one view is quite wrong. It might be shown, for example, to be inconsistent, or incoherent in some other way. But this is not the case with either of these views. Each would have a certain amount of explaining and adjusting to do, but each could perfectly consistently be carried through. More important, each is *reasonable*. Instead of trying to demonstrate that one is quite right and the other quite wrong, it is more instructive to see how both are reasonable, how both represent different ways of being impressed by the facts.

As a point of departure here, it is reasonable to take related cases of what are indisputably false statements and then set beside them the disputed case, so that we can see how one party is more impressed by the resemblances, the other by the differences, between the disputed case and the undisputed cases. The relevant undisputed cases are obviously of two kinds. One is that of an utterance in which an identifying reference is successfully made, and all the conditions of a satisfactory or all-round successful act of empirical assertion are fulfilled except that the particular item identifyingly referred to and declared to be thus-and-so is, as a matter of fact, *not* thus-and-so. It is said of Mr Smith, the new tenant of the Grange, that he is single, when he is in fact married: a statement satisfactory in all respects except that it is, indisputably, false. The other relevant case is that in which an explicit assertion of existence and uniqueness is made. It is said, say, that there is one and not more than one island in Beatitude Bay. And this is false because there is none at all or because there are several.

Now, it might be said on the one side, how vastly different from the ways in which things go wrong in either of these undisputed cases of falsity is the way in which things go wrong in the case of radical reference-failure. A judgement as to truth or falsity is a judgement on what the speaker asserts. But we have already noted the uncontroversial point that the existence-condition which fails in the case of radical reference-failure is not something asserted, but something presupposed, by the speaker's utterance. So his statement cannot be judged as a false existential assertion. Nor, evidently, can it be judged as an assertion false in the same way as the first undisputed example, i.e. false as being a *mis*-characterization of the particular item referred to. For there is no such item for it to be a mischaracterization of. In general, where there *is* such an item as the speaker refers to, and the speaker asserts, with regard to that item, that it is thus-and-so, his assertion is rightly assessed as true if the item is thus-and-so, as false if it is not. In the case of radical reference-failure, the speaker, speaking in good faith, *means* his statement to be up for assessment in this way; he takes himself similarly to be asserting with regard to a particular item, that it is thus-and-so. But in fact the conditions of his making an assertion such as he takes himself to be making are not fulfilled. We can acknowledge the character of his intentions and the nature of his speech-performance by saying that he makes a statement; but we must acknowledge, too, the radical character of the way in which his intentions are frustrated by saying that his statement does not qualify as such an assertion as he takes it to be, and hence does not qualify for assessment as such an assertion. But then it does not qualify for truth-or-falsity assessment at all. The whole assertive enterprise is wrecked by the failure of its presupposition.

But now, on the other side, it could be said that what the disputed case has in common with the undisputed cases of falsity is far more important than the differences between them. In all the cases alike, we may take it a genuine empirical statement is made; a form of words is used such that if there were as a matter of fact in the world (in Space and Time) a certain item, or certain items, with certain characteristics – if, to put it differently, certain complex circumstances did as a matter of fact obtain in the world (in Space and Time) – then the statement would be true. The important distinction is between the case in which those complex circumstances do obtain and the case in which they don't. This distinction is the distinction we *should* use the words 'true' and 'false' (of statements) to mark, even if we do not consistently do so. And this distinction can be drawn equally in the disputed and the undisputed cases. A false empirical statement is simply any empirical statement whatever which fails for *factual* reasons, i.e. on account of circumstances in the world being as they are and not otherwise, to be a true one. Cases of radical reference-failure are simply one class of false statements.

It no longer seems to me important to come down on one side or the other in this dispute. Both conceptions are tailored, in the ways I have just indicated, to emphasize different kinds of interest in statement; and each has its own merits. My motives in bringing up the issue are three, two of which have already partially shown themselves. First, I want to disentangle this issue of controversy from other questions with which it is sometimes confused. Second, I want to dispel the illusion that the issue of controversy can be speedily settled, one way or the other, by a brisk little formal argument. Third, I want to indicate one way – no doubt there are more – in which, without positive commitment to either rival theory, we may find the issues they raise worth pursuing and refining. I shall say something on all three points, though most on the third.

First, then, the issue between the truth-value gap theory and the falsity theory, which has loomed so large in this whole area of discussion, has done so in a way which might be misleading, which might give a false impression. The impression might be given that the issue between these two theoretical accounts was the *crucial* issue in the whole area – the key, as it were, to all positions. Thus it might be supposed that anyone who rejected the view that the Theory of Descriptions gives an adequate general analysis, or account of the functioning, of definite descriptions was committed, by that rejection, to uncompromising adherence to the truth-value gap theory and uncompromising rejection of the falsity theory for the case of radical reference-failure. But this is not so at all. The distinction between identifying reference and uniquely existential assertion is something quite undeniable. The sense in which the existence of something answering to a definite description used for the purpose of identifying reference, and its distinguishability by an audience from anything else, is presupposed and not asserted in an utterance containing such an expression, so used, stands absolutely firm, whether or not one opts for the view that radical failure of the presupposition would deprive the statement of a truth-value. It remains a decisive objection to the Theory of Descriptions, regarded as embodying a generally correct analysis of statements containing definite descriptions, that, so regarded, it amounts to a denial of these undeniable distinctions. I feel bound to labour the point a little, since I may be partly responsible for the confusion of these two issues by making the word 'presupposition' carry simultaneously the burden both of the functional distinction and of the truth-value gap theory. Only, at most, partly responsible; for the line-up is natural enough, though not inevitable; and though there is no logical compulsion one way, there is logical compulsion the other. One who accepts the Theory of Descriptions as a correct analysis is bound to accept the falsity theory for certain cases and reject the truth-value gap theory. One who accepts the truth-value gap theory is bound to reject the Theory of Descriptions as a generally correct analysis. But it is perfectly consistent to reject the view that the Theory of Descriptions is a generally correct analysis, on the grounds I have indicated, and also to withhold assent to the truth-value gap theory.

Now for my second point. I have denied that either of the two theories can be decisively refuted by short arguments, and I shall support this by citing and commenting on some specimen arguments which are sometimes thought to have this power. First, some arguments for the truth-value gap theory and against the falsity theory:

A (1) Let *Fa* represent a statement of the kind in question. If the falsity theory is correct, then the contradictory of *Fa* is not -*Fa*, but the disjunction of -*Fa* with a negative existential statement. But the contradictory of *Fa is* -*Fa*. Therefore the falsity theory is false.

(2) If 'false' is used normally, then from *It is false that S is P* it is correct to infer *S is not P*. But it is agreed on both theories that *S is not P* is true only if there is such a thing as *S*. Hence, if 'false' is used normally, *It is false that S is P* is true only if there is such a thing as *S*. Hence, if 'false' is used normally in the statement of the falsity theory, that theory is false.

(3) The question *Is S P?* and the command *Bring it about that S is P* may suffer from exactly the same radical reference failure as the statement *S is P*. But if an utterance which suffers from this radical reference failure is thereby rendered false, the question and command must be said to be false. But this is absurd. So the falsity theory is false.

Now arguments on the other side:

B (1) Let *Fa* represent a statement of the kind in question (e.g. *The king of France is bald*). Then there may be an equivalent statement, *Gb* (e.g. *France has a bald king*) which is obviously false if there is no such thing as *a*. But the two statements are equivalent. So *Fa* is false if there is no such thing as *a*. So the truth-value gap theory is false.

(2) Let *P* be a statement which, on the truth-value gap theory, is neither true nor false. Then the statement that *P* is true is itself

false. But if it is false that P is true, then P is false. In the same way we can derive from the hypothesis the conclusion that P is true, hence the conclusion that P is both true and false. This is self-contradictory, hence the original hypothesis is so too.

The defender of either view will have little difficulty in countering these arguments against it. Thus to B2 the reply is that if a statement lacks a truth-value, any statement assessing it as true *simpliciter* or as false *simpliciter* similarly lacks a truth-value. So no contradiction is derivable. To B1 the reply is that the argument is either inconclusive or question-begging. If 'equivalent' means simply 'such that if either is true, then necessarily the other is true', it is inconclusive. If it also means 'such that if either is false, then necessarily the other is false', it is question-begging. To A3 the reply is that there is no reason why what holds for statements should hold also for questions and commands. To A2 the reply is that the inference is not strictly correct, though it is perfectly natural that we should normally make it. To A1 the reply is that it is question-begging, though again it is perfectly intelligible that we should be prone to think of contradictories in this way.

It is just an illusion to think that either side's position can be carried by such swift little sallies as these. What we have, in the enthusiastic defence of one theory or the other, is a symptom of difference of direction of interest. One who has an interest in actual speech-situations, in the part that stating plays in communication between human beings, will tend to find the simpler falsity theory inadequate and feel sympathy with – though, as I say, he is under no compulsion, exclusively or at all, to embrace – its rival. One who takes a more impersonal view of statement, who has a picture in which the actual needs, purposes, and presumptions of speakers and hearers are of slight significance – in which, as it were, there are just statements on the one side and, on the other, the world they should reflect – he will naturally tend to brush aside the truth-value gap theory and embrace *its* simpler rival. For him, one might say, the subject of every statement is just the world in general. For his opponent, it is now this item, now that; and perhaps sometimes – rarely and disconcertingly enough – nothing at all.

And now for the third matter, which we shall find not unconnected with this last thought. It seems to be a fact which advocates of either, or of neither, theory can equally safely acknowledge, that the intuitive appeal, or prima facie plausibility, of the truth-value gap theory is not constant for all example-cases of radical reference-failure which can be produced or imagined. We can, without commitment to either theory, set ourselves to explain this variation in the intuitive appeal of one of them – which is also an inverse variation in the intuitive appeal of the other. The attempt to explain this fact may bring into prominence other facts which bear in interesting ways upon speech-situations in general, and those involving identifying reference in particular. I shall draw attention to but one factor – no doubt there are more – which may contribute to the explanation of this fact in some cases. In doing so, I shall invoke another platitude to set beside, and connect with, the platitudes we already have.

First, we may note that the truth-value gap theory can be expressed, in terms of the familiar idea of predication, in such a way as to secure for it a certain flexibility in application. Let us call an expression *as and when used in a statement with the role of identifying reference* – whether or not it suffers in that use from radical reference-failure – a *referring expression*. Then any statement containing a referring expression, E, can be regarded as consisting of two expression-parts, one the expression E itself, to be called the subject-expression or subject-term, and the other the remainder of the statement, to be called the predicate-expression or predicate-term. In the case of a statement containing more than one, say two, referring expressions, it is to be open to us to cast one of these for the role of subject-expression, while the other is regarded as absorbed into the predicate-term which is attached to the subject-term to yield the statement as a whole. The adherent of the truth-value gap view can then state his view as follows.[1] The statement or predication as a whole is true just in the case in which the predicate-term does in fact apply to (is in fact 'true of') the object which the subject-term (identifyingly) refers to. The statement or predication as a whole is false just in the case where the negation of the predicate-term applies to that object, i.e. the case where the predicate-term can be truthfully denied of that object. The case of radical reference-failure on the part of the subject-term is of neither of these two kinds. It is the case of the truth-value gap.

[1] This way of stating it is in fact implicit in the fundamental definition of predication which Quine gives on p. 96 of *Word and Object*.

Now consider a statement consisting of two referring expressions one of which is guilty of reference-failure while the other is not. Then it is open to us to carve up the statement in two different ways; and different decisions as to carving-up procedure may be allowed to result in different assessments of the statement for truth-value. Thus (1) we can see the guilty referring expression as absorbed into a predicate-term which is attached to the innocent referring expression to make up the statement as a whole; or (2) we can see the innocent referring expression as absorbed into a predicate-expression which is attached to the guilty referring expression to make up the statement as a whole. Now if we carve up the statement in the second way, we must say – according to our current statement of the truth-value gap theory – that the statement lacks a truth-value. But if we carve it up in the first way, we *may* say that it is false (or, sometimes – when negative in form – that it is true). For to carve it up in the first way is to think of the statement as made up of the satisfactory or innocent referring expression together with one general term or predicate into which the guilty referring expression has been absorbed. The question whether that predicate does or does not apply to the object referred to by the satisfactory referring expression remains a perfectly answerable question; and the fact that the predicate has absorbed a guilty referring expression will, for most predicates affirmative in form, merely have the consequence that the right answer is 'No'. Thus, if we look at such a statement in this way, we can naturally enough declare it false or untrue, and naturally enough affirm its *negation* as true, on the strength of the reference-failure of the guilty referring expression.

In this way, it might seem, the truth-value gap theory can readily modify itself to take account of certain examples which may seem intuitively unfavourable to it. For example, there is no king of France; and there is, let us say, no swimming-pool locally. But there is, let us say, an Exhibition in town; and there is, let us say, no doubt of Jones's existence. If we consider the statements

    (1) that Jones spent the morning at the local swimming-pool
and (2) that the Exhibition was visited yesterday by the king of
         France

it may seem natural enough to say (1) that it is quite untrue, or

G

is false, that Jones spent the morning at the local swimming-pool, since there isn't one; that, however Jones spent the morning, he did *not* spend it at the local swimming-pool, since there's no such place; and similarly (2) that it is quite untrue, or is false, that the Exhibition was visited yesterday by the king of France; that, whoever the Exhibition was visited by yesterday, it was *not* visited by the king of France, since there is no such person. And the modified truth-value gap theory accommodates these intuitions by allowing the guilty referring expressions, 'the local swimming-pool', 'the king of France', to be absorbed into the predicate in each case.

This modification to the truth-value gap theory, though easy and graceful, will scarcely seem adequate. For one thing, it will not be available for all intuitively unfavourable examples, but only for those which contain more than one referring expression. For another, it will remain incomplete inside its own domain unless some *principle of choice* between alternative ways of carving up a statement is supplied. The theory might resolve the latter question self-sacrificially, by declaring that the carving-up operation was always to be so conducted as to permit the assignment of a truth-value whenever possible. But this move might be too self-sacrificial, turning friends into enemies, turning intuitively favourable cases into unfavourable ones.

So let us consider further. Confronted with the classical example, 'The king of France is bald', we may well feel it natural to say, straight off, that the question whether the statement is true or false doesn't arise because there is no king of France. But suppose the statement occurring in the context of a set of answers to the question: 'What examples, if any, are there of famous contemporary figures who are *bald*?' Or think of someone compiling a list in answer to the question, 'Who has died recently?' and including in it the term 'the king of France'. Or think of someone including the statement 'The king of France married again' in a set of statements compiled in reply to the question: 'What outstanding events, if any, have occurred recently in the social and political fields?' In the first two cases the king of France appears to be cited as an *instance* or example of an *antecedently introduced class*. In the last case the statement as a whole claims to report an event as an instance of an *antecedently introduced class*. The question in each case represents the antecedent centre of interest as a certain class – the class of bald notables, the class of recently deceased notables, the class of notable recent events in a certain field – and the question is as to what items, if any, the classes include. Since it is certainly false that the classes, in each case, include any such items as our answers claim they do, those answers can, without too much squeamishness, be simply marked as wrong answers. So to mark them is not to reject them as answers to questions which don't arise, but to reject them as wrong answers to questions which do arise. Yet the answers need include only *one* referring expression for a particular item, viz. the one guilty of reference-failure; and the questions need not contain any at all.

This suggests a direction in which we might look for the missing principle of choice in the case of our previous examples, those about the swimming-pool and the Exhibition, which contained two referring expressions. The point was not, or was not solely, that each contained an extra and satisfactory referring expression. It was rather that we could easily see the centre of interest in each case as being the question, e.g. *how Jones spent the morning* or *what notable visitors the Exhibition has had*, or *how the Exhibition is getting on*. And the naturalness of taking them in this way was increased by the device of putting the satisfactory referring expression *first*, as grammatical subject of the sentence, and the unsatisfactory one last. We might, for example, have felt a shade more squeamish if we had written 'The king of France visited the Exhibition yesterday' instead of 'The Exhibition was visited yesterday by the king of France'. We feel very squeamish indeed about 'The king of France is bald' presented abruptly, out of context, just because we don't naturally and immediately think of a context in which interest is centred, say, on the question *What bald notables are there?* rather than on the question *What is the king of France like?* or *Is the king of France bald?* Of course, to either of *these* two questions the statement would not be just an incorrect answer. *These* questions have no correct answer and hence, in a sense, no incorrect answer either. They *are* questions which do not arise. This does not mean there is no correct *reply* to them. The correct reply is: 'There is no king of France'. But this reply is not an answer to, but a rejection of, the question. The question about bald notables, on the other hand, *can* be answered, rightly or wrongly. Any answer which purports to mention someone included in the class, and fails to do so, is wrong; and it is still wrong even if there is no such person at all as it purports to mention.

I should like to state the considerations I have been hinting at a little more generally, and with less dependence upon the notion of a question. Summarily my suggestions are as follows.

(1) First comes the additional platitude I promised. Statements, or the pieces of discourse to which they belong, have subjects, not only in the relatively precise senses of logic and grammar, but in a vaguer sense with which I shall associate the words 'topic' and 'about'. Just now I used the hypothesis of a *question* to bring out, with somewhat unnatural sharpness, the idea of the topic or centre of interest of a statement, the idea of what a statement could be said, in this sense, to be about. But even where there is no actual first-order question to pinpoint for us with this degree of sharpness the answer to the higher-order question, 'What is the statement, in this sense, about'?, it may nevertheless often be possible to give a fairly definite answer to this question. For stating is not a gratuitous and random human activity. We do not, except in social desperation, direct isolated and unconnected pieces of information at each other, but on the contrary intend in general to give or add information about what is a matter of standing or current interest or concern. There is a great variety of possible types of answer to the question what the topic of a statement is, what a statement is 'about' – about baldness, about what great men are bald, about which countries have bald rulers, about France, about the king, etc. – and not every such answer excludes every other in a given case. This platitude we might dignify with the title, the Principle of Relevance.

(2) It comes to stand beside that other general platitude which I announced earlier under the title, the Principle of the Presumption of Knowledge. This principle, it will be remembered, is that statements, in respect of their informativeness, are not generally self-sufficient units, free of any reliance upon what the audience is assumed to know or to assume already, but commonly depend for their effect upon knowledge assumed to be already in the audience's possession. The particular application I made of this principle was to the case of identifying reference, in so far as the performance of this function rests on the presumption of identifying knowledge in the possession of the audience. When I say that

the new platitude comes to stand beside the old one, I mean that the spheres of (*a*) what a statement addressed to an audience is *about* and (*b*) what, in the making of that statement, the audience is assumed to have some knowledge of already, are spheres that will often, and naturally, overlap.

But (3) they need not be co-extensive. Thus, given a statement which contains a referring expression, the specification of that statement's topic, what it is about, would very often involve mentioning, or seeming to mention, the object which that expression was intended to refer to; but sometimes the topic of a statement containing such an expression could be specified without mentioning such an object. Let us call the first type of case Type 1 and the second type of case Type 2. (Evidently a statement could be of Type 1 relative to one referring expression it contained and of Type 2 relative to another.)

Now (4) assessments of statements as true or untrue are commonly, though not only, topic-centred in the same way as the statements assessed; and when, as commonly, this is so, we may say that the statement is assessed *as* putative information *about its topic*.

Hence (5), given a case of radical reference-failure on the part of a referring expression, the truth-value gap account of the consequences of this failure will seem more naturally applicable if the statement in question is of Type 1 (relative to that referring expression) than if it is of Type 2. For if it is of Type 2, the failure of reference does not affect the topic of the statement, it merely affects what purports to be information *about its topic*. We may still judge the statement as putative information *about its topic* and say, perhaps, that the failure of reference has the consequence that it is *mis*informative *about its topic*. But we cannot say this if it is a case of Type 1. If it is a case of Type 1, the failure of reference affects the topic itself and not merely the putative information about the topic. If we know of the reference-failure, we know that the statement cannot really have the topic it is intended to have and hence cannot be assessed as putative information about that topic. It can be seen neither as correct, nor as incorrect, information *about its topic*.

But, it might be said, this account is self-contradictory. For it implies that in a Type 1 case of radical reference-failure the statement does not really *have* the topic which by hypothesis it does have; it implies that a statement which, by hypothesis, is *about* something is really about nothing. To this objection we must reply with a distinction. If I believe that the legend of King Arthur is historical truth, when there was in fact no such person, I may in one sense make statements *about* King Arthur, *describe* King Arthur and make King Arthur my *topic*. But there is another sense in which I cannot make statements about King Arthur, describe him or make him my topic. This second sense is stronger than the first. I may suppose myself to be making statements about him in the second, stronger sense; but I am really only making statements about him in the first and weaker sense. If, however, my belief in King Arthur were true and I really was making statements about him in the second sense, it would still be true that I was making statements about him in the first sense. This is why the first is a weaker (i.e. more comprehensive) sense than the second and not merely different from it.

Bearing this distinction of sense in mind, we can now frame a recipe for distinguishing those cases of reference-failure which are relatively favourable to the truth-value gap theory from those cases which are relatively unfavourable to it. The recipe is as follows. Consider in its context the statement suffering from reference-failure and frame a certain kind of description of the speech-episode of making it. The description is to begin with some phrase like 'He (i.e. the speaker) was saying (describing) . . .' and is to continue with an interrogative pronoun, adjective, or adverb, introducing a dependent clause. The clause, with its introductory conjunction, specifies the topic of the statement, what it can be said (at least in the weaker, and, if there is no reference-failure, also in the stronger, sense) to be *about*; while *what is said about its topic* is eliminated from the description in favour of the interrogative expression. Examples of such descriptions based on cases already mentioned would be:

He was describing *how Jones spent the morning*
He was saying *which notable contemporaries are bald*
He was saying *what the king of France is like*.

If the peccant referring expression survives in the clause introduced by the interrogative, the clause which specifies what the original statement was about, then we have a case relatively favourable to the truth-value gap theory. If the peccant referring expression is eliminated, and thus belongs to what purports to be information about the topic of the original statement, then we have a case relatively unfavourable to the truth-value gap theory. There can be no true or false, right or wrong, descriptions-of-what-the-king-of-France-is-like, because there is no king of France. But there can be right or wrong descriptions-of-how-Jones-spent-the-morning, and the description of him as having spent it at the local swimming-pool is wrong because there is no such place.

It is easy to see why the relevance of these factors should have been overlooked by those philosophers, including myself, who, considering a few example sentences in isolation from possible contexts of their use, have been tempted to embrace, and to generalize, the truth-value gap theory. For, first, it often is the case that the topic of a statement is, or includes, something referred to by a referring expression; for such an expression invokes the knowledge or current perceptions of an audience, and what is of concern to an audience is often what it already knows something about or is currently perceiving. And, second, it often is the case that the placing of an expression at the beginning of a sentence, in the position of grammatical subject, serves, as it were, to announce the statement's topic. The philosopher, thinking about reference-failure in terms of one or two short and isolated example sentences beginning with referring expressions, will tend to be influenced by these facts without noticing *all* of what is influencing him. So he will tend to attribute his sense of something more radically wrong than falsity to the presence alone of what is alone obvious, viz. a referring expression which fails of reference; and thus will overlook altogether these considerations about aboutness or topic which I have been discussing.

Let me remark that I do not claim to have done more than mention one factor which may sometimes bear on the fact that a truth-value gap theory for the case of radical reference-failure is apt to seem more intuitively attractive in some instances than it does in others.

5. The Asymmetry of Subjects and Predicates

I

In *Analysis* for December 1965 Miss Anscombe says:

> What signally distinguishes names from expressions for predicates is that expressions for predicates can be negated, names not. I mean that negation, attached to a predicate, yields a new predicate, but when attached to a name it does not yield any name.[1]

In the *Philosophical Review* for the same year Geach says:

> What distinguishes predicates from subjects, I suggest, is ... that by negating a predicate we can get the negation of the proposition in which it was originally predicated (plainly there is nothing analogous for subject terms);[2]

and in *Reference and Generality* he has a somewhat longer passage to the same or a similar effect:

> When a proposition is negated, the negation may be taken as going with the predicate in a way in which it cannot be taken as going with the subject. For predicables always occur in contradictory pairs; and by attaching such a pair to a common subject, we get a contradictory pair of propositions. But we never have a pair of names so related that by attaching the same predicates to both we always get a pair of contradictory propositions.[3]

These remarks do not perhaps all come to quite the same thing. But they come nearly enough to the same thing to give the thing a name. I shall call it the *thesis of the asymmetry of subjects and predicates regarding negation*, or, for short, the asymmetry thesis.

I shall not dispute the truth of the asymmetry thesis, but shall, instead, try to explain why it is true. Of course, in undertaking

[1] p. 33.   [2] p. 461.   [3] p. 32.

such an attempt at explanation, I am disputing – if anyone upholds it – a different contention, viz. the contention that the asymmetry thesis of itself expounds or makes clear the nature of the distinction between subject and predicate, so that there is simply no room for the question *why* the thesis is true. But this would not be a very plausible contention. In any case, the best rebuttal of the view that there is no room for a certain question is to produce a satisfactory answer to that question. So I will not linger further on this view now.

II

Instead, I shall begin a little obliquely by considering a possible objection to the asymmetry thesis, an objection which would rightly be held by upholders of the thesis to miss its point altogether. But it may clarify the nature of the thesis a little to see just this. Consider the following three remarks about Tom, his camera, and the relations between them:

> If anyone has sold his camera, it is not Tom.
> If Tom has disposed of (or otherwise modified his relation to) his camera, it is not by selling it.
> If Tom has sold anything, it is not his camera.

As regards their truth-conditions, these remarks appear to be equivalent to each other and to the negation of

> Tom has sold his camera,

i.e. to

> Tom has not sold his camera.

Indeed by varying the distribution of stress in our pronouncing of the last sentence, we could confer upon it the force of each of the three previous remarks in turn (first stress 'Tom', then 'sold', then 'camera'). We could then perfectly properly characterize the difference in force between the three remarks, as made in the second way, i.e. with shifting stress, by saying that negation was to be taken in each case with a different part of the proposition which is negated alike in them all. Introducing now the terminology of subject and predicate; and making one presumably acceptable application of it, we could add that in none of the instanced cases was negation to be taken with the predicate as a whole; in one case it was to be taken with one part of the predicate, viz. '. . . sold . . .', in another with another part, viz.

'. . . his camera', and in the remaining case with the subject, viz. 'Tom'. In general, the argument concludes, negation has no natural affinity for one part rather than another of a negated subject-predicate proposition. Its attachments may vary from part to part, depending on the force with which the proposition is propounded; or it may simply attach to the proposition as a whole.

The upholder of the asymmetry thesis will reply that the facts adduced in this objection are quite beside the point. The sense, invoked in the objection, in which negation may be taken now with one part, now with another part, of a proposition belongs to a different level of theory altogether from that to which the asymmetry thesis belongs. The thesis is not at all concerned with differences in the force with which a proposition or its negation may be propounded, but with the common propounded thing, the proposition or its negation. The point is that negation can never be taken together with the subject of the negated proposition *as yielding a new expression of the same kind, or having the same role*, as the subject of the original proposition; whereas negation can always be taken together with the predicate of the negated proposition *as yielding a new expression of the same kind, or having the same role*, as the predicate of the original proposition. But this reply, though it may be perfectly correct, merely sharpens our sense of the need for an explanation.

III

Before embarking on the explanation of the asymmetry of subjects and predicates regarding negation, we should note that this is not the only asymmetry we shall have to explain. Asymmetry regarding negation (negatability) carries with it as a consequence a certain asymmetry regarding composition (compoundability). To see that this is so, let us regard the original asymmetry thesis as supplying a *test* for subjects and predicates, and a test which we sufficiently well understand to be satisfied that when applied to a proposition such as 'Tom is tall', it yields 'Tom' as subject and 'is tall' as predicate; i.e. we are to be supposed to understand the requirement about sameness of kind of expression sufficiently well to appreciate that when we introduce 'not' into the original proposition so as to yield its negation, we can take 'not' together with 'is tall' to yield a new expression of the same kind as 'is tall', whereas, even if it is allowable in some sense to take 'not' with

'Tom', we should not thereby obtain an expression of the same kind as 'Tom'.

Consider now the following four propositions:

(1) Tom is either tall or bald
(2) Tom is both tall and bald
(3) Both Tom and William are tall
(4) Either Tom or William is tall

Each of (1) to (4) is, evidently, equivalent to some disjunction or conjunction of two of the three (atomic) propositions 'Tom is tall', 'Tom is bald', 'William is tall'. If we apply our test to the first two of the four numbered propositions, we seem to come out with the satisfactory result that 'Tom' is the subject in each case and 'is either tall or bald' and 'is both tall and bald' are compound predicates. This result is satisfactory because we see at once the possibility of a smooth and coherent formal theory of the logic of propositions with simple and compound predicates, a theory in which the relations of 'Tom is tall and bald', 'Tom is tall', and 'Tom is either tall or bald' can be clearly exhibited.

But now what of propositions (3) and (4), i.e. 'Both Tom and William are tall' and 'Either Tom or William is tall'. We might be inclined unreflectively to say that what we have here is a pair of propositions with compound subjects just as what we have in the other case is a pair of propositions with compound predicates. The logical relations these propositions have to each other and to 'Tom is tall' are just as intuitively clear as the logical relations which the propositions with compound predicates have to each other and to 'Tom is tall'. There should be no impediment to constructing as satisfactory a formal theory for propositions with compound subjects as can be constructed for propositions with compound predicates.

This optimism, however, receives a decisive check as soon as we bring the asymmetry thesis regarding negation to bear on the propositions with putative compound subjects. For the negation of 'Both Tom and William are tall' is not 'Both Tom and William are not tall' but 'Not both Tom and William are tall' and the negation of 'Either Tom or William is tall' is not 'Either Tom or William is not tall' but 'Neither Tom nor William is tall'. That is to say, there is a clear and unexceptionable sense in which negation *must* be taken with the putative subjects, rather than the putative

predicates, of the original propositions in order to yield the negations of these propositions. Thus 'is tall' and 'are tall' fail the test
for being predicates of these putative subjects and their failure
carries with it the failure of the putative subjects to qualify as
subjects of their putative predicates.

What, then, does the asymmetry thesis license our saying about
these propositions? Should we say that 'Both Tom and William'
and 'Either Tom or William' pass the tests for predicates, and
hence that 'is tall' and 'are tall' should be allowed as subjects of
these predicates? There are fatal objections to this: (i) it is highly
counter-intuitive; (ii) so far from advancing the prospects for a
smooth logical theory capable of exhibiting the logical relationships of all the propositions concerned, it would put an obstacle
in the way of those prospects; and (iii) it is not sanctioned by the
asymmetry test itself. What kind of understanding of the notion
of 'same kind of expression' would we have to possess in order
confidently to disallow 'not Tom' as an expression of the same kind
as 'Tom' while confidently allowing 'not both Tom and William'
as an expression of the same kind as 'Tom and William'?

Of course the adherent of the asymmetry thesis has not come
to the end of his resources. There is something else he can say. He
can say that the appearance of symmetry between propositions (1)
and (2) on the one hand and propositions (3) and (4) on the other
is misleading. The expressions 'is either tall or bald' and 'is both
tall and bald' are indeed compound predicates, disjunctive and
conjunctive respectively, whereas the expressions 'Both Tom
and William' and 'Either Tom or William' are not predicates at all
and hence not compound predicates: but they are not compound
subjects either; for there are no such things as compound (conjunctive or disjunctive) subjects. Alongside the asymmetry of
subjects and predicates regarding negation, we must install
another asymmetry regarding conjunctive or disjunctive composition. Compound predicates have a place in logical theory, compound subjects have not. This does not mean that we are at a loss
for anything at all to say about propositions (3) and (4). One thing
we could say, for example, is that 'Both Tom and William are tall'
is simply a linguistically legitimate abbreviation of the compound
(conjunctive) *proposition*, 'Tom is tall and William is tall' and that
'Not both Tom and William are tall' is the corresponding abbreviation of the negation of the compound proposition. In the case

of propositions (1) and (2), on the other hand, there is no need for any such resource. For while propositions (1) and (2) are also equivalent to compound propositions, the terms 'is both tall and bald' and 'is either tall or bald' have a place in logical theory as they stand, as compound predicate-terms; whereas no such place is available for the expressions 'Both Tom and William' and 'Either Tom or William'. These last are not logical-subject-terms, but only pseudo-logical-subject-terms.

So, then if the asymmetry thesis regarding negation is true, we must accept a further asymmetry between subjects and predicates as regards composition. There are compound predicates but no compound subjects. Evidently it would be satisfactory if we could see this restriction not merely as an imposed consequence of the acceptance of the asymmetry thesis but as something intrinsically acceptable. It would be more satisfactory still if the reasons why the asymmetry thesis regarding negation is true proved to have a certain harmony with, to be reasons of the same general kind as, the reasons why there are compound predicates but no compound subjects.

IV

I shall argue that we can find such harmonizing reasons for these asymmetries if and only if we attend to certain other asymmetries; and that these other and underlying asymmetries require for their description a more extended terminology than that of *formal* logic alone. To find these underlying asymmetries we must attend in the first place to propositions of a certain class, which I shall describe somewhat artificially as follows. In any proposition of this class there are presented as assigned to each other a specified empirical particular (or spatiotemporal individual) and a specified general character or kind of empirical particulars. I speak, in symmetrical style, of the particular individual and the general character or kind being presented as *assigned to each other* because asymmetries of direction of fit do not here concern us. I speak of their being *presented as* assigned to each other because the question whether such a proposition is *asserted* or introduced into discourse in some other way is equally irrelevant.

Of course different empirical particulars may be presented as assigned to the same general character, and different general characters may be presented as assigned to the same empirical particular. So far there is still symmetry; but there are also asymmetries. Every general character is such that, whatever individual particular it may be presented as assigned to, there is some other general character, or range of characters, the possession of which, or of any member of which, by the individual in question would be *incompatible* with its possession of the specified character. It is not the case, however, that every (or indeed any) individual particular is such that, whatever general character it may be presented as assigned to, there is some other individual or range of individuals the possession by which, or by any member of which, of the character in question would be incompatible with its being possessed by the specified individual. In brief: Every general character competes for location, in any and every particular individual it might belong to, with some other general character. But it is not the case that every particular individual competes for possession of any and every general character it might possess with some other particular individual. Indeed no particular individual does so. We might speak of this asymmetry as *asymmetry between particulars and general characters of particulars in respect of the possession of incompatibility-ranges*.

Now for another asymmetry. This is of the same family as the first though it cannot be stated quite so simply. We may express it roughly by saying that it is typical of general characters of particulars to stand to other general characters of particulars in certain relations which can be expressed in the terminology of necessary and sufficient conditions; whereas no symmetrical sense can be found in which particulars can be said to stand to other particulars in such relations. These relations between general characters are of different degrees of complexity. It will be sufficient for the immediate purpose to mention the simplest kind of case. This is the case exemplified by any general character – and there are many – which is such that, whatever individual particular it is presented as assigned to, either there is some other general character (or characters) the possession of which by the specified individual would be *sufficient* for that individual's possession of the assigned character or there is some other general character (or characters) the possession of which by the specified individual would be *necessary* for that individual's possession of the assigned character. Neither for this simplest case nor for the more complex cases is it possible to find any symmetrically explicable relationships between particular individuals. It is not the case that *any* particular individual at all is such that, whatever general character is presented as assigned to it, either there is some other individual (or individuals) the possession by which of the specified character would be *sufficient* for the assigned individual's possession of that character or there is some other individual (or individuals) the possession by which of the specified character would be *necessary* for the assigned individual's possession of that character. We might speak of this asymmetry as *asymmetry between particulars and general characters of particulars in respect of the possession of sufficient and/or necessary conditions.*

To express these asymmetries differently: We are considering the class of propositions in each of which a specified particular individual *i* and a specified general character *g* are presented as assigned to each other. Then for all *g*, for all *i*, by keeping *i* constant and varying *g*, we can obtain a proposition (or propositions) incompatible with the proposition we started with, and, for some *g*, for all *i*, by keeping *i* constant and varying *g*, we can obtain a proposition (or propositions) related to the original proposition in one direction or the other by the relation of one-way entailment. But it is not even the case that for *some i*, for all *g*, by keeping *g* constant and varying *i* we can obtain a proposition (or propositions) incompatible with the original proposition; and it is not the case that for some *i*, for all *g*, by keeping *g* constant and varying *i*, we can obtain a proposition (or propositions) related to the original proposition in one direction or the other by the relation of one-way entailment. General characters, we may say, come in groups the members of which are related by relations of mutual exclusiveness or (sometimes) of one-way involvement *vis-à-vis* any and every particular they may be assigned to. But particular individuals do not come in groups the members of which are related by relations of mutual exclusiveness or of one-way involvement *vis-à-vis* any and every general character they may be assigned to.

These asymmetries seem to be as obvious and (nearly) as fundamental as anything can be in philosophy.

V

Let us now simply *appropriate* the expressions 'subject' and 'predicate' as follows. In any proposition in which a specified individual particular and a specified general character are presented as assigned to each other, the expression which has the function of specifying the assigned particular (say, a proper name of that particular) is the subject; and, in any such proposition, the expression which, whatever other function it may also have, has the function of specifying the assigned general character, is the predicate. We now ask whether, given this appropriation of the expressions 'subject' and 'predicate', the asymmetries just remarked on explain and vindicate, for this class of propositions, the asymmetries of subjects and predicates in respect of negation and composition. I think they do.

Let us begin with the case of asymmetry as regards negation. Consider any proposition in which a specified particular individual i and a specified general character g_1 are presented as assigned to each other. Call this proposition P_1:

$$P_1 \quad \text{ass } (i \ g_1)$$

Because of one of the features of general characters just remarked on, we know that by replacing the predicate of P_1 by an expression specifying some other suitably chosen character, say g_2, and leaving its subject unchanged, we can obtain a proposition incompatible with P_1, say P_2. (The incompatibility of P_1 and P_2 is represented below by the symbol 'X'.):

$$P_1 \quad \text{ass } (i \ g_1)$$
$$\text{X}$$
$$P_2 \quad \text{ass } (i \ g_2)$$

We can describe the incompatibility of P_1 and P_2 by saying that they have the same subject and incompatible predicates; and we can represent this relation between the predicates as under:

$$P_1 \quad \text{ass } (i \ \begin{vmatrix} g_1 \\ \text{X} \\ g_2 \end{vmatrix} \ )$$
$$P_2$$

Now consider the negations of P_1 and P_2. They are the propositions, we may say, in which the individual in question and the relevant character are presented, not as assigned to, but as withheld from (or negatively assigned to), each other. Call them P_1' and P_2'. Negative assignment we may represent by putting a negation sign above 'ass' thus:

$$P_1' \; \overline{\text{ass}} \; (i \; g_1)$$
$$P_2' \; \overline{\text{ass}} \; (i \; g_2)$$

Since P_1 and P_2 are incompatible with each other, P_1 entails P_2' and P_2 entails P_1'. Thus we have, using '→' for 'entails':

Fig. I
$$P_1 \quad \text{ass } (i \,|\, g_1 \,|) \to \overline{\text{ass}} \; (i \; g_2) \; P_2'$$
$$\times \qquad\qquad \times$$
$$P_2 \quad \text{ass } (i \,|\, g_2 \,|) \to \overline{\text{ass}} \; (i \; g_1) \; P_1'$$

The fact that P_1 and P_2 are incompatible with each other is, as we have seen, really identical with (or dependent upon) the fact that they have the same subjects and incompatible predicates. And the fact that P_1 entails P_2' and P_2 entails P_1' is really identical with (or dependent upon) the fact that P_1 is incompatible with P_2. These identities (or dependences) are clearly registered if, in the case of each negating or withholding proposition, we take negation, together with the predicate of the proposition of which it is the negation, as forming a new, a negative, predicate, i.e. if, in Figure I, we transfer the negation sign in P_2' and P_1' from 'ass' to 'g_2' and 'g_1' respectively:

Fig. II
$$P_1 \text{ ass } (i \,|\, g_1 \,|) \to \text{ass } (i \,|\, \overline{g}_2 \,|) \quad P_2'$$
$$\times \qquad\qquad \times$$
$$P_2 \text{ ass } (i \,|\, g_2 \,|) \to \text{ass } (i \,|\, \overline{g}_1 \,|) \quad P_1'$$

Incompatibility of predicates in the case of P_1 and P_2 then appears as the same thing as the *entailment (involvement) of the negative predicate* of P_1' by the predicate of P_2 and the *entailment (involvement) of the negative predicate* of P_2' by the predicate of P_1. In this way we do justice to the logical (but nor formally logical) relations of incompatibility and entailment in which the members of any such pair of propositions as P_1 and P_1' (i.e. a proposition of our chosen class and its negation) stand to other propositions (e.g. P_2 and P_2') in virtue of the logical relatedness (incompatibility) of general characters. Here we have an argument for taking negation with the predicate; but we can construct no parallel argument for taking negation with the *subject* of the original proposition in each case as forming a new, a negative, subject. We could construct such an argument only if there were such things as incompatible subjects in a sense symmetrical with the sense in which there are incompatible predicates; only, that is to say, if by keeping g_1

H

constant, *whatever it was*, we could always form another proposition incompatible with P_1 by replacing the designation of i, whatever i was, with an expression specifying a different particular individual. But the fact that we can always perform the operation with changing characters and not with changing particular individuals is precisely the asymmetry we started with.

The relations I have been speaking of can be presented in a simplified figure. Thus we have:

$$\text{Fig. III} \quad i \begin{cases} g_1 \;\; \text{X} \;\; g_2 \\ \;\;\downarrow \quad\;\; \downarrow \\ \overline{g_2} \quad\;\; \overline{g_1} \end{cases}$$

where g_1 and g_2 are incompatible general characters and i represents any particular to which either might be assigned. Taking the character-specifying part of any proposition in which either of them is so assigned as the predicate of that proposition, we then have the entailment (involvement) of the relevant negative predicate in each case represented by the downward arrows.

There is no counterpart diagram we can draw in which 'g' replaces 'i' and 'i_1', 'i_2' replace 'g_1', 'g_2'.

The argument can be clinched by considering the limiting case, and bearing in mind that it is only the limiting case, of the kind of relationships just described. This is the case which we have when there are a pair of characters g_1 and g_2 which are not only incompatible but complementary. That is to say, it is the case in which, given a proposition P_1 in which g_1 and some specified particular i are presented as assigned to each other, and a proposition P_2 obtained from P_1 by replacing the expression specifying g_1 by an expression specifying g_2, there is no logical room for a third proposition incompatible with both and obtained from either by replacing the expression specifying g_1 or g_2, as the case may be, with an expression specifying a third character g_3. Perhaps the expressions 'is stationary' and 'is moving' may be regarded as specifying complementary characters in this sense. And there are many pairs of expressions which might be tentatively offered, involving such prefixes or suffixes as 'non-', 'un-', '-less': e.g. harmful, harmless; happy, unhappy; toxic, non-toxic; obtrusive, unobtrusive, and so on. It may well be that our need for nuances makes this class rather less extensive than we might at first be inclined to think. Certainly there are enormous and varied ranges of character-specifying expressions for which ordinary language offers no plausible candidates as their complementaries: e.g. asparagus, elephant, red, two inches long, and so on.

Given, then, that g_1 and g_2 are complementary characters and allowing, as before, that P_1' and P_2' are the negations of P_1 and P_2, then we not only have the relations we had before, viz. that, since P_1 is incompatible with P_2, P_1 entails P_2' and P_2 entails P_1', we also have the converses of these last relations. (We can add, in these cases, upward arrows to our last diagram.) And here the case for taking negation, in P_1' or P_2', together with the original predicate of P_1 or P_2, as forming a new, a negative, predicate – a term of the same kind – is too clear for it to be worthwhile setting it out in form. It reflected, of course, in ordinary language in the use of the negative prefixes and suffixes just mentioned, where a formal sign of negation is absorbed into a character-specifying expression. But it must be pointed out that the case *is* a limiting case and that the *general* justification of taking negation as part of the predicate in propositions of our chosen class rests on the prior identification of predicates with the character-specifying expressions which figure in such propositions. Because every general character is incompatible, in the required sense, with some other, there is at least the possibility of complementary characters. Because there is no symmetrical sense in which any particular individual is incompatible with any other, there is no sense in the notion of complementary particular individuals.

VI

Now we pass to asymmetry as regards composition. I expressed the underlying asymmetry in this case by saying that while characters may typically stand in the relations of being sufficient or necessary conditions of other characters, there is no symmetrical sense in which particular individuals may be said to stand in such relations. Note that in denying that there are any such relations in the case of particular individuals, I am not claiming that there are no particular individuals such that there are no ways of specifying those individuals such that there are no general characters at all such that a proposition assigning a general character to one of those individuals entails or is entailed by a proposition assigning that general character to the other. Thus suppose there is a chair C, made of pure gold. Then the proposition that C is of pure gold entails the proposition that the seat of C is of pure gold. But of course the proposition that C weighs twenty pounds does not entail the proposition that the seat of C weighs twenty pounds. So it would be a great misunderstanding of the general principle to suppose that any such case constitutes a counter-example to it; but I will not linger tediously on the point.

Because we can sensibly speak of characters standing in these necessary-or-sufficient-condition relations to other characters, we can sensibly define certain more complex relations in which characters might stand to other characters. Thus I define two triadic relations as follows: (1) g_3 is the conjunctive character of g_1 and g_2 when g_1 and g_2 are jointly sufficient and singly necessary for g_3 and neither is sufficient or necessary for the other; (2) g_3 is the disjunctive character of g_1 and g_2 when each is singly sufficient for g_3 and each is necessary in the absence of the other. We can not only define such relations, we can find examples of them. Thus the character expressed by 'is a deaf-mute' is the conjunctive character of the characters expressed by 'is deaf' and 'is dumb'. The character expressed by 'has a sibling' is the disjunctive character of the characters expressed by 'has a brother' and 'has a sister'.

Ordinary language perhaps provides relatively few examples of expressions, not formally compound, which signify conjunctive or disjunctive characters of other characters; but it would be possible vastly to extend the class of such expressions. Consider any two characters, e.g. tall, bald, such that there is a class of particular individuals such that each character could, independently of the other, be consistently assigned to one and the same specified particular individual of that class. Then the definitions just given of disjunctive or conjunctive characters in general seem to provide us with the means of defining the disjunctive or conjunctive character of those two characters (though we must stipulate also, in the case of conjunctive characters, that the two characters are not incompatible with each other). But then again, we can dispense with any such definitions by utilizing some standard formal means of representing the relationships which would be invoked in such definitions. This we do by linking the character-specifying expressions concerned by the same signs as are used in the formation of conjunctive or disjunctive propositions. Given our decision about the appropriation of the terms 'subject' and 'predicate' in the case of propositions in which a specified particular individual and a specified general character are presented as assigned to each other, we obviously need no further argument for counting a formally compound expression specifying a disjunctive or conjunctive character as the predicate of a proposition in which that character and a specified individual are presented as assigned to each other.

The case for compound predicates is complete. For compound subjects, on the other hand, there can be nothing but the illusion of a case. We can indeed take the *first* step towards framing the idea of a compound (i.e. conjunctive or disjunctive) particular individual. That is to say, we can consider two particulars, say Tom and William, such that there is a class of characters such that each of the two particular individuals could, independently of the other, be consistently assigned to any character of that class. But no basis exists for taking the *second* step, i.e. the step which would correspond to defining the conjunctive or disjunctive character of two characters. For this step could be taken only if we could speak of one particular individual being a necessary or sufficient condition of another in a sense which symmetrically corresponds to that in which we can speak of one general character being a necessary or sufficient condition of another. And, as we have seen, there is no such sense.

How does the illusion of a case for compound subjects arise? It arises, evidently, from the fact that we can legitimately frame sentences with the following characteristics: (1) their *grammatical* subjects are compounds of expressions specifying particular individuals and their grammatical predicates are expressions specifying general characters of particulars; (2) they express propositions equivalent to conjunctions or disjunctions of propositions of which the several individual subjects are those which appear as compounded in the sentences with apparent compound subjects, and of which the predicates specify the same general characters as those specified by the grammatical predicates of those sentences. And here we have a deceptive analogy with the case of compound predicates. That it is no more than a deceptive analogy we see as soon as we set up the conditions, symmetrically analogous to those for compound characters, which would have to be satisfied by conjunctive or disjunctive individuals, and see the senselessness of supposing that they could be satisfied. Hence we are obliged to rule, with regard to such sentences, that their grammatical subjects are not logically compound subjects and their grammatical predicates are no true logical predicates to such subjects. Instead we read them as permitted and linguistically natural abbreviations of compound propositions of which the constituents have different subjects and share the same predicate. But this conclusion we arrive at now, not as a consequence of accepting the asymmetry thesis regarding negation, but by an independent argument based upon the provisional decision about the identification of subject and predicate in a proposition in which a specified particular individual and a specified general character are presented as assigned to each other. Given that decision, it follows by independently statable, though consilient, arguments *both* that in the negation of such a proposition negation is properly taken with the predicate of the original proposition as forming a new predicate *and* that compound predicates are admissible whereas compound subjects, like negative subjects, are inadmissible.

There may remain a lingering doubt about compound subjects. Could we not, after all, it might be said, find direct analogues among individuals for disjunctive or conjunctive characters – by recognizing slightly unusual types of individual? Why not, to take the more promising-looking case, a conjunctive individual? Might not *a couple* be, in precisely the required sense, a conjunctive individual? Jane is handsome and Thomas is handsome. They are a handsome couple. The possession of this character by Jane (i_1) and its possession by Thomas (i_2) are jointly sufficient and singly necessary to its possession by the third individual (i_3), the couple. So far, if a little shakily, so good. But suppose Jane has seven children and Thomas has seven children. Does it follow that the couple has seven children? In one sense (as a couple) they may have none; in another the couple may have (between them) fourteen – or any smaller number down to seven. Or suppose that they are a very diverse couple. Does it follow that Jane is very diverse? or that Thomas is? So much for the couple as a conjunctive individual of two individuals. I am tempted to pass over in silence the disjunctive individual as unlikely to appeal to anyone. But lest it should seem that I am avoiding a possible difficulty, let it suffice to point out that in order for it to be true that either Tom or William is always on duty it is not necessary, if Tom is not always on duty, that William should be, or if William is not, that Tom should be.[1]

VII

I have been arguing that, given *our* choice of a certain class of propositions and given *our* appropriations of the expression 'subject' and 'predicate' in relation to propositions of that class, then we have an adequate explanation and vindication of the asymmetry thesis regarding subjects and predicates, both in respect of negation and in respect of composition, *so far as propositions of that class are concerned*. But to say that the explanation and vindication are *so far* adequate is not to say that they are adequate

[1] I have, surprisingly, found that the hankering for disjunctive or conjunctive particulars is not always dispelled by these arguments. Surely – I have heard it said – we can just *define* an individual particular as the disjunctive particular of the two others (say, Tom and William); or as their conjunctive particular. So let me just illustrate some consequences of such attempts.

(1) Take Tom and William and their supposed disjunctive particular, Tilliam.

Suppose the following proposition is true:

Tom is taller than William.

Since from the fact that Tom has a certain property it follows that Tilliam has it, and from the fact that William has a certain property it also follows that Tilliam has it, it follows that Tilliam is taller than himself.

(2) Take Tom and William and their supposed conjunctive particular, Tolliam.

Suppose Tom and William are both in the drawing-room. Then since Tolliam has all and only the properties that both Tom and William have, Tolliam is in the drawing-room too. Suppose, however, that Tom (and every part of him) is in the eastern half of the drawing-room and that William (and every part of him) is in the western half of the drawing-room. Then where in the drawing-room is Tolliam? He is not in the eastern half, for William is not there. And he is not in the western half, for Tom is not there. Nor does he straddle both halves, for neither Tom nor William does. So he is not in the drawing-room at all. So he both is and is not in the drawing-room.

The idea of the complementary particular of a given particular has not seemed so attractive, perhaps because the general difficulties are more obvious in this case, e.g. if the given particular possesses a certain determinate member of a range of incompatible characters (as a certain shape, or size, or age), it also possesses the complementary character of each of the other members of the range. Hence the supposed complementary of the given particular would have to possess the complementaries of all those complementary characters, i.e. it would have to possess all but one of the incompatible characters of the range.

in *general*. For, in the first place, even if we restrict our attention to propositions of the *fa* form – singular subject-predicate propositions – not all such propositions are propositions in which an individual spatiotemporal particular and a general character of particulars are presented as assigned to each other. In the second place, even if we succeed in generalizing our explanation for propositions of the *fa* form, there arises the question of whether our logical conception of subject and predicate should not be extended beyond propositions of the *fa* form. This second question has many ramifications and I shall not discuss it in this paper. But I should, in conclusion, like to say something about the problem of generalizing our explanation for propositions of the *fa* form.

Let us look back to the underlying asymmetries invoked in our explanation for the chosen class of propositions. One way in which I stated them was as follows:

> *general characters* come in groups the members of which are related by relations of mutual exlusiveness or (sometimes) of one-way involvement *vis-à-vis* any and every *individual particular* they may be presented as assigned to;
> but *individual particulars* do not come in groups related by relations of mutual exclusiveness or one-way involvement *vis-à-vis* any and every *general character* they may be presented as assigned to. Let us write this, for short:
> *general characters* come in exclusiveness/involvement groups *vis-à-vis individual particulars*;
> *individual particulars* do not come in exclusiveness/involvement groups *vis-à-vis general characters*.

But here we have a generalizable form of contrast. Let us substitute '*y*' for '*general character*' and '*x*' for '*individual particular*', thus obtaining a general form of statement of a certain condition which we will call the '*x/y* condition'. Suppose we have any proposition which can be viewed as a proposition in which an *x* and a *y* are presented as assigned to each other, where it is understood that *x*s and *y*s fall, relatively to each other, under the *x/y* condition. Then we *already* have a vindication of the thesis that the *x*-specifying part and the y-specifying part of that proposition are asymmetrical in respect of negation and compoundability in just the ways we have been concerned with. For generalizing the condition automatically generalizes the argument based upon the condition. So one way – I do not say the only, or even the best way, but certainly the quickest way – of obtaining a generalization of our explanation is this. Simply take 'Expressions e and e' are respectively subject and predicate of proposition P' to be equivalent to: 'Proposition P can be viewed as a proposition in which an x and a y are presented as assigned to each other (where it is understood that xs and ys fall, relatively to each other, under the x/y condition) and expression e is the x-specifying part and expression e' of the y-specifying part of proposition P.'

To illustrate the application of the generalized definition to one type of proposition not belonging to our originally chosen class: I take as an example the proposition, 'Happiness is found in all stations in life'. The expression 'is found in all stations in life' specifies a character of characters which has its own incompatibility and involvement ranges in relation to any and every character such that that character and it may be presented as assigned to each other. Thus *being found in all stations in life* is this way incompatible with *being found in few stations in life* and entails (involves) *being found in most stations in life*. But it is not the case that the character-specifying expression 'happiness' specifies a character which has its own incompatibility and involvement ranges in relation to any and every character of characters such that it and that character of characters can be presented as assigned to each other. If we consider, say, *happiness*, *misery*, and *bliss* (or being in a state of bliss) in relation to individual particulars to which they may be presented as assigned, then we may indeed say that happiness is incompatible with misery and is involved or entailed by bliss. But if we consider them in relation to characters of characters to which they may be presented as assigned, then we can say no such thing. 'Happiness is found in all stations in life' is not incompatible with 'Misery is found in all stations in life' and 'Happiness is of short duration' is not entailed by 'Bliss is of short duration'.[1] Our definition, then, yields 'Happiness' as the subject

[1] It might be suggested that the involvement relation holds in the other direction, on the ground that 'Happiness is of short duration' entails 'Bliss is of short duration'. But no such relation holds in this direction either. For 'Happiness is found in all stations in life' does not entail 'Bliss is found in all stations in life'. And 'Bliss is more rarely enjoyed by the old than by the young' neither entails nor is entailed by 'Happiness is more rarely enjoyed by the old than by the young'.

and 'is found in all stations in life' as the predicate of our proposition.

VIII

Suppose it granted that the general criterion, or definition, of subject and predicate contains the underlying ground of the originally alleged asymmetries regarding negation and composition. Then why, it might finally be asked, should we present that definition *as* a generalization from a particular kind of case, viz. the case of the proposition in which a specified empirical particular and a specified general character of particulars are presented as assigned to each other? One might answer simply that the underlying asymmetries stand out with peculiar clarity in this kind of case. But this answer is too weak. It is not simply that these cases present very good *examples* or *illustrations* of the general thesis. These cases – or rather these cases together with *relational* propositions about specified particulars, which I neglected for the sake of expository simplicity – really are the fundamental cases of predication. They really are the model for the rest. For every other kind of subject-predicate proposition presupposes them and they presuppose no other kind of subject-predicate proposition. I will not try to argue this case now, though the evidence for it seems to me overwhelming. (I suspect, in any case, that few would wish to dispute it.) I will simply point out – to put it loosely – that the appearance of any type of item other than a particular in the role of subject is dependent upon, or presupposes, its capacity to appear in another propositional role.[1] We could not predicate anything of happiness unless we could predicate happiness of people. We could not predicate anything of a number unless we could predicate having a certain number of a set. We could not predicate anything of propositions unless we framed propositions in which nothing was predicated of propositions. The propositional role of the particular, on the other hand, is – with one dubious exception – always that of subject. The dubious exception is the case which I have elsewhere described[2] as that of a

[1] This is to put it very loosely. Strictly: the introduction or presentation of any type of item other than a particular by means of an expression having the role of subject is dependent upon, or presupposes, the possibility of introducing or presenting an item of that type by means of an expression having another propositional role.

[2] *Individuals*, Ch. 5, pp. 167 ff. (Methuen); pp. 168 ff. (Doubleday).

proposition in which a dependent and an independent particular are presented as 'attributively tied' to each other, for example, 'That shout was John's'. In such a case, it might be held, the dependent particular (the shout) and the independent particular (John) respectively satisfy, as far as incompatibility-ranges are concerned, the x-part and the y-part of the x/y condition; so the independent particular has a predicative role. Few would dispute, however, that this type of formation is derivative from the type exemplified by 'John shouted'. So even if we allow the dubious exception, we must add that the particular's capacity to appear in this type of case as a predicate is dependent upon, or presupposes, its capacity to appear elsewhere as a subject. Hence we still have the result that the appearance of any type of item other than a particular in the subject-role is dependent upon, or presupposes, its capacity to appear in another propositional role, while the appearance of a particular in the predicate-role, if admitted at all, is dependent upon its capacity to appear in the subject-role. So particular-specifying expressions really are the basic logical subjects, and the class which I selected as the base class of subject-predicate propositions really is the base class of such propositions.

6. Propositions, Concepts, and Logical Truths

The main purpose of Professor Quine's article, *Two Dogmas of Empiricism*, is to discredit a certain group of non-extensional notions, which includes those of logical necessity, logical impossibility, and synonymity or identity of meaning. His article contains, besides arguments directed to this aim, a certain characterization of truths of logic. I shall try to show that this characterization is coherent only if we suppose that it makes implicit use of one or more of the notions which it is the main purpose of the article to discredit.

I

Quine describes the truths of logic as follows: 'If we suppose a prior inventory of logical particles, comprising "no", "un-", "not", "if", "then", "and", etc., then in general a logical truth is a statement which is true and remains true under all reinterpretations of its components other than the logical particles.'[1] Elsewhere we learn that *reinterpreting the components* of a statement means *making substitutions as we please upon its component words and phrases*.[2] Evidently the apparent liberality of the expression 'as we please' is not to be taken too seriously. For suppose we take an example of an undoubted logical truth – say, 'If Socrates is wise, then Socrates is wise'. We might be pleased to replace the phrase 'Socrates is wise' in its second occurrence with the phrase 'Plato is foolish', while leaving it untouched in its first occurrence. But few people would want to say that 'If Socrates is wise, then Plato is foolish' expressed a truth of any kind; and fewer still would want to say that the fact that it was obtainable by means of *this* kind of substitution from 'If Socrates is wise, then Socrates is wise', showed that the latter did not, after all, express a logical truth. We clearly need some restrictive provision about uniformity of substitution, something, perhaps, like this: 'always

[1] *From a Logical Point of View*, pp. 22–3.
[2] *Methods of Logic*, p. xv.

provided that if one of the words or phrases for which we make a substitution occurs more than once in the original true statement, then the same substitution is made for every one of its occurrences'. But now the question arises: What counts as *the same* here? or, What are the criteria of identity of substitutions?

Let us for the moment confine our attention to the cases, such as the example just considered, where we make substitutions for phrases which could stand by themselves as complete sentences. Now what counts as making the same substitution twice in such a case? Is it enough that the *sentences* should be the same in each case, i.e. should consist in each case of the same words in the same order? Or, better, since there may be some dangerous ambiguities in the word 'word', is it enough that, were the substitutions written down, they should be found to consist of the same letters arranged in the same groupings in the same order? We may speak of this condition as that of 'typographical identity', for short. Now is typographical identity an adequate criterion of identity of substitutions in the cases in question? One could scarcely claim that it is. For consider two typographically identical occurrences of the sentence 'He is sick'. In one occurrence the sentence might be used to attribute a condition of mind to one person, in the other occurrence to attribute a condition of body to a different person. (Nor is this fact altered by replacing the pronoun 'he' by a proper name, say, 'John'.) If now, keeping in mind two such uses for this expression, we frame the sentence 'If he is sick, then he is sick', we obtain something which may be used to make statements some of which would be true and others false. Evidently, then, we have to make a choice between admitting that typographical identity is not an adequate criterion of identity for our purposes, and accepting the conclusion that there are no logical truths at all. For if it is insisted that typographical identity *is* a sufficient condition of the identity we seek, then, for every given candidate for logical truth, we could find a reinterpretation of the components other than the logical particles, such that the resulting statement was false. The example just produced destroys the claims of 'If Socrates is wise, then Socrates is wise', of any other statement of this form. Candidates for logical truth not belonging to the propositional logic are equally easily disposed of. For Quine's own example, 'No unmarried man is married', a suitable counter-example might be, for instance, 'No unilluminated book is illuminated'. It is not difficult to imagine circumstances in which one might make a false statement in these words.

One way that might occur to us of supplementing the condition of typographical identity is the following. We are to require, in the case of identical substitutions for sentence-like clauses, not only that sentences substituted should be identical (in the typographical sense), but that they should – in the context of use of the resulting total sentence – be used to make the same statement, or express the same proposition, or whatever else we choose to call those linguistically expressed things of which we predicate truth or falsity. This requirement is not quite correctly phrased. For in uttering a conditional sentence, for example, it is not the case that we use both of the constituent clauses to make statements; we make only one statement, by the use of the whole sentence. Nevertheless we can recognize that there is either present or absent a relation of identity between what is expressed by two identically phrased clauses of a conditional, and that this relation is exactly parallel to the relation of identity which holds between two identically phrased but uncompounded sentences (or sentence-instances) when these are used to make the same statement. So we need not perhaps press this point about phrasing; or, alternatively, we could allow the vaguer phrase 'express the same proposition' to apply to both relations of identity, i.e. to both the case where it would be correct to speak of 'making the same statement' and the case where it would, strictly speaking, be incorrect. But there is another point that we *must* press, if this revised criterion of identity is offered. That is, we must ask what it is for two sentences or two clauses (whether typographically identical or not) to be used to make the same statement, express the same proposition. We must, that is, inquire about the criterion of identity of statements or propositions. One kind of answer which suggests itself, at any rate as a beginning, is the following: two expressions are used to make the same statement (express the same proposition) when it is logically impossible that the statement made or proposition expressed by one should be true, while the statement made or proposition expressed by the other was false. This requirement may well, by itself, seem too liberal, and it could accordingly be supplemented by some requirement, more or less stringent according to taste, of an at least partly typographical kind – ranging from the most stringent requirement of typographical identity down through various degrees of isomorphism. This is a minor point. The major point is that though the criterion offered is such as I, for one, should consider perfectly reasonable – at least as a beginning – it is also such as Quine could not for a moment consider accepting. For it rests fairly and squarely upon the notion of logical impossibility, upon a member, that is, of the group of notions which he is concerned to discredit and to show to be superfluous. So this way out of Quine's difficulty is, for him, a blind alley, and not a way out at all.

Let us take a brief look up another blind alley, though one that may turn out to have a further opening leading off it. (I shall return to this possibility later.) You will have noticed that in the example I introduced to make difficulties for Quine, the difficulties were of two different kinds. In the first place, the sentences 'He is sick' and 'He is sick', though typographically identical, did not, as we crudely say, have the same meaning. Or, if you like, the one sentence 'He is sick' has two different meanings or senses – a physical sense and a psychological sense. This is a quite general point about the sentence (or sentences) – a point which one could make if, for example, one came across the sentence as an isolated specimen for translation into another language, and quite without considering any particular historical applications that might be made of it. The second kind of difficulty, however, had nothing to do with differences of *meaning*, and everything to do with differences of application or reference. In the cases imagined, the word 'he' did not exhibit any variation of meaning: it was just doing its single, standard job of referring to a male person, though, of course, a different person in each case. Now surely the difficulties about reference can easily be met simply by stipulating that where the same referring expression occurs in the same positions within two typographically identical substitution-clauses which are required also to be identical in the further sense we are seeking, then the referring expression, in both its occurrences, shall be taken to have the same reference, i.e. to refer to the same person, object, etc. This stipulation seems to involve no difficulty and raise no mystery. There remains the first kind of difficulty to be dealt with – that which arises from difference of *meaning* between sentences. And it seems tempting to meet this difficulty by stipulating that in the case where identical clause-substitutions are to be made, the clauses or sentences shall not only be typographically identical, but also identical in meaning, i.e. synonymous. I say this stipulation seems tempting; but, of course, it will not tempt Quine in the least, for the notion of sentence-synonymy is just one more of those discreditable notions which we should learn to get on without.

It might now seem better, from Quine's point of view, to change the whole approach to the problem. Instead of starting with typographical identity, and trying to remedy its deficiencies with additional stipulations about identity of statements or propositions or sentence-meanings – all too obviously intensional notions – one might try casting around for some safely extensional substitute, for some kind of extensional identity which involves none of these troublesome difficulties. What extensional substitute can we find for the idea of the sense of a sentence? Remembering now Frege and his followers, we might clutch at the notion of a truth-value; and suggest that the only kind of identity required in our sentence-substitutions is that the substituted items should have identical truth-values. But this must surely be the least attractive suggestion so far. Certainly it has one merit: it wards off the menace of the conclusion that there are no logical truths at all. Everything to which we are at present willing to award the status will, it seems, preserve it. But it has other and less appealing features. Suppose, for instance, we ask the question: how are we to know when the new requirement of identity in truth-value of the substituted items is to be enforced? Presumably if we test a proffered statement for logical truth, we shall sometimes have to observe this restriction of permitted substitutions, and sometimes not. Which cases are which? In view of the character of the restriction, the most natural answer might seem to be this: that whenever the candidate-statement contains two or more sub-statements of identical truth-value, then any statements substituted for these sub-statements must also be of identical truth-value. But the application of this rule will yield an unwelcome expansion of the class of logical truths. For example, any statement containing the one logical particle '⊃' or the one logical particle '≡' and two sub-statements of identical truth-values will turn out to be a logical truth (e.g. 'Socrates is a Greek ⊃ Eisenhower is an American' and 'Eisenhower is a Greek ≡ Socrates is an American'). For any such statement will be true already and will remain true under all the permitted substitutions.

Suppose, then, we return to typographical identity, and say that the restriction to substitutions identical in truth-value is to be enforced only in the case of typographically identical sub-statements of the statement to be tested. This rule, it is true, would give us results closer to those we want. But now the *rule* seems capricious. For we have already seen that, for example, typographical identity of the two clauses of an 'If . . . then . . .' (or a '. . . ⊃ . . .') statement is simply not a guarantee of identity of truth-value of its two sub-statements. To make typographical identity, then, the condition of applying a rule requiring the substitution of statements of identical truth-value would seem to be invoking a condition irrelevant to this rule. Surely the point of any such rule, whatever its form, must be to preserve some kind of identity *already present* in the components for which the substitutions are to be made. We might of course try just adding this condition (of typographical identity) to the one already considered, and insisting on both being fulfilled. But this procedure, besides having something arbitrary-looking and *ad hoc* about it, would still leave us in the situation of having to acknowledge as logical truths statements which are nothing of the kind. For example, any statement made in the words 'If he is sick, then he is sick', so long as it is true, would count as a logical truth, even if what the speaker meant by it could be otherwise expressed in the words 'If John is ill, then William is depressed', and even though, had the speaker used *these* words to convey his message, he would not, on the suggested tests, have uttered a logical truth.

One last desperate suggestion, before we abandon this unprofitable line. It might be suggested that the restriction on statement-substitutions should be simply this: that in every case of statement-substitution whatever, the replacing statement should have the same truth-value as the replaced statement. But obviously, unless we hedge this rule about with restrictions which make it idle, it will yield the result that any statement which is true is a logical truth.

Let us give up this solemn game for a moment and take a more general look at the facts. Obviously in the logician's examples of logical truths – in such examples as 'If Socrates is wise, then Socrates is wise' – typographical identity of sentences plays a very important part. It symbolizes or represents some kind of identity or other, the presence of which is an essential feature of the logical

I

truth in question, whatever that logical truth may be. This same role, of representing or symbolizing some kind of identity or other, is played in the schemata of logic by recurrences of the letters *p, q, r,* etc. Now what is the kind of identity thus represented? For reasons sufficiently indicated already, it cannot be just typographical identity itself. Not, at any rate, as far as actual languages are concerned. Nor can the question be evaded by saying that the logician's examples are to be treated as belonging to an ideal language. For if this is said, we must simply ask what typographical identity of sentences in an ideal language corresponds to in actually spoken languages, since it evidently does not correspond to typographical identity. The apparently unavoidable answer to these questions is that typographical identity of sentences or recurrences of sentence-letters (as Quine calls them) represent or symbolize identity of *statements* or *propositions* or whatever we call those things which are true or false. (The terminology of 'sentence-letters' is objectionable in so far as it obscures this important fact.) If this apparently unavoidable answer is right, then we have no adequate characterization of logical truth until we have an adequate criterion of identity of statements or propositions. (We have already seen some reason for preferring the word 'proposition' in this connection.) But we have not so far found any adequate criterion of this kind which does not involve an appeal to notions which Quine finds inadmissible, such as those of sentence-synonymy or logical impossibility. As for the suggestion that the kind of identity in question is no more than identity in truth-value, this is obviously untenable. If it were no more than this, we should do better to drop the symbolism of '$p \supset p$' in favour of '$T \supset T$' and '$F \supset F$', to which there would then be no reason for not adding '$F \supset T$'. We should then, as far as the propositional logic is concerned, be in the position of counting every truth-functionally compounded *truth* as a logical truth – which is certainly not the intention of those who speak of logical truth.

The attempt to represent identity of truth-values as a satisfactory extensional substitute for identity of propositions is, then, a failure. But it does not follow from this that *no* satisfactory extensional substitute can be found. There is one more direction in which the attempt can be made. I have remarked already that the difficulties which arose over the original typographical criterion were of two kinds. Some arose from the fact that typographical identity does not guarantee identity of sentence-meaning; others arose from the fact that typographical identity does not guarantee identity of reference on the part of the referring expressions of a sentence, the expressions which replace the individual variables of the logician's schemata. (The distinction here is, for a number of fairly obvious reasons, a good deal less neat and clear than this formulation suggests. But, for present purposes, no matter.) If we assume the adequacy of the logician's schematization of the parts of a sentence, other than the logical particles, by means of individual variables on the one hand and predicate-letters on the other, we may simplify this statement by eliminating the reference to sentence-synonomy. We may, that is to say, characterize the difficulties as follows. Some arise from the fact that typographical identity of referring expressions does not guarantee identity of reference; others arise from the fact that typographical identity of predicate expressions does not guarantee identity of sense. And this suggests the following general stipulation for the cases where substitution-identity is required: viz. (1) that where identity of substitutions of referring expressions is required, the referring expressions substituted shall *at least* have the same reference; (2) that where identity of substitutions of predicate expressions is required, the predicate expressions substituted shall *at least* have the same sense; and (3) that where identity of substitutions of statement-clauses is required, both the above conditions *at least* shall be satisfied. This stipulation has the merit that it is quite general, i.e. covers all the reinterpretations we have to consider. (The function of the words 'at least' throughout is to leave open for the moment the question whether typographical identity of substituted expressions is also required.) The objection to it from Quine's point of view is that it turns once more, in part, on a notion he objects to, the notion, this time, of predicates *having the same sense*, or of *predicate-synonymy*.

It seems, however, that there might be available a suitable extensional substitute for predicate-synonymy in the notion of extensional agreement or equivalence of predicates. Two predicates are said to agree extensionally or to be extensionally equivalent when they are true of just the same objects: an example of Quine's is the pair of predicates 'creature with a heart' and 'creature with kidneys', or, more simply, 'has a heart' and 'has kidneys'. Let us try, therefore, to frame a suitable rule with the use of this substitute. There seem to be a number of alternative possibilities. First we might try ignoring the condition of typographical identity altogether. Then the relevant part of our characterization of logical truth would run as follows: A statement is a logical truth if it is true and remains true under all reinterpretations, etc., provided that predicates extensionally equivalent to each other are always replaced by predicates extensionally equivalent to each other. Presumably this is not what is wanted. It has, immediately, the result that '(x) x has a heart ⊃ x has kidneys' is a logical truth, and that '(x) x is a dragon ⊃ x is a unicorn' is a logical truth. It looks as though we shall have to bring in typographical identity once more and amend our provision to read: 'provided that predicates which are both typographically identical with each other and extensionally equivalent to each other are always replaced by predicates which are extensionally equivalent to each other'. (Whether we insist that the *replacing* predicates should also be typographically identical, or not, does not make much difference; what is here crucial is the question of which *candidates* for logical truth the provision is to be applied to.) Let us then apply the new characterization to one of the difficult cases – a case, that is, of an ambiguous predicate. We may return to our old example, 'If he is sick, he is sick', when someone uttering this sentence uses it with the force of 'If he is ill, he is depressed'. Evidently someone uttering the sentence with this force may be saying something true or something false. Our hope must be that the effect of our new rule is such that even when the statement made is true, it is ruled out from being a logical truth. Cases where the word 'he' has a different reference in the two clauses are already covered by a stipulation which does not mention meanings, and is therefore innocuous from Quine's point of view. It might now seem that the new extensionally phrased provision deals equally satisfactorily with the case where 'sick' is used in two different senses. For surely the word 'sick' in its first use has a different extension from, is not extensionally equivalent to, the word 'sick' in its second use. Therefore the restrictive provision, about substituting only extensionally equivalent predicates, does not apply; and so we shall have no difficulty in finding permitted reinterpretations which are false, and thus no difficulty in showing the statement in question not to be a logical truth. But we must pause over this reasoning. Clearly it turns on distinguishing *the word 'sick' in its first use* from *the word 'sick' in its second use*. But what exactly are the items so distinguished? What are the criteria of identity for these two items? What is *a word in a certain use*? Clearly here we cannot be speaking of two tokens belonging exclusively to a particular historical utterance. A word, taken in this most limited of possible senses, is not something which has an extension, so we cannot even raise the question what its extension is; or, if we do raise and insist on pressing this mistaken question in this sense of 'word', then I think we could only answer that the token-extensions (what the two tokens are truly uttered of) are in fact the same in the two cases, since the two tokens (*these* two tokens) are truly applied (on the assumption that the statement is true) to one and the same individual, and to nothing else (for *they* are not applied to anything else). If by *a word in a certain use*, then, we are not here to understand an historically unique token, what are we to understand by it? 'Well, surely', one is inclined to answer, 'the expression declares itself clearly enough. We are speaking, are we not, of *a word as used in a certain sense, with a certain meaning*?' But this answer will be no more acceptable to Quine than any of those we are trying to replace. For if we adopt it, then our characterization at once forfeits its extensional character. If the condition of identifying extensions is the prior identification of meanings or senses, then we might as well stop talking about identical extensions and talk instead about identical senses. We shall not have brought in anything we are not committed to anyway.

'But surely', someone might say, 'there just *are* two different extensions here, aren't there? Can't we just speak directly of them, without mentioning meanings or senses?' But of course this is just the point. An extension must be an extension *of* something, of some expression. If we just speak of the extension of the word 'sick', without qualification, where the criterion of identity of the word is, once more, typographical, then, because we have just one word, we have just one extension, ambiguity notwithstanding. And in our sample sentence, too, the word will have just one extension, ambiguity notwithstanding: an extension comprising both the ill and the depressed. There will, therefore, be no question of the word having different extensions in its two occurrences, the restrictive provisions on substitution will apply and the statement, if true, will stand as a logical truth. One might now be inclined to clutch at a straw. Certainly the restrictive provisions will apply, one might say, and certainly therefore one will be able to substitute only predicates identical in extension in the permitted reinterpretations. But these, as the foregoing argument indicates, will include similarly ambiguous predicates, e.g. 'has a lot of vices'. And among the resulting sentences, therefore, will be some, some uses of which (as in the case of our sample sentence) will issue in false statements. Therefore the claims of the sample statement to be a logical truth will be disallowed. But to clutch at this straw is to bring the whole dubious house down. For evidently the argument can be as well applied in the case of statements whose status as logical truths we wish to preserve as in the case of statements whose claims to logical truth we wish to disallow. So the argument merely reveals, more nakedly than ever, the inadequacy of the extensional substitute.

The suggestion I have just been considering will be my last attempt to find a statement of the kind, and conditions, of identity-substitutions which shall both fit Quine's characterizations of logical truth and shall not involve an appeal to intensional notions of the kind he considers disreputable. Like the other attempts, it fails; and it was of course my purpose to demonstrate the failure of such attempts and to draw, or at least to encourage, the inference that Quine's characterization of logical truth can be made coherent, and made to do its job, only by implicit use of notions belonging to the group which he wishes to discredit.

II

The concern throughout has been with certain kinds of identity present in, and essential to, logical truths. I have maintained, first, that no account of logical truth is complete which does not state what these identities are; and, second, that it does not appear possible to state what these identities are in terms acceptable to Quine. Now it is perhaps incumbent upon me to state more explicitly what I conceive those identities to be, and how I take them to be related to the usual mode of representation of logical truth. This I can perhaps best do, in the present context, by formulating an amendment to Quine's original characterization. As a first step, then, towards formulating this amendment, I shall say that a logical truth is a statement which is true and remains true under all reinterpretations of the components other than the logical particles, provided that in any reinterpretation of propositional components certain propositional identities are preserved in the reinterpretation, and that in any reinterpretation of non-propositional components certain identities of sense and reference are preserved in the reinterpretation. (When I speak of preserving identities, I mean of course not that the identity of the propositions, concepts, and references in question is to be unchanged in the reinterpretation, but that propositions, concepts, and references identical with each other in the original statement are replaced by propositions, concepts, and references identical with each other in the reinterpretation.) The characterization I have just produced, of course, does not have the nature of a definition; for I speak of preserving *certain* identities without specifying which ones. Evidently the identities in question are represented in logicians' schemata by recurrences of what Quine calls sentence-letters, predicate-letters, and variables. But this fact alone does not tell us what they are. We need to know more about the conventions governing the use of these letters. Consider, for example, the sentence, 'If the king is dead, then the king is deceased'. If we assume identity of reference, then any statement made by the use of this sentence would be true, and what most would be ready to call a necessary truth. Since the concept expressed by 'dead' is identical with that expressed by 'deceased', the two sub-propositions may be said (on *one* criterion) to be identical, and the whole statement to be, to that extent, a candidate for being counted as a statement of the form 'If p, then p'. Yet few would want to say it was a truth of logic. Or consider the statement that if Sir Walter Scott is snobbish, then the author of Waverley is snobbish. Here, we have identity of reference and identity of concept. If we took these as a sufficient condition of the proper use of recurrent variables and sentence-letters, we should have to say we have a statement of the form 'If Fx, then Fx' and hence a truth of logic. But, of course, though we have here a truth, we have not even a necessary truth, let alone a truth of logic. To discover which identities are in question, therefore, we must turn not simply to the logician's schemata, but to his examples. And to turn to these is to return, though with a difference, to our starting-point. For the identities in question are there represented by typographical identity of words and phrases. And this is not merely, as the above phrasing might seem to suggest, a conventional method of *representing* the identities in question. Rather, there exists an entirely reasonable and non-arbitrary convention that we do not speak of, we do not *have*, truths of logic *unless* the relevant identities are so represented. Whether or not we have to do with a truth of logic is not simply a question of what the statement says, but of how it is expressed. So our characterization must be once more re-expressed, as follows: 'A statement is a truth of logic if it is true, and remains true under all reinterpretations of the components other than the logical particles, provided that, in any reinterpretation of propositional components (clauses), all those propositional identities which are represented in the original statement by typographically identical clauses are preserved in the reinterpretation, and in any reinterpretation of non-propositional components all those identities of sense and reference which are represented in the original statement by typographically identical predicate expressions and referring expressions are preserved in the reinterpretation.' This characterization is, I think, satisfactory in this sense. On the one hand, it rules out those statements which create difficulties for Quine, like some uses of the sentence, 'If he is sick, then he is sick'; for in these cases one of the conditions of the restriction on reinterpretation (viz. the existence of propositional or conceptual identity) is not satisfied. On the other hand, it does not admit examples such as the two I have just produced; for in their case, another of the conditions of the restriction on reinterpretation (viz. the condition that the identities should be expressed in typographically identical expressions) is not satisfied.

The justification of the convention whereby we speak of logical truths only in the cases when the condition of typographical identity is fulfilled is not hard to see, though it is hard to state precisely. We may be helped in trying to explain it by reverting to that old – in itself unclear – characterization of the propositions of logic as propositions true in virtue of their form alone. What does this mean? Does it mean that their truth is solely the result of their containing the logical particles they do contain? Evidently not. For this ignores the whole question of identities with which we have been concerned. A closer approximation would be this. Their truth is quite independent of what the concepts, references, and sub-propositions actually *are* which they contain; it depends solely on the logical particles together with the relations of identity which exist among these concepts, references, and sub-propositions. But of course the fact that certain relations of identity obtain between references made in statements may be an empirical matter, as it is an empirical matter that Scott is the author of *Waverley*; or it may be a matter of language, but a matter of language relating to particular expressions in a statement besides the logical particles, as it is such a matter that 'dead' means the same as 'deceased'. In such cases, then, when the truth of a statement depends on the existence of such identities, and the existence of the identities depends on such matters of fact or language, it is hard to maintain that we have a concrete example of a statement true in virtue of its form alone. To produce such an example, we must surely exploit some quite *general* linguistic convention for representing the identities in question. And here typographical identity offers itself as the only plausible candidate. For though the conventions of reference are various and complex, there is at least a strong assumption that in the context of utterance of a single sentence, typographically identical referring expressions will have the same reference; while, on the other hand, it seems almost a condition of the possibility of communication that ambiguity of predicate-expressions should be an exceptional feature, a 'quirk of language'. So, then, there is nothing arbitrary about the insistence that only in those cases where the typographical condition is fulfilled do we have an example of a truth of logic.

The point I have tried to establish in this paper is that Quine's account of logical truth cannot be made to yield the results he (or anyone else) desires, unless it is taken to make implicit use of certain notions which elsewhere he attacks, declaring them to be superfluous and to embody mythical distinctions. In the particular form taken by my amendment to his account, the notions made use of were those of identity of propositions and of concepts. And these two notions are members of that group of inter-explainable ideas which includes logical impossibility, synonymity, necessity and inconsistency.

7. *Grammar and Philosophy*[1]

I

One who speaks his native language fluently and correctly has acquired over a period of time that mastery of the language which he now has. During this period he was exposed, no doubt, to many sentences produced by others and to some correction of sentences he produced himself. But his mastery of the language does not consist merely in his being able to reproduce the sentences produced by others and, in their corrected forms, the sentences earlier produced by himself. It consists in his being able also to produce indefinitely many new sentences, knowing what they mean, and in being able to understand indefinitely many new sentences which are produced to him. It consists also in his being able to distinguish between sentences of his language which are fully 'correct' and literally significant sentences – however elaborate or stylistically unusual they may be – and sentences which deviate, in various ways or degrees, from full 'correctness' or literal significance; and perhaps to remark, with more or less explicitness, on how the sentences which deviate from correctness do so deviate.

It seems entirely reasonable to say that the possession, on the part of the fluent and correct speaker of a language, of these abilities to construct, interpret, and criticize sentences implies the existence of a set or system of rules which the speaker has, in some sense, mastered. This does not imply that he consciously constructs or interprets sentences by the light of any such rules, nor that he could even begin to formulate such rules with any approach to full explicitness or to the maximum of system. Such rules may 'govern' his exercise of his abilities of sentence-

---

[1] It will be obvious to any auditor of Professor Chomsky's John Locke lectures, delivered in Oxford in the summer of 1969 after the present paper was written, that he has moved from, or modified, some of the positions here attributed to him on the basis of his publications. However, with occasional qualifications, I have allowed the attributions to stand; the written, checkable word provides a firmer basis for discussion than the spoken, uncheckable word.

construction and interpretation, and even of sentence-criticism, without his approaching full consciousness of such rules as governing such exercise. We should not expect of the fluent and correct speaker of a language, just because he is one, that he can state the theory of his practice.

Nevertheless the practice is there. And so it should be possible, for those who are minded to do so, to extract the theory and to state it with full explicitness and the maximum of system. This the aim which the new grammarians set themselves, the exponents of transformational generative grammar. A fully explicit and maximally systematic statement of the rules which 'govern' the fluent speaker's exercise of his capacities will supply the *theory* of that speaker's language. Such a theory may be called, in an extended sense of the word, a *grammar* of the language. It will contain three parts or components: a syntactic part; a semantic part; and a phonological part. Very roughly, and rather misleadingly, these parts may be said to be concerned respectively with structure, with sense and with sound; rather misleadingly, in so far as structure is itself quite largely determinant of sense. It is, on the whole, the syntactic or structural part which has received the most emphasis and aroused the most interest in the work of the transformational grammarians.

We are familiar, from traditional grammar, with some of the terms which are used in the new grammar to express facts about the structure of sentences. We are familiar, that is to say, with such grammatical *class-* or *category*-names as those of noun and noun-phrase, verb, preposition, adverb, and adjective; and with the names of such grammatical *relations* as those of subject of sentence, subject of verb, object of verb, modifier of subject, modifier of verb, and so on. Quite obviously a grasp of facts about structure, about grammatical relations in a sentence, enters into our understanding of sentences. To appreciate the difference in sense between 'John loves Mary' and 'Mary loves John' or between 'The old man sings a song' and 'The man sings an old song' *is* to grasp those structural facts which are expressed in the terminology of grammar by saying that 'John' is the subject and 'Mary' the object of the verb in the first sentence and vice versa in the second or that the adjective 'old' stands in attributive combination with 'man' in the third sentence and with 'song' in the fourth. In the kind of grammatical analysis which we do (or did) at school, we set out, in a prescribed form, facts of this kind about the grammatical relations which hold within the sentences we analyse. To that extent we set out their structure. Of course we may be rather bad at this exercise while perfectly well appreciating the differences in sense between such sentences; which illustrates merely the point that grasp of structure is not the same thing as ability to state explicitly what is grasped.

Grammatical structure, then, as well as the senses of individual words, is determinant of the sense or semantic interpretation of sentences. The central thesis of the transformational grammarians, the step which conditions the whole character of their theories, is the insistence that any adequate grammatical theory must recognize a distinction between the superficial syntactic structure of a sentence and its basic structure, between its deep grammar and its surface grammar. The motivation of this distinction goes very deep indeed, as we shall see hereafter. But we can easily be induced to see reason for it by noting, for example, that two sentences may be very similar in their superficial syntactic structure while, so to speak, the structure of their sense is very different; that in our understanding of such sentences we allow for differences in the grammatical relations of their elements which are simply not marked in the sentences as they stand. Chomsky gives as an example of this the pair of sentences, 'They persuaded John to leave' and 'They expected John to leave'. In our understanding of these sentences 'John' has a subject-like relation to the verb 'leave' in both; but while it also has an object-like relation to the main verb ('persuaded') of the first sentence, it has no such relation to the main verb ('expected') of the second. Thus we understand the elements of the sentences as differently related in the two cases; but there is no *manifest* structural difference between the sentences as they stand, corresponding to this understood difference. Again, a perhaps more striking way of making the distinction between deep and surface structure acceptable is to point to certain syntactically or structurally ambiguous sentences such as – to adapt an older example – 'The principal thing in his life was the love of women'. Though the ambiguity might well be removed by the context, the sentence, as it stands, leaves us uncertain as to whether it is his loving women or women loving him that is in question. Now both the unmanifest structural differences exemplified in the first kind of case and the syntactic ambiguities exemplified in the second would, it is held, be clearly and systematically exhibited in the representation of the deep, as opposed to the surface, structure of sentences. For *every* syntactic or structural relation between sentence-elements would be represented with total explicitness. A grammar of the desired kind will therefore assign at least two different deep structures to a syntactically ambiguous sentence, and will assign patently different deep structures to sentences which have a merely superficial identity of structure.

Looking for a moment beyond the confines of a single language, we may glimpse another and older kind of motivation for such a distinction. Just as surface similarity may conceal deep difference, so surface difference may conceal deep identity. Given two sentences in different languages, the one an accurate and adequate translation of the other, we may easily find grammatical constructions in the one which are absent in the other. But may we not want to say that the *fundamental* structural relationships thus differently displayed on the surface are exactly the same in both? The question how far we are prepared to press this thought has a bearing on the question whether we are prepared to entertain, and, if so, how we are prepared to use, the notion of a universal grammar. Evidently such a thought cannot be without interest for philosophers.

But this is to anticipate. Let us turn now to the question how facts about structure are actually presented by the transformational grammarians. Any answer I can give to this question in the present context must necessarily be incomplete and grossly simplified; but not, I hope, misleadingly so in relation to the further questions I wish to raise.

The syntactic component, then, of a grammar or theory of a language consists of a system of rules, permissive or mandatory, which operate, finally, on certain elements. These terminal materials are to be thought of as the minimal meaning units of the language, the atoms to be structured, as it were, by the syntax of the language. Chomsky calls these items formatives. No easy identification of formatives with any familiar idea is possible; but we need not concern ourselves here with their exact nature. Formatives are of two kinds, lexical and non-lexical. The first we may think of as corresponding to those general terms or proper names of the language of which the meaning is not in any way syntactically derived – such as the verbs 'sing' or 'love', the adjective 'red', the name 'Mary'. The latter are a more heterogeneous bunch and will include, for example, a formative named *Past*, for Past Tense.

The rules which operate, finally, on these materials are such that, for any sentence of the language, there is a path through the application of these rules the following of which path will yield us a complete exhibition both of the deep structure and of the surface structure of that sentence. This must not be misunderstood. It means no more than it says. It does not mean, for example, that the grammar provides us with a mechanical procedure for *finding* the deep structure of an antecedently given sentence or for *producing* a given sentence.[1] It means only that, in a complete grammar of the kind in question, there *is* some path through the rules which will yield these results. From what has already been said it will be clear that the rules are themselves of two kinds: those which yield deep structures and those which transform these into surface structures. With rules of the latter kind I shall not be much concerned. But I must say a little more about deep structure rules or rules of the base.

The terms in which the fundamental type of base-rules are framed have reassuring familiarity. They are the names of grammatical *classes* or *categories*, such as Sentence, Noun-Phrase, Predicate-Phrase, Noun, Verb, Adjective, Verbal Auxiliary, Prepositional Phrase, etc. The results of applying the rules can be most easily represented by a kind of inverted tree-structure, in producing which we start from the basic symbol *S* (for Sentence) and branch out into constituent grammatical categories, then into constituents of those constituents and so on until we reach a point at which all the terminal category names are such that we can enter formatives directly under them. The rules permit the production of very simple diagrams of this kind – such as the diagram, say, for 'John smiled' – and, again, of diagrams of any degree of complexity. For they permit the reintroduction of the symbol *S* under a suitable constituent structure heading, such as nounphrase, where it acts, in turn, as the head of another, subordinate branching diagram. The deep or base structure diagram of some actual sentence of the language is completed when, under the terminal category headings are entered appropriate formatives,

[1] See Chomsky, *Aspects of the Theory of Syntax*, p. 141.

the resulting string or sequence of formatives constituting the terminal sequence of the structure. Thus the non-lexical formative *Past* can be entered under the category heading *Verbal Auxiliary*. Lexical formatives are listed in a lexicon which assigns them to lexical categories like Noun, Verb, and Adjective.

From a completed diagram of this kind, setting out a terminal sequence together with the pattern of its derivation, we can read off, with total explicitness, all those facts of grammatical structure which bear on the interpretation of the sentence whose deep structure it represents. The reason why we can do so – and this is a point of absolutely central importance – is that all those syntactical *relations* which, as we already know, are so largely determinant of the sense (or semantic interpretation) of sentences are *defined* in terms of the grammatical *categories* or *classes* and their permitted concatenations in deep structure diagrams. Chomsky is quite explicit on this important point. If we set aside the lexicon, the primary function of the rules of the base so far described is, he says, 'that of defining the grammatical relations that are expressed in the deep structure and that therefore determine the semantic interpretation of a sentence'.[1] Here, I repeat, we have a point of central importance. Most of the detail of what I have been saying can be safely forgotten if this is remembered.

The syntactic component of the theory, then, yields us both deep and surface structures of sentences. Now a word – no more – about their relations to the remaining components, the semantic and the phonological. The rules of the phonological component of the theory are applied to surface structures to yield the actual sound-rendering of a sentence. The information contained in the semantic component about the meanings of individual lexical items is supposed to combine with the structural information contained in the deep structure diagram to determine the full semantic interpretation of the sentence.[2]

[1] Op. cit., p. 99. See also pp. 69, 117, 120, 141.

[2] This is one important point on which Chomsky has modified his views. He now allows that surface structure also may bear on semantic interpretation; so that two sentences with exactly the same deep structure diagram may nevertheless differ in meaning, the difference appearing only at the level of the transformations which yield surface structure. However, he adheres to his original view as regards those aspects of semantic interpretation which depend on the *grammatical relations*; and it is with these that the present paper is concerned.

II

So much by way of a sketch of the type of theory of a language envisaged by some transformational grammarians. Now I began this paper by summarizing the linguistic ability of an ideally fluent and correct speaker of a language as the ability to understand, produce, and criticize indefinitely many new sentences of his language. The theorists of transformational grammar, at least in their more cautious moments, do not claim that the possession of these linguistic abilities by an idealized speaker-hearer can be completely and adequately explained simply by crediting him with a 'tacit mastery' – or even by crediting him with an 'internal representation' – of such a system of rules as such a theory would provide. They concede, or, rather, insist, that more is required for an adequate explanation. Let us, for the moment, postpone consideration of the question how the grammarians themselves think the provision of such a theory needs supplementing if the demand for adequate explanation is to be met; and let us consider, instead, a condition in respect of which a non-specialist critic might find that such a theory fell short of *his* demand for understanding. I shall name this the condition of perspicuousness.

Here we must turn once more to the consideration of the deep structures of sentences, so decisive, as Chomsky says, for their semantic interpretation. Deep structures are generated by the base rules of the syntactic component. If we set aside that part of the base (including the lexicon) which allows the completion of deep structures with terminal sequences, we are left essentially with the branching rules which introduce grammatical categories (Noun-Phrase, Verb, Prepositional Phrase, etc.) in various permitted concatenations. As remarked, Chomsky says that the importance of these rules and of the grammatical categories which they introduce consists primarily in the fact that they supply the basis for the definition of those grammatical *relations* which, as far as structural considerations go, are of decisive, though not exclusive, importance for the semantic interpretation of sentences. This is why the grammatical categories and the rules framed in terms of them *matter*. They matter because together they provide the terms in which the grammatical relations (subject-of, predicate-of object-of, modifier-of, etc.) can be defined for the given language. And these relations matter because of their decisive bearing on the semantic interpretation of sentences. But so far, if we keep the lexicon on one side, the grammar gives us no information about the significance of these grammatical relations independent of their definition in terms of the grammatical categories. The symbols for the grammatical categories, and the rules for framing structure diagrams containing them, are said to point forward to the grammatical relations, so important for understanding sentences; but the names of the grammatical relations point back, by definition, to the symbols for the grammatical categories and their arrangement; and, since the grammar is a fully explicit statement of rules, we must not suppose ourselves equipped with *any* understanding of *either* of these kinds of term except such as is given by the explicit rules of the grammar itself.

Of course the grammar, or theory of the language, as a whole, provides a way out of this circle of technical terms. It provides a way out because it contains a lexicon which, in its syntactic part, assigns lexical formatives to grammatical categories; and because it contains a semantic component which we may think of as containing all the remaining information about elements of the language which anyone must possess who understands the language. Now it is true, as critics have urged and grammarians acknowledged, that no satisfactory theoretical account has yet been given of the semantic component. But this point, thus generally stated, is not one I wish to labour. Let us simply assume that grasp of the rules of the theory, including grasp of the semantic component, would carry with it a complete grasp of the sense of all formatives, lexical and non-lexical alike. Then, since the grammar assigns individual formatives to grammatical categories, we see that the grammar provides for the immediate linking of the senses of formatives with grammatical categories; and hence it provides, mediately, for the linking of the senses of formatives with possible grammatical relations in deep structure, the relations which help to determine the sense of sentences. But – and this is the point on which my criticisms bear – of this apparently crucial set of connections there is, in the grammar, no general theory whatever. There is simply the list of items in the lexicon without any account of general principles determining the assignment of those items to grammatical categories. Yet it is above all of this set of connections that we might expect a general

K

theory if we hoped that the grammar might satisfy the condition of perspicuousness.

It is worth while dwelling once more on the reasons why we might expect this. We are to remember that the primary importance of the grammatical categories and their permitted orderings in the deep structures of a language lies in the fact that they provide the terms in which the underlying grammatical functions and relations of elements in sentences can be defined – for the given language. And these functions and relations are functions and relations which any ordinary speaker of the language grasps implicitly in understanding the sentences he hears and produces. He grasps them implicitly, having – we may suppose – no explicit training in the grammar. Now how is his implicit grasp of these functions and relations connected with his knowledge of the meaning of the elements of his language? It is not to be supposed that his knowledge of the meaning of these elements is something quite separate from his grasp of the power of these elements to figure in those grammatical functions and in those grammatical relations which he must have an implicit grasp of in order to understand the sense of the sentences he hears and produces. His grasp of the meanings of the elements of the language, it seems, must include at least some grasp of their potential roles in the grammatical relations of base structures. Suppose, then, there are intrinsic and general connections between types of element-meaning and potentialities of grammatical role in deep, or base, structure. In stating the principles of such connection, we should, obviously, be linking semantic and syntactic considerations. Might we not also be laying the foundations, or some part of the foundations, of a general theory of grammar? In any case, a grammar which rested on, or incorporated, such principles would have a better claim than one which did not, to satisfy the condition of perspicuousness.

III

Thus, at least, we might reason. A little later I shall have to refine on this notion of perspicuousness. First, let us return, briefly, to Chomsky. As I have already hinted, he himself is the first to acknowledge that what he calls a '*descriptively* adequate' generative grammar of a language – such a theory as I described, in barest outline, in Section I of this paper – would not by itself satisfy the condition of *explanatory* adequacy. To satisfy this condition we should need, he says, a theory of linguistic universals characteristic of human language in general; and we should need to show that this theory was related in a certain way to our descriptively adequate grammar, picking it out, as it were, from other possible grammars consistent with the 'primary linguistic data'. Now regarding these requirements we may be disposed to ask two questions. First, would their fulfilment finally yield a *complete* explanation of the idealized hearer-speaker's possession of his linguistic abilities – including it must be remembered, his ability to *understand* the indefinitely many sentences of the language? And, second, would their fulfilment involve – besides, doubtless, much else – the linking of semantic and syntactic considerations in somewhat the way just alluded to?

To neither question is the official answer entirely clear. But, as regards the first question, we may suppose that the fulfilment of the stated requirements would take us at least nearer to a complete explanation of the speaker-hearer's abilities.[1] And, in view of this, we may be surprised by the character of Chomsky's answer to the second question. For though he admits that 'there is no reason to rule out *a priori*' the possibility that 'substantive characterizations' of 'the universal vocabulary from which grammatical descriptions are constructed' might ultimately have to refer 'to semantic concepts of one sort or another',[2] yet his references to any such possibility are markedly cool. Thus he speaks of 'vague and unsupported assertions about the "semantic basis for syntax" ' which 'make no contribution to the understanding of these questions'.[3] Vague and unsupported assertions, of course, do not make much of a contribution to the understanding of anything. But if a general direction of inquiry seems promising, if indeed one can see no alternative to it, one should surely seek in that direction for assertions which are not vague and which one can support.

Chomsky himself remarks that it would be natural to expect that the ultimate framework for the characterization of the universal categories of grammar should be found in some features of the base. He has in mind what he calls *formal* features of the base.

[1] Leaving, one must suppose, a certain amount of work for psychologists and physiologists still to do.

[2] Op. cit., pp. 116–17.

[3] Op. cit., p. 78.

But the base includes the lexicon. And the lexicon includes lists of items capable of being entered directly under lexical category-headings in base structures. These items will be far less numerous than the entries in an ordinary dictionary of the language. For example, they will not include, in the category of nouns, formatives corresponding to our ordinary abstract nouns, 'sincerity' and 'destruction'; 'sincerity' and 'destruction' appear in sentences only as a result of a nominalizing transformation.[1] Would it not seem very natural, then, to survey the restricted list of items in the lexicon with a certain question in mind, viz. what semantical types of items are to be found in the lexicon, such that they can combine into sentences of which the deep structure requires minimum transformation to yield surface structure? And what correlations can be found between the semantical types of those items and the grammatical or syntactic categories to which they are there assigned? Or consider a more specific question. The grammatical category, Sentence, is basically divided, in the models of trans-formational grammar put forward by Chomsky, into Noun-Phrase and Predicate-Phrase, and this division immediately yields us, by definition, for basic structures, the relations of subject and predicate of a sentence. This point seems to bring us to the very brink of the question: What general semantic types of expression qualify for the basic subject- and predicate-roles in simplest sentences? and why? An answer to this question, it might seem, could very well be at least a beginning towards a perspicuous characterization of this apparently fundamental grammatical relation; helping us, e.g. to understand its extension, via nominalizations, to other, less simple cases. Yet no move is made towards confronting these questions, either in the more general or a more specific form.

[1] It appears from the John Locke lectures that Chomsky no longer holds (or holds for all cases) that such abstract nouns appear as the result of a nominalizing transformation. Rather, he holds that there are underlying semantic or lexical elements, in themselves neither nominal nor, for example, verbal or adjectival, but capable of appearing in deep structures in either role. Nevertheless, there would appear to be gounds for awarding *some kind* of syntactical primacy to the verbal, or adjectival, over the nominal, role in such cases; and such an award will serve my present purpose, in whatever theoretical terms it is ultimately to be understood. My own guess, for what it is worth, is in line with Chomsky's later position, in so far as I see no reason why we should not, and much reason why we should, have a use for a notion of *nominalization* which does not depend on that of *transformation*.

IV

I have said that it would seem natural enough, given their ultimate theoretical concerns, for transformational grammarians to move in the direction I have indicated. Yet, on the other hand, there are reasons why it is natural that they should not. More than this: there are reasons why the questions I have just indicated as natural, though they are in the right spirit, are not yet in the right form. It is probably true that if genuinely explanatory foundations are to be provided for grammar, an attempt must be made to close the explanation-gap between semantico-logical features on the one hand and syntactic classifications and relations on the other. It is probably false that this attempt is best undertaken by first framing questions directly in terms of traditional syntactic categories and relations, such as those of noun and verb, object of the verb, etc. Let me first try to explain the grammarians' reluctance to undertake the necessary enterprise before explaining why the form of the enterprise is not to be so simply understood. The two points are closely, and subtly, interconnected.

First, let us recall that just as, on the one hand, the transformational grammarians tend to be severe critics of the philosophers of ordinary language for being insufficiently systematic, so, on the other, they are no less severe critics of those philosophers of language who derive their inspiration from formal logic and practise, or advocate, the construction of ideal languages; and their criticism of these last is that, though they are indeed systematic, they are insufficiently empirical.[1] For though the approach of the transformational grammarians is in one way highly abstract and theoretical, it is in another way thoroughly empirical. They are empirical linguists, grammarians – though in aspiration generalizing grammarians – of actually given languages, inclined to be suspicious of theoretical notions except in so far as they can be used in *the construction of systems, or mechanisms, of rules* which will yield what is actually found in accepted sentences and will regularly mark the deviations in deviant ones. Thus, though it is characteristic of the transformational grammarian that he is willing to view the thought of a universal grammar, a general theory of language, with favour, yet he would – the example of Chomsky suggests – prefer to view the concepts which enter into such a

[1] See, for example, on both points, Katz, *Philosophy of Language*, Ch. 3.

theory as capable of being elucidated entirely in terms of the contribution they make to such working rule-mechanisms. Any other view of them is likely to be, from the grammarian's point of view, too vague and intuitive to satisfy his ideal of empirical clarity.

Thus the grammarian is apt to be inhibited from adopting an approach which the philosopher may be more ready to adopt, and which perhaps must be adopted if truly explanatory foundations are to be provided for grammar. Certain of the fundamental ideas of the transformational grammarians – the distinction between deep and surface structures, the notion of systematic transformational relations between them, the hint of a suggestion that the basic forms of functional relation are to be found in the simplest forms of deep structures – these will strike a responsive chord in the breast of any philosopher who has tried to reach through surface similarities of grammatical form to the semantico-logical differences which lie below them; that is, in any philosopher whatever. But when the question of explanatory foundations for grammar is raised against this background of shared ideas, the philosopher's response, it seems to me, should, at least at first, be to make the maximum use of his disreputable liberty from empirical constraints. Thus he need not be at all concerned, at least to begin with, with the actual formal arrangements by means of which functional relations are actually represented, whether in the base or at any other level, in a particular language. He will have, as the grammarian has, a conception of meaning-elements (the atoms to be structured) on the one hand; and of semantically significant modes of combination of them (syntactical relations) on the other. But he will be prepared from the start to use a vocabulary which is overtly semantic or, in a broad sense, logical, for the classification of elements, abstractly conceived; and this vocabulary will from the start stand in perspicuous connection with his vocabulary of modes of combination or grammatical relations. Given these perspicuous connections, he may next consider possible formal arrangements by means of which the combining functions might be discharged; and may finally relate these theoretical models of language to what is actually found in empirically given languages.

Here, then, is a programme for research in non-empirical linguistics, which may perhaps in the end pay empirical dividends. The procedure to be followed in pursuing such a programme will in some ways be reminiscent of the setting up of ideal languages by the logicians; but the purpose will be less restricted than that of the logicians. Quine says somewhere: don't expose more structure than you need expose. But the non-empirical grammarian will be concerned with every point at which structure is needed to contribute to overall meaning. Structure must be exposed at every point and understood at every point.

To say now a little more about details of procedure. Practically speaking it is inevitable that one should start with relatively simple models of language-types and work up to more complex ones. The vital distinction to be observed throughout is that between the intrinsic or essential grammar of a language-type and the alternative or variable grammars of that language-type. A language-type is defined by specifying (1) the semantic or broadly logical type of meaning-elements it contains and (2) the types of significant combinations into which they can enter to form sentences. These specifications determine *a priori* the essential grammar of the language-type, on the assumption that each sentence, at least in the base, must permit of a syntactically unambiguous reading. The rules of essential grammar will require that all combinations must somehow or other be indicated and, when necessary, differentiated; that if, for example, a sentence contains a number of elements which could be significantly clustered into different attributive groupings, then it must somehow be indicated which elements are to be taken with which; or, again, that in the case of an element signifying a non-symmetrical relation in combination with elements or clusters signifying its terms, the ordering of the term-signifying elements or clusters must somehow be indicated. These are requirements of essential grammar. But the essential grammar of a language-type in no way stipulates *how* such requirements are to be fulfilled. There lies open a choice among different ways of using such various formal devices as those of, for example, element-positioning, inflection, affixing or the use of special syntactic markers. In choosing one among various possible sets of formal arrangements adequate to the requirements of essential grammar, we should be choosing one of the possible variable or alternative grammars for the language-type in question. When such a choice is made and codified, we have a complete and completely perspicuous grammar (or form of grammar) for that language-type; at the cost, of course, of not having the grammar of an actual language at all, but only of an ideally simplified type of language.

If we press these researches even a little way, we find that we need quite an elaborate vocabulary, or set of interrelated vocabularies, of theoretical notions. Thus we need, first, what might be called an ontological vocabulary. We need, second, a semantic vocabulary, or vocabulary for naming semantic types of elements and even for describing individual elements (elements being throughout, as already said, rather abstractly conceived). Third, we need a functional vocabulary for naming the kinds of combination or relation into which elements may enter in sentences and the kinds of role which elements or combinations of elements may play in sentences. Fourth, and finally, we need a vocabulary of formal devices. Between, and within, the first three vocabularies, or batteries of notions, there are close interrelations and dependences. The fourth vocabulary stands rather apart from the rest in that we need to invoke it only when we move from essential to variable grammar. Specimen items belonging to the fourth vocabulary I have already mentioned, in referring to element-positioning, inflection, etc. Specimen items belonging to the ontological vocabulary might include space, time, particular continuant, situation, general character or relation; and some sub-classifications of these last, as, perhaps, of general characters into sorts, states, actions, properties, and of relations into, at least, symmetrical and non-symmetrical. Readiness to employ some such notions as these is inseparable from the use of the functional and semantic vocabularies. The functional notions must include those of major linkage of major sentence-parts into sentences and, for any language-type which is not of an idiotic simplicity, the notion of minor linkages of elements into sentence-parts. Major and minor linkages alike will have to be further distinguished into kinds, as also will the roles which elements or parts may play, and the different relations in which they may stand to each other, inside these different combinations. The internal relations, the interlockings and overlappings of the functional vocabulary are most complex, and I shall not attempt to illustrate them here. The semantic vocabulary for a fairly restricted language-type might include three main classes of elements: (1) proper names for continuant particulars; (2) elements signifying general characters and relations; and (3) deictic elements. At least the second and third classes would be subdivided for a language-type of any richness, the second on lines already indicated in the ontological vocabulary, the third perhaps into elements for temporal deixis, for spatial deixis, for interlocutory deixis and for what might be called merely contextual deixis.

Now it will be noted that in listing these specimen items from the interrelated vocabularies of essential grammar, I have made no mention of any of the traditional syntactic categories of noun, verb, adjective, preposition, etc. And this is no accident of selection or omission. The more complex the language-type, the more complex, certainly, will be the interrelated vocabularies necessary to specify the type and to state, as consequences of the specification, the requirements of its essential grammar. But, however complex those vocabularies become, they will never, so long as we remain at the level of essential grammar, include the traditional syntactic classifications I have mentioned. For those classifications, as understood by conventional modern grammarians, involve an essential reference to the formal arrangements by means of which grammatical relations are represented in variable grammar. The more rigorous the grammarian, the more he strives to explain such categories as noun and verb in terms of formal criteria: in terms of the types of inflection which expressions may undergo and their distribution in sentences, the positions they may standardly occupy in sentences relative to expressions of other categories. The statement of such criteria can, perhaps never be entirely purged of semantic notions; and it must be framed with some looseness if the traditional categories are to be applied over a range of languages. But the point remains that the conventional categories reflect the interaction, in actual languages, of semantic and functional factors with actually found formal factors; and therefore have no place in the study of essential grammars. This will not prevent the student of perspicuous grammar from observing how natural it is that certain types of formal arrangement, and hence perhaps certain conventional syntactic categories, should enter at the level of variable grammar. But it will be at that level that they will enter, and not before. And what holds for the conventional syntactic *categories* will hold also for the conventional syntactic *relations* in so far as their characterization is inseparable from that of the conventional syntactic categories.

It will now, I hope, be clear why I earlier remarked that the task of finding explanatory foundations for grammar is not best approached by trying to establish direct links between semantico-logical notions and such traditional, or at least traditionally named, syntactic categories as the transformational grammarians employ in imagining base structures. If the names have anything like their normal significance, we must go behind or below them, to essential functions and classifications; and if they do not, it would be better to drop them in favour of a more perspicuous nomenclature. Some incidental advantages of emancipating ourselves, as we must, from these traditional categories are indeed obvious. We shall be readier for the discovery that such categories cannot be readily forced on some (from our point of view) remoter languages; and correspondingly less prone to draw from such a discovery romantic conclusions about profound differences between the conceptual schemes of speakers of such languages and our own.

Many questions arise about such a programme as I have sketched. The notion of an essential grammar is, evidently, a relative notion: an essential grammar is the essential grammar *of a specified language-type*. We may set aside the obvious fact that the only practicable way of proceeding is to start from relatively simple specifications and build up to more complex ones, essential and alternative grammars themselves becoming more complex at every stage. There are more fundamental questions to be faced regarding the specifications of relatively basic types of element and combination, the selection of basic functional and logico-semantic vocabularies. It is admitted that these selections cannot be wholly independent of each other, that every semantico-logical type carries with it a certain potentiality of syntactic function. Is it not to be feared (supposed) that any such selection as the theorist of perspicuous grammars will make is likely to be restrictively conditioned by features of those languages with which he is most familiar? that, at worst, the ontology which was to enter into the explanatory foundations of grammar will be nothing but the abstract reflection of the base of the ontologist's native and local grammar? And, if so, how does it stand with the idea of a *general* theory of human language – nothing less than which will satisfy the full demand for explanation?

To these questions I can give only dogmatic answers. First, even if such fears are to some extent justified, it by no means follows that there is nothing to be gained by pursuing the suggested approach. To achieve any fairly rich models of perspicuous grammar would, I think, be to achieve a great deal. Even though it did not directly supply us with substantive linguistic universals of a general theory, it might help us to look for them. It is no new thing to work towards a comprehensive theory by way of theories which are less than comprehensive, to reach an adequate explanation by way of discarding inadequate explanations. But, second, it seems to me that such fears are likely to be exaggerated. We are all animals of the same species with fundamentally similar nervous and cerebral organizations and it is not to be supposed either that the most general categories for the organization of human experience are widely different or, correspondingly, that the basic logico-semantic types of element to be detected in human languages are so very widely different either. (This is not to say that detection will be easy.) The linguistic evidence may indeed *seem* to point to some fairly basic variations;[1] and it simply cannot be said, in advance of a much greater development of theory and research, what the best way of handling such apparent problems of variation will be. But no language could even set us a definite problem unless it were *understood* by some theorist of grammar; so it is scarcely to be feared (or hoped) that any which does set a definite problem could for ever escape the embrace of a unified theory.

One of the transformational grammarians suggests that a general theory of language, conceived as a quite self-contained empirical-linguistic study, would contain the solutions to a great range of traditional philosophical problems.[2] I have been suggesting that a general theory of language should not be above receiving help from philosophy as well as offering help to it. One of the most striking things about the transformational approach to grammar is that it does point so markedly in the direction I have indicated. To follow this direction does not seem to be a departure from empiricism, generously conceived, even though

[1] It may *seem* to suggest, for example, that in certain areas in which *we* are inclined to number concepts of sorts of objects among our *primary* concepts, the most nearly corresponding *primary* concepts of other language-speakers *may* be of a different and possibly more primitive kind, not yet determined either as concepts of certain sorts of objects or as concepts of sorts of activities or situations in which such objects may be typically involved.

[2] See Katz, loc. cit.

the proper title for such an endeavour might well be held to be, as I suggested earlier, Research in Non-Empirical Linguistics. Of course the empirical value of the constructions of the philosophical student of perspicuous grammars is finally subject to the checks of psychologists and linguists, working separately and in combination. But where these two very different studies meet, the philosopher, at least for a time, may also find a role; and that not the least promising which is at present available to him. And, finally, whatever the ultimate empirical value of his constructions, and even if they have none, he may be sure of finding them a fruitful source of a kind of question and answer which he characteristically prizes.

8. Intention and Convention in Speech Acts

I

In this paper I want to discuss some questions regarding J. L. Austin's notions of the illocutionary force of an utterance and of the illocutionary act which a speaker performs in making an utterance.[1]

There are two preliminary matters I must mention, if only to get them out of the way. Austin contrasts what he calls the 'normal' or 'serious' use of speech with what he calls 'etiolated' or 'parasitical' uses. His doctrine of illocutionary force relates essentially to the normal or serious use of speech and not, or not directly, to etiolated or parasitical uses; and so it will be with my comments on his doctrine. I am not suggesting that the distinction between the normal or serious use of speech and the secondary uses which he calls etiolated or parasitical is so clear as to call for no further examination; but I shall take it that there is such a distinction to be drawn and I shall not here further examine it.

My second preliminary remark concerns another distinction, or pair of distinctions, which Austin draws. Austin distinguishes the illocutionary force of an utterance from what he calls its 'meaning' and distinguishes between the illocutionary and the locutionary acts performed in issuing the utterance. Doubts may be felt about the second term of each of these distinctions. It may be felt that Austin has not made clear just what abstractions from the total speech act he intends to make by means of his notions of meaning and of locutionary act. Although this is a question on which I have views, it is not what the present paper is about. Whatever doubts may be entertained about Austin's notions of meaning and of locutionary act, it is enough for present purposes to be able to say, as I think we clearly can, the following about their relation to the notion of illocutionary force. The meaning of a (serious) utterance,

---

[1] All references, unless otherwise indicated, are to *How To Do Things with Words* (Oxford, 1962).

as conceived by Austin, always embodies some limitation on its possible force, and sometimes – as, for example, in some cases where an explicit performative formula, like 'I apologize', is used – the meaning of an utterance may exhaust its force; that is, there may be no more to the force than there is to the meaning; but very often the meaning, though it limits, does not exhaust, the force. Similarly, there may sometimes be no more to say about the illocutionary force of an utterance than we already know if we know what locutionary act has been performed; but very often there is more to know about the illocutionary force of an utterance than we know in knowing what locutionary act has been performed.

So much for these two preliminaries. Now I shall proceed to assemble from the text some indications as to what Austin means by the force of an utterance and as to what he means by an illocutionary act. These two notions are not so closely related that to know the force of an utterance is the same thing as to know what illocutionary act was actually performed in issuing it. For if an utterance with the illocutionary force of, say, a warning is not understood in this way (that is, as a warning) by the audience to which it is addressed, then (it is held) the illocutionary act of warning cannot be said to have been actually performed. 'The performance of an illocutionary act involves the securing of uptake'; that is, it involves 'bringing about the understanding of the meaning and of the force of the locution' (pp. 115–16).[1] Perhaps we may express the relation by saying that to know the force of an utterance is the same thing as to know what illocutionary act, *if any*, was actually performed in issuing it. Austin gives many examples and lists of words which help us to form at least a fair intuitive notion of what is meant by 'illocutionary force' and 'illocutionary act'. Besides these, he gives us certain general clues to these ideas, which may be grouped, as follows, under four heads:

1. Given that we know (in Austin's sense) the meaning of an utterance, there may still be a further question as to *how what was said was meant* by the speaker, or as to *how the words spoken were used*, or as to *how the utterance was to be taken* or *ought to have been taken* (pp. 98–9). In order to know the illocutionary force of the utterance, we must know the answer to this further question.

[1] I refer later to the need for qualification of this doctrine.

2. A locutionary act is an act *of* saying something; an illocutionary act is an act we perform *in* saying something. It is what we *do*, *in* saying what we *say*. Austin does not regard this characterization as by any means a satisfactory test for identifying kinds of illocutionary acts since, so regarded, it would admit many kinds of acts which he wishes to exclude from the class (p. 99 and Lecture X).

3. It is a sufficient, though not, I think, a necessary, condition of a verb's being the name of a *kind* of illocutionary act that it can figure, in the first person present indicative, as what Austin calls an explicit performative. (This latter notion I shall assume to be familiar and perspicuous.)

4. The illocutionary act is 'a conventional act; an act done as conforming to a convention' (p. 105). As such, it is to be sharply contrasted with the producing of certain effects, intended or otherwise, by means of an utterance. This producing of effects, though it too can often be ascribed *as an act* to the speaker (his *perlocutionary* act), is in no way a conventional act (pp. 120–1). Austin reverts many times to the 'conventional' nature of the illocutionary act (pp. 103, 105, 108, 115, 120, 121, 127) and speaks also of 'conventions of illocutionary force' (p. 114). Indeed, he remarks (pp. 120–1) that though acts which can properly be called by the same names as illocutionary acts – for example, acts of warning – can be brought off non-verbally, without the use of words, yet, in order to be properly called by these names, such acts must be *conventional* non-verbal acts.

II

I shall assume that we are clear enough about the intended application of Austin's notions of illocutionary force and illocutionary act to be able to criticize, by reference to cases, his general doctrines regarding those notions. It is the general doctrine I listed last above – the doctrine that an utterance's having such and such a force is a matter of convention – that I shall take as the starting-point of inquiry. Usually this doctrine is affirmed in a quite unqualified way. But just once there occurs an interestingly qualified statement of it. Austin says, of the use of language with a certain illocutionary force, that 'it may . . . be said to be *conventional* in the sense that at least it could be made explicit by the performative formula' (p. 103). The remark has a certain authority in that it is the first explicit statement of the conventional nature of the illocutionary act. I shall refer to it later.

Meanwhile let us consider the doctrine in its unqualified form. Why does Austin say that the illocutionary act is a conventional act, an act done as conforming to a convention? I must first mention, and neutralize, two possible sources of confusion. (It may seem an excess of precaution to do so. I apologize to those who find it so.) First, we may agree (or not dispute) that any speech act is, as such, at least in part a conventional act. The performance of any *speech* act involves at least the observance or exploitation of some *linguistic* conventions, and every illocutionary act is a speech act. But it is absolutely clear that this is not the point that Austin is making in declaring the illocutionary act to be a conventional act. We must refer, Austin would say, to linguistic conventions to determine what *locutionary* act has been performed in the making of an utterance, to determine what the *meaning* of the utterance is. The doctrine now before us is the further doctrine that where force is *not* exhausted by meaning, the fact that an utterance has the further unexhausted force it has is also a matter of convention; or, where it is exhausted by meaning, the fact *that* it is, is a matter of convention. It is not just as being a speech act that an illocutionary act – for example, of warning – is conventional. A non-verbal act of warning is, Austin maintains, conventially such in just the same way as an illocutionary – that is, verbal – act of warning is conventionally such.

Second, we must dismiss as irrelevant the fact that it can properly be said to be a matter of convention that an act of, for example, warning is correctly called by this name. For if this were held to be a ground for saying that illocutionary acts were conventional acts, then any describable act whatever would, as correctly described, be a conventional act.

The contention that illocutionary force is a matter of convention is easily seen to be correct in a great number of cases. For very many kinds of human transaction involving speech are governed and in part constituted by what we easily recognize as established conventions of procedure additional to the conventions governing the *meanings* of our utterances. Thus the fact that the word 'guilty' is pronounced by the foreman of the jury in court at the proper moment constitutes his utterance as the act of bringing in a verdict;

and that this is so is certainly a matter of the conventional procedures of the law. Similarly, it is a matter of convention that if
the appropriate umpire pronounces a batsman 'out', he thereby
performs the act of *giving the man out*, which no player or spectator
shouting 'Out!' can do. Austin gives other examples, and there
are doubtless many more which could be given, where there
clearly exist statable conventions, relating to the circumstances of
utterance, such that an utterance with a certain meaning, pronounced by the appropriate person in the appropriate circumstances, has the force it has *as* conforming to those conventions.
Examples of illocutionary acts of which this is true can be found
not only in the sphere of social institutions which have a legal
point (like the marriage ceremony and the law courts themselves)
or of activities governed by a definite set of rules (like cricket and
games generally) but in many other relations of human life. The
act of *introducing*, performed by uttering the words 'This is Mr
Smith', may be said to be an act performed as conforming to a
convention. The act of surrendering, performed by saying
'*Kamerad!*' and throwing up your arms when confronted with a
bayonet, may be said to be (to have become) an act performed as
conforming to an accepted convention, a conventional act.

But it seems equally clear that, although the circumstances of
utterance are always relevant to the determination of the illocutionary force of an utterance, there are many cases in which it is
not as conforming to an accepted *convention* of any kind (other than
those linguistic conventions which help to fix the meaning of the
utterance) that an illocutionary act is performed. It seems clear,
that is, that there are many cases in which the illocutionary force
of an utterance, though not exhausted by its meaning, is not owed
to any *conventions* other than those which help to give it its meaning. Surely there may be cases in which to utter the words 'The ice
over there is very thin' to a skater is to issue a warning (is to say
something with the *force* of a warning) without its being the case
that there is any statable convention at all (other than those which
bear on the nature of the *locutionary* act) such that the speaker's act
can be said to be an act done as conforming to that convention.

Here is another example. We can readily imagine circumstances
in which an utterance of the words 'Don't go' would be correctly
described not as a request or an order, but as an entreaty. I do
not want to deny that there may be conventional postures or

L

procedures for entreating: one can, for example, kneel down, raise one's arms and *say*, 'I entreat you'. But I do want to deny that an act of entreaty can be performed only as conforming to some such conventions. What makes X's words to Y an *entreaty* not to go is something – complex enough, no doubt – relating to X's situation, attitude to Y, manner, and current intention. There are questions here which we must discuss later. But to suppose that there is always and necessarily a convention conformed to would be like supposing that there could be no love affairs which did not proceed on lines laid down in the *Roman de la Rose* or that every dispute between men must follow the pattern specified in Touchstone's speech about the countercheck quarrelsome and the lie direct.

Another example. In the course of a philosophical discussion (or, for that matter, a debate on policy) one speaker *raises an objection* to what the previous speaker has just said. X says (or proposes) that p and Y *objects* that q. Y's utterance has the force of an objection to X's assertion (or proposal) that p. But where is the *convention* that constitutes it an objection? That Y's utterance has the force of an objection may lie partly in the character of the dispute and of X's contention (or proposal) and it certainly lies partly, in Y's *view* of these things, in the bearing which he takes the proposition that q to have on the doctrine (or proposal) that p. But although there may be, there does not have to be, any convention involved other than those linguistic conventions which help to fix the meanings of the utterances.

I do not think it necessary to give further examples. It seems perfectly clear that, if at least we take the expressions 'convention' and 'conventional' in the most natural way, the doctrine of the conventional nature of the illocutionary act does not hold generally. Some illocutionary acts are conventional; others are not (except in so far as they are locutionary acts). Why then does Austin repeatedly affirm the contrary? It is unlikely that he has made the simple mistake of generalizing from some cases to all. It is much more likely that he is moved by some further, and fundamental, feature of illocutionary acts, which it must be our business to discover. Even though we may decide that the description 'covential' is not appropriately used, we may presume it worth our while to look for the reason for using it. Here we may recall that oddly qualified remark that the performance of an illocutionary act, or the use of a sentence with a certain illocutionary force, 'may be said to be conventional in the sense that at least it *could* be made explicit by the performative formula' (p. 103). On this we may first, and with justice, be inclined to comment that there is no such *sense* of 'being conventional', that if this is a *sense* of anything to the purpose, it is a sense of 'being *capable* of being conventional'. But although this is a proper comment on the remark, we should not simply dismiss the remark with this comment. Whatever it is that leads Austin to call illocutionary acts in general 'conventional' must be closely connected with whatever it is about such acts as warning, entreating, apologizing, advising, that accounts for the fact that *they* at least *could* be made explicit by the use of the corresponding first-person performative form. So we must ask what it is about them that accounts for this fact. Obviously it will not do to answer simply that they are acts which can be performed by the use of words. So are many (perlocutionary) acts, like convincing, dissuading, alarming, and amusing, for which, as Austin points out, there is no corresponding first-person *performative* formula. So we need some further explanation.

III

I think a concept we may find helpful at this point is one introduced by H. P. Grice in his valuable article on *Meaning* (*Philosophical Review*, LXVII, 1957), viz. the concept of *someone's non-naturally meaning something by an utterance*. The concept does not apply only to speech acts – that is, to cases where that by which someone non-naturally means something is a *linguistic* utterance. It is of more general application. But it will be convenient to refer to that by which someone, S, non-naturally means something as S's *utterance*. The explanation of the introduced concept is given in terms of the concept of intention. S non-naturally means something by an utterance x if S intends (i_1) to produce by uttering x a certain response (r) in an audience A and intends (i_2) that A shall recognize S's intention (i_1) and intends (i_3) that this recognition on the part of A of S's intention (i_1) shall function as A's reason, or a part of his reason, for his response r. (The word 'response', though more convenient in some ways than Grice's 'effect', is not ideal. It is intended to cover cognitive and affective states or attitudes as well as actions.) It is, evidently, an important feature of this definition that the securing of the response r is intended to be mediated by the securing of another (and always cognitive) effect in A; viz. recognition of S's intention to secure response r.

Grice's analysis of his concept is fairly complex. But I think a little reflection shows that it is not quite complex enough for his purpose. Grice's analysis is undoubtedly offered as an analysis of a situation in which one person is trying, in a sense of the word 'communicate' fundamental to any theory of meaning, to communicate with another. But it is possible to imagine a situation in which Grice's three conditions would be satisfied by a person S and yet, in this important sense of 'communicate', it would not be the case that S could be said to be trying to communicate by means of his production of x with the person A in whom he was trying to produce the response r. I proceed to describe such a situation.

S intends by a certain action to induce in A the belief that p; so he satisfies condition (i_1). He arranges convincing-looking 'evidence' that p, in a place where A is bound to see it. He does this, knowing that A is watching him at work, but *knowing also that* A *does not know that* S *knows that* A *is watching him at work*. He realizes that A will not take the *arranged* 'evidence' as genuine or natural evidence that p, but realizes, and indeed intends, that A will take his arranging of it as grounds for thinking that he, S, intends to induce in A the belief that p. That is, he intends A to recognize his (i_1) intention. So S satisfies condition (i_2). He knows that A has general grounds for thinking that S would not wish to make him, A, think that p unless it were known to S to be the case that p; and hence that A's recognition of his $(S$'s$)$ intention to induce in A the belief that p will in fact seem to A a sufficient reason for believing that p. And he intends that A's recognition of his intention (i_1) should function in just this way. So he satisfies condition (i_3).

S, then, satisfies all Grice's conditions. But this is clearly not a case of attempted *communication* in the sense which (I think it is fair to assume) Grice is seeking to elucidate. A will indeed take S to be trying to bring it about that A is aware of some fact; but he will not take S as trying, in the colloquial sense, to 'let him know' something (or to 'tell' him something). But unless S at least brings it about that A takes him (S) to be trying to let him (A) know something, he has not succeeded in communicating with A; and if, as in our example, he has not even *tried* to bring this about, then he has not even *tried* to communicate with A. It seems a minimum further condition of his trying to do this that he should not only intend A to recognize his intention to get A to think that p, but that he should also *intend* A *to recognize his intention to get* A *to recognize his intention* to get A to think that p.

We might approximate more closely to the communication situation if we changed the example by supposing it not only clear to both A and S that A was watching S at work, but also clear to them both that it *was* clear to them both. I shall content myself, however, with drawing from the actually considered example the conclusion that we must add to Grice's conditions the further condition that S should have the further intention (i_4) that A should recognize his intention (i_2). It is possible that further argument could be produced to show that even adding this condition is not *sufficient* to constitute the case as one of attempted communication. But I shall rest content for the moment with the fact that this addition at least is necessary.

Now we might have expected in Grice's paper an account of what it is for A to *understand* something by an utterance x, an account complementary to the account of what it is for S to *mean* something by an utterance x. Grice in fact gives no such account, and I shall suggest a way of at least partially supplying this lack. I say 'at least partially' because the uncertainty as to the sufficiency of even the modified conditions for S's non-naturally *meaning* something by an utterance x is reflected in a corresponding uncertainty in the sufficiency of conditions for A's understanding. But again we may be content for the moment with necessary conditions. I suggest, then, that for A (in the appropriate sense of 'understand') to understand *something* by utterance x, it is necessary (and perhaps sufficient) that there should be *some* complex intention of the (i_2) form, described above, which A takes S to have, and that for A to understand the utterance correctly, it is necessary that A should take S to have *the* complex intention of the (i_2) form which S does have. In other words, if A is to understand the utterance correctly, S's (i_4) intention and hence his (i_2) intention must be fulfilled. Of course it does not follow from the fulfilment of these intentions that his (i_1) intention is fulfilled; nor, consequently, that his (i_3) intention is fulfilled.

It is at this point, it seems, that we may hope to find a possible point of connection with Austin's terminology of 'securing uptake'. If we do find such a point of connection, we also find a possible starting-point for an at least partial analysis of the notions of illocutionary force and of the illocutionary act. For to secure uptake is to secure understanding of (meaning and) illocutionary force; and securing understanding of illocutionary force is said by Austin to be an essential element in bringing off the illocutionary act. It is true that this doctrine of Austin's may be objected to.[1] For surely a man may, for example, actually have made such and such a bequest, or gift, even if no one ever reads his will or instrument of gift. We may be tempted to say instead that at least *the aim, if not the achievement*, of securing uptake is an essential element in the performance of the illocutionary act. To this, too, there is an objection. Might not a man really have made a gift, in due form, and take some satisfaction in the thought, even if he had no expectations of the fact ever being known? But this objection at most forces on us an amendment to which we are in any case obliged,[2] viz. that the aim, if not the achievement, of securing uptake is essentially *a standard, if not an invariable*, element in the performance of the illocutionary act. So the analysis of the aim of securing uptake remains an essential element in the analysis of the notion of the illocutionary act.

IV

Let us, then, make a tentative identification – to be subsequently qualified and revised – of Austin's notion of uptake with that at least partially analysed notion of understanding (on the part of an audience) which I introduced just now as complementary to Grice's concept of somebody non-naturally meaning something by an utterance. Since the notion of audience understanding is introduced by way of a fuller (though partial) analysis than any which Austin gives of the notion of uptake, the identification is equivalent to a tentative (and partial) analysis of the notion of uptake and hence of the notions of illocutionary act and illocutionary force. If the identification were correct, then it would follow that to say something with a certain illocutionary force is

[1] I owe the objections which follow to Professor Hart.

[2] For an illocutionary act *may* be performed *altogether* unintentionally. See the example about redoubling at bridge, p. 166 below.

at least (in the standard case) to have a certain complex intention of the (i_4) form described in setting out and modifying Grice's doctrine.

Next we test the adequacy and explanatory power of this partial analysis by seeing how far it helps to explain other features of Austin's doctrine regarding illocutionary acts. There are two points at which we shall apply this test. One is the point at which Austin maintains that the production of an utterance with a certain illocutionary force is a conventional act in that unconventional sense of 'conventional' which he glosses in terms of general suitability for being made explicit with the help of an explicitly performative formula. The other is the point at which Austin considers the possibility of a general characterization of the illocutionary act as what we *do*, *in* saying what we say. He remarks on the unsatisfactoriness of this characterization in that it would admit as illocutionary acts what are not such; and we may see whether the suggested analysis helps to explain the exclusion from the class of illocutionary acts of those acts falling under this characterization which Austin wishes to exclude. These points are closely connected with each other.

First, then, we take the point about the general suitability of an illocutionary act for performance with the help of the explicitly performative formula for that act. The explanation of this feature of illocutionary acts has two phases; it consists of, first, a general, and then a special, point about intention. The first point may be roughly expressed by saying that in general a man can speak of his intention in performing an action with a kind of authority which he cannot command in predicting its outcome. What he intends in doing something is up to him in a way in which the results of his doing it are not, or not only, up to him. But we are concerned not with just any intention to produce any kind of effect by acting, but with a very special kind of case. We are concerned with the case in which there is not simply an intention to produce a certain response in an audience, but an intention to produce that response by means of recognition on the part of the audience of the intention to produce that response, this recognition to serve as part of the reason that the audience has for its response, and the intention that this recognition should occur being itself intended to be recognized. The speaker, then, not only has the general authority on the subject of his intention that any agent has; he also has a motive, inseparable from the nature of his act, for making that intention clear. For he will not have secured understanding of the illocutionary force of his utterance, he will not have performed the act of communication he sets out to perform, unless his complex intention is grasped. Now clearly, for the enterprise to be possible at all, there must exist, or he must find, means of making the intention clear. If there exists any conventional linguistic means of doing so, the speaker has both a right to use, and a motive for using, those means. One such means, available sometimes, which comes very close to the employment of the explicit performative form, would be to attach, or subjoin, to the substance of the message what looks like a force-elucidating *comment* on it, which may or may not have the form of a self-ascription. Thus we have phrases like 'This is only a suggestion' or 'I'm only making a suggestion'; or again 'That was a warning' or 'I'm warning you'. For using such phrases, I repeat, the speaker has the *authority* that anyone has to speak on the subject of his intentions and the *motive* that I have tried to show is inseparable from an act of communication.

From such phrases as these – which have, *in appearance*, the character of comments on utterances other than themselves – to the explicit performative formula the step is only a short one. My reason for *qualifying* the remark that such phrases have the character of comments on utterances other than themselves is this. We are considering the case in which the subjoined quasi-comment is addressed to the same audience as the utterance on which it is a quasi-comment. Since it is *part* of the speaker's audience-directed intention to make clear the character of his utterance as, for example, a warning, and since the subjoined quasi-comment directly subserves this intention, it is better to view the case, appearances notwithstanding, *not* as a case in which we have two utterances, one commenting on the other, but as a case of a single unitary speech act. Crudely, the addition of the quasi-comment 'That was a warning' is *part* of the total act of warning. The effect of the short step to the explicitly performative formula is simply to bring appearances into line with reality. When that short step is taken, we no longer have, even in appearance, two utterances, one a comment on the other, but a single utterance in which the first-person performative verb *manifestly* has that peculiar logical character of which Austin rightly made so much, and which we may express in the present context by saying that the verb serves not exactly to *ascribe* an intention to the speaker but rather, in Austin's phrase, to *make explicit* the type of communication intention with which the speaker speaks, the type of force which the utterance has.

The above might be said to be a deduction of the general possibility and utility of the explicitly performative formula for the cases of illocutionary acts not essentially conventional. It may be objected that the deduction fails to show that the intentions rendered explicit by the use of performative formulae *in general* must be of just the complex form described, and hence fails to justify the claim that just this kind of intention lies at the core of all illocutionary acts. And indeed we shall see that this claim would be mistaken. But before discussing why, we shall make a further application of the analysis at the second testing point I mentioned. That is, we shall see what power it has to explain why some of the things we may be *doing, in* saying what we say, are not illocutionary acts and could not be rendered explicit by the use of the performative formula.

Among the things mentioned by Austin which we might be doing in saying things, but which are not illocutionary acts, I shall consider the two examples of (1) showing off and (2) insinuating. Now when we show off, we are certainly trying to produce an effect on the audience: we talk, indeed, for effect; we try to impress, to evoke the response of admiration. But it is no part of the intention to secure the effect *by means of* the recognition of the intention to secure it. It is no part of our total intention to secure recognition of the intention to produce the effect at all. On the contrary: recognition of the intention might militate against securing the effect and promote an opposite effect, for example, disgust.

This leads on to a further general point not explicitly considered by Austin, but satisfactorily explained by the analysis under consideration. In saying to an audience what we do say, we very often intend not only to produce the primary response *r* by means of audience recognition of the intention to produce that response, but to produce further effects by means of the production of the primary response *r*. Thus my further purpose in informing you that *p* (that is, aiming to produce in you the primary cognitive response of knowledge or belief that *p*) may be to bring it about thereby that you adopt a certain line of conduct or a certain attitude. In saying what I say, then, part of what I am *doing* is trying to influence your attitudes or conduct in a certain way. Does this part of what I am doing in saying what I say contribute to determining the character of the illocutionary act I perform? And if not, why not? If we take the first question strictly as introduced and posed, the answer to it is 'No'. The reason for the answer follows from the analysis. We have no complex intention (i_4) that there should be recognition of an intention (i_2) that there should be recognition of an intention (i_1) that the further effect should be produced; for it is no part of our intention that the further effect should be produced by way of recognition of our intention that it should be; the production in the audience of belief that p is intended to be itself the means whereby his attitude or conduct is to be influenced. We secure uptake, perform the act of communication that we set out to perform, if the audience understands us as *informing* him that p. Although it is true that, in saying what we say, we are in fact *trying* to produce the further effect – this is part of what we are doing, whether we succeed in producing the effect or not – yet this does not enter into the characterization of the illocutionary act. With this case we have to contrast the case in which, instead of aiming at a primary response and a further effect, the latter to be secured through the former alone, we aim at a complex primary response. Thus in the case where I do not simply inform, but warn, you that p, among the intentions I intend you to recognize (and intend you to recognize as intended to be recognized) are not only the intention to secure your belief that p, but the intention to secure that you are on your guard against p-perils. The difference (one of the differences) between showing off and warning is that your recognition of my intention to put you on your guard may well contribute to putting you on your guard, whereas your recognition of my intention to impress you is not likely to contribute to my impressing you (or not in the way I intended).[1]

---

[1] Perhaps trying to impress might sometimes have an illocutionary character. For I might try to impress you with my *effrontery*, intending you to recognize this intention and intending your recognition of it to function as part of your reason for being impressed, and so forth. But then I am not *merely* trying to impress you; I am *inviting* you to be impressed. I owe this point to Mr B. F. McGuinness.

Insinuating fails, for a different reason, to be a type of illocutionary act. An essential feature of the intentions which make up the illocutionary complex is their overtness. They have, one might say, essential avowability. This is, in one respect, a logically embarrassing feature. We have noticed already how we had to meet the threat of a counter-example to Grice's analysis of the communicative act in terms of three types of intention – (i_1), (i_2), and (i_3) – by the addition of a further intention (i_4) that an intention (i_2) should be recognized. We have no proof, however, that the resulting enlarged set of conditions is a complete analysis. Ingenuity might show it was not; and the way seems open to a regressive series of intentions that intentions should be recognized. While I do not think there is anything necessarily objectionable in this, it does suggest that the complete and rounded-off set of conditions aimed at in a conventional analysis is not easily and certainly attainable in these terms. That is why I speak of the feature in question as logically embarrassing. At the same time it enables us easily to dispose of insinuating as a candidate for the status of a type of illocutionary act. The whole point of insinuating is that the audience is to *suspect*, but not more than suspect, the intention, for example, to induce or disclose a certain belief. The intention one has in insinuating is essentially non-avowable.

Now let us take stock a little. We tentatively laid it down as a necessary condition of securing understanding of the illocutionary force of an utterance that the speaker should succeed in bringing it about that the audience took him, in issuing his utterance, to have a complex intention of a certain kind, viz. the intention that the audience should recognize (and recognize as intended to be recognized) his intention to induce a certain response in the audience. The suggestion has, as we have just seen, certain explanatory merits. Nevertheless we cannot claim general application for it as even a partial analysis of the notions of illocutionary force and illocutionary act. Let us look at some reasons why not.

V

I remarked earlier that the words 'Don't go' may have the force, *inter alia*, either of a request or of an entreaty. In either case the primary intention of the utterance (if we presume the words to be uttered with the *sense* 'Don't go *away*') is that of inducing the person addressed to stay where he is. His staying where he is is the primary response aimed at. But the only other intentions mentioned in our scheme of partial analysis relate directly or indirectly to recognition of the primary intention. So how, in terms of that scheme, are we to account for the variation in illocutionary force between requests and entreaties?

This question does not appear to raise a major difficulty for the scheme. The scheme, it seems, merely requires supplementing and enriching. *Entreaty*, for example, is a matter of trying to secure the primary response not merely through audience recognition of the intention to secure it, but through audience recognition of a complex attitude of which this primary intention forms an integral part. A wish that someone should stay may be held in different ways: passionately or lightly, confidently or desperately; and it may, for different reasons, be part of a speaker's intention to secure recognition of *how* he holds it. The most obvious reason, in the case of entreaty, is the belief, or hope, that such a revelation is more likely to secure the fulfilment of the primary intention.

But one may not only request and entreat; one may *order* someone to stay where he is. The words 'Don't go' may have the illocutionary force of an order. Can we so simply accommodate in our scheme *this* variation in illocutionary force? Well, we can accommodate it; though not so simply. We can say that a man who issues an order typically intends his utterance to secure a certain response, that he intends this intention to be recognized, and its recognition to be a reason for the response, that he intends the utterance to be recognized as issued in a certain social context such that certain social rules or conventions apply to the issuing of utterances in this context and such that certain consequences may follow in the event of the primary response not being secured, that he intends *this* intention too to be recognized, and finally that he intends the recognition of these last features to function as an element in the reasons for the response on the part of the audience.

Evidently, in this case, unlike the case of entreaty, the scheme has to be extended to make room for explicit reference to social convention. It can, with some strain, be so extended. But as we move further into the region of institutionalized procedures, the strain becomes too much for the scheme to bear. On the one hand, one of its basic features – viz. the reference to an intention to secure a definite response in an audience (over and above the securing of uptake) – has to be dropped. On the other, the reference to social conventions of procedure assumes a very much greater importance. Consider an umpire giving a batsman out, a jury bringing in a verdict of guilty, a judge pronouncing sentence, a player redoubling at bridge, a priest or a civil officer pronouncing a couple man and wife. Can we say that the umpire's primary intention is to secure a certain response (say, retiring to the pavilion) from a certain audience (say, the batsman), the jurymen's to secure a certain response (say, the pronouncing of sentence) from a certain audience (say, the judge), and then build the rest of our account around this, as we did, with some strain, in the case of the order? Not with plausibility. It is not even possible, in other than a formal sense, to isolate, among all the participants in the procedure (trial, marriage, game) to which the utterance belongs, a particular audience to whom the utterance can be said to be addressed.

Does this mean that the approach I suggested to the elucidation of the notion of illocutionary force is entirely mistaken? I do not think so. Rather, we must distinguish types of case; and then see what, if anything, is common to the types we have distinguished. What we initially take from Grice – with modifications – is an at least partially analytical account of an act of communication, an act which might indeed be performed non-verbally and yet exhibit all the essential characteristics of a (non-verbal) equivalent of an illocutionary act. We gain more than this. For the account enables us to understand how such an act may be linguistically conventionalized right up to the point at which illocutionary force is exhausted by meaning (in Austin's sense); and in this understanding the notion of wholly overt or essentially avowable intention plays an essential part. Evidently, in these cases, the illocutionary act itself is not *essentially* a conventional act, an act done as conforming to a convention; it may be that the act is conventional, done as forming to a convention, only in so far as *the means to perform it* are conventional. To speak only of those conventional means which are also *linguistic* means, the extent to which the act is one done as conforming to conventions may depend solely on the extent to which conventional linguistic meaning exhausts illocutionary force.

At the other end of the scale – the end, we may say, from which Austin began – we have illocutionary acts which *are* essentially conventional. The examples I mentioned just now will serve – marrying, redoubling, giving out, pronouncing sentence, bringing in a verdict. Such acts could have no existence outside the rule- or convention-governed practices and procedures of which they essentially form parts. Let us take the standard case in which the participants in these procedures know the rules and their roles, and are trying to play the game and not wreck it. Then they are presented with occasions on which they have to, or may, perform an illocutionary act which forms part of, or furthers, the practice or procedure as a whole; and sometimes they have to make a decision within a restricted range of alternatives (for example, to pass or redouble, to pronounce sentence of imprisonment for some period not exceeding a certain limit). Between the case of such acts as these and the case of the illocutionary act not essentially conventional, there is an important likeness and an important difference. The likeness resides in the fact that, in the case of an utterance belonging to a convention-governed practice or procedure, the speaker's utterance is standardly *intended* to further, or affect the course of, the practice in question in some one of the alternative ways open, and intended to be recognized as so intended. I do not mean that such an act could *never* be performed *unintentionally*. A player might let slip the word 'redouble' without *meaning* to redouble; but if the circumstances are appropriate and the play strict, then he *has* redoubled (or he may be *held* to have redoubled). But a player who continually did this sort of thing would not be asked to play again, except by sharpers. Forms can take charge, in the absence of appropriate intention; but when they do, the case is *essentially* deviant or non-standard. There is present in the standard case, that is to say, the same element of wholly overt and avowable intention as in the case of the act not essentially conventional.

The difference is a more complicated affair. We have, in these cases, an act which is conventional in two connected ways. First, if things go in accordance with the rules of the procedure in question, the act of furthering the practice in the way intended is an act required or permitted by those rules, an act done as falling under the rules. Second, the act is identified as the act it is just because it is performed by the utterance of a form of words conventional for the performance of that act. Hence the speaker's utterance is not only *intended* to further, or affect the course of, the practice in question in a certain conventional way; in the absence of any breach of the conventional conditions for furthering the procedure in this way, it cannot fail to do so.

And here we have the contrast between the two types of case. In the case of an illocutionary act of a kind not essentially conventional, the act of communication is performed if *uptake* is secured, if the utterance is taken to be issued with the complex overt intention with which it is issued. But even though the act of communication is performed, the wholly overt intention which lies at the core of the intention complex may, *without any breach of rules or conventions*, be frustrated. The audience response (belief, action, or attitude) may simply not be forthcoming. It is different with the utterance which forms part of a wholly convention-governed procedure. Granted that uptake is secured, then any frustration of the wholly overt intention of the utterance (the intention to further the procedure in a certain way) must be attributable to a breach of rule or convention. The speaker who abides by the conventions can avowably have the intention to further the procedure in the way to which his current linguistic act is conventionally appropriated *only* if he takes it that the conventional conditions for so furthering it are satisfied and hence takes it *that his utterance will not only reveal his intentions but give them effect*. There is nothing parallel to this in the case of the illocutionary act of a kind not essentially conventional. In both cases, we may say, speakers assume the responsibility for making their intentions overt. In one case (the case of the convention-constituted procedure) the speaker who uses the explicitly performative form also explicitly assumes the responsibility for making his overt intention effective. But in the other case the speaker cannot, in the speech act itself, explicitly assume any such responsibility. For there are no conditions which can conventionally guarantee the effectiveness of his overt intention. Whether it is effective or not is something that rests with his audience. In the one case, therefore, the explicitly performative form *may* be the name of the very act which is performed if and only if the speaker's overt intention is effective; but in the other case it cannot be the name of this act. But of course – and I shall recur to this thought – the sharp contrast I have here drawn between two extreme types of case must not blind us to the existence of intermediate types.

Acts belonging to convention-constituted procedures of the

kind I have just referred to form an important part of human communication. But they do not form the whole nor, we may think, the most fundamental part. It would be a mistake to take them as the model for understanding the notion of illocutionary force in general, as Austin perhaps shows some tendency to do when he both insists that the illocutionary act is essentially a conventional act and connects this claim with the possibility of making the act explicit by the use of the performative formula. It would equally be a mistake, as we have seen, to generalize the account of illocutionary force derived from Grice's analysis; for this would involve holding, falsely, that the complex overt intention manifested in any illocutionary act always includes the intention to secure a certain definite response or reaction in an audience over and above that which is necessarily secured if the illocutionary force of the utterance is understood. Nevertheless, we can perhaps extract from our consideration of two contrasting types of case something which is common to them both and to all the other types which lie between them. For the illocutionary force of an utterance is essentially something that is intended to be understood. And the understanding of the force of an utterance in all cases involves recognizing what may be called broadly an audience-directed intention and recognizing it as wholly overt, as intended to be recognized. It is perhaps this fact which lies at the base of the general possibility of the explicit performative formula; though, as we have seen, extra factors come importantly into play in the case of convention-constituted procedures.

Once this common element in all illocutionary acts is clear, we can readily acknowledge that the types of audience-directed intention involved may be very various and, also, that different types may be exemplified by one and the same utterance.

I have set in sharp contrast those cases in which the overt intention is simply to forward a definite and convention-governed practice (for example, a game) in a definite way provided for by the conventions or rules of the practice and those cases in which the overt intention includes that of securing a definite response (cognitive or practical) in an audience over and above that which is necessarily secured if uptake is secured. But there is something misleading about the sharpness of this contrast; and it would certainly be wrong to suppose that all cases fall clearly and neatly into one or another of these two classes. A speaker whose job it is to do so may offer information, instructions, or even advice, and yet be overtly indifferent as to whether or not his information is accepted as such, his instructions followed, or his advice taken. His wholly overt intention may amount to no more than that of making available – in a 'take it or leave it' spirit – to his audience the information or instructions or opinion in question; though again, in some cases, he may be seen as the mouthpiece, merely, of another agency to which may be attributed at least general intentions of the kind that can scarcely be attributed, in the particular case, to him. We should not find such complications discouraging; for we can scarcely expect a general account of linguistic communication to yield more than schematic outlines, which may almost be lost to view when every qualification is added which fidelity to the facts requires.

M

9. *Meaning and Truth*

During the last quarter of a century Oxford has occupied, or reoccupied, a position it last held, perhaps, six hundred years ago: that of a great centre of philosophy in the Western world. During the same period my predecessor in this Chair, Professor Gilbert Ryle, has been the centre of this centre. We owe much to his vision, his enterprise, and his devotion as a kind of overseer – a wholly non-autocratic overseer – of the subject's development and organization; we owe much more to his fertility, his brilliance, and his originality as a philosopher.

It is characteristic of philosophers to reflect on their own activity in the same spirit as they reflect on the objects of that activity; to scrutinize philosophically the nature, the aims, and the methods of philosophical scrutiny. When he has written in this meta-philosophical vein, Professor Ryle has sometimes presented the model philosopher in a somewhat austere light: as one whose role is to correct a slack, habitual mental stance; or to disentangle the traffic-jams of ideas; or to prescribe the right exercises for our intellectual cramps and confusions. Professor Ryle has done his share of this work of necessary correction. But when we survey his philosophical output as a whole, the impression is not of austerity, but of abundance; of profusion of insight, vividness of illustration, and readiness of devisal. Each recalcitrant topic in turn is brilliantly illuminated by a method in which detail, imagery, contrast, and generalization are powerfully combined. The topics cover a wide range; many of them fall in the broad regions of the philosophy of meaning and the philosophy of mind; and if I may, tentatively, express a judgement of preference here, I would select his treatment of *thinking*, on which he has already written much and on which he is still engaged, as perhaps the most subtle and sensitive of all his philosophical explorations.

In Professor Ryle's work, as in that of few other philosophers, the thought and the style are one: the accumulation of image and epigram, the sharp antithesis, the taut and balanced sentences are not decorative additions to his argument, but the very form of his thought. If one has to name a single quality as supremely charac-

teristic of that thought and of that style, it will be one I have, per-
force, named twice already: *brilliance*. His writings form a brilliant
and lasting contribution, not only to philosophy, but also – which
is as great a thing – to English letters.

What is it for anything to have a *meaning* at all, in the way, or in
the sense, in which words or sentences or signals have meaning?
What is it for a particular sentence to have the meaning or
meanings it does have? What is it for a particular phrase, or a
particular word, to have the meaning or meanings it does have?
These are obviously connected questions. Any account we give
of meaning in general (in the relevant sense) must square with the
account we give of what it is for particular expressions to have
particular meanings; and we must acknowledge, as two complementary truths, first, that the meaning of a sentence in general
depends, in some systematic way, on the meanings of the words
that make it up and, second, that for a word to have a particular
meaning is a matter of its making a particular systematic contribution to the meanings of the sentences in which it occurs.
I am not going to undertake to try to answer these so obviously
connected questions. That is not a task for one lecture; or for one
man. I want rather to discuss a certain conflict, or apparent conflict, more or less dimly discernible in current approaches to these
questions. For the sake of a label, we might call it the conflict
between the theorists of communication-intention and the
theorists of formal semantics. According to the former, it is impossible to give an adequate account of the concept of meaning
without reference to the possession by speakers of audience-
directed intentions of a certain complex kind. The particular
meanings of words and sentences are, no doubt, largely a matter
of rule and convention; but the general nature of such rules and
conventions can be ultimately understood only by reference to the
concept of communication-intention. The opposed view, at least
in its negative aspect, is that this doctrine simply gets things the
wrong way round or the wrong way up, or mistakes the contingent for the essential. Of course we may expect a certain regularity
of relationship between what people intend to communicate by
uttering certain sentences and what those sentences conventionally
mean. But the system of semantic and syntactical rules, in the
mastery of which knowledge of a language consists – the rules

which determine the meanings of sentences – is not a system of rules *for* communicating at all. The rules can be exploited for this purpose; but this is incidental to their essential character. It would be perfectly possible for someone to understand a language completely – to have a perfect linguistic competence – without having even the implicit thought of the function of communication; provided, of course, that the language in question did not contain words explicitly referring to this function.

A struggle on what seems to be such a central issue in philosophy should have something of a Homeric quality; and a Homeric struggle calls for gods and heroes. I can at least, though tentatively, name some living captains and benevolent shades: on the one side, say, Grice, Austin, and the later Wittgenstein; on the other, Chomsky, Frege, and the earlier Wittgenstein.

First, then, as to the theorists of communication-intention. The simplest, and most readily intelligible, though not the only way of joining their ranks is to present your general theory of meaning in two stages: first, present and elucidate a primitive concept of *communication* (or communication-intention) in terms which do not presuppose the concept of *linguistic meaning*; then show that the latter concept can be, and is to be, explained in terms of the former.[1] For any theorist who follows this path, the fundamental concept in the theory of meaning is that of a speaker's, or, generally, an utterer's, *meaning something by* an audience-directed utterance on a particular occasion. An utterance is something produced or executed by an utterer; it need not be vocal; it could be a gesture or a drawing or the moving or disposing of objects in a certain way. What an utterer means by his utterance is incidentally specified in specifying the complex intention with which he produces the utterance. The analysis of the kind of intention in question is too complex to be given in detail here, so I shall confine myself to incomplete description. An utterer might have, as one of his intentions in executing his utterance, that of bringing his audience to think that he, the utterer, believes some proposition, say the proposition that *p*; and he might intend this

---

[1] Not the *only* way; for to say that a concept ϕ cannot be adequately elucidated without reference to a concept ψ is not the same thing as to say that it is possible to give a classical analysis of ϕ in terms of ψ. But the *simplest* way; for the classical method of analysis is that in terms of which, in our tradition, we most naturally think.

intention to be wholly overt, to be clearly recognized by the audience. Or again he might have the intention of bringing his audience to think that he, the utterer, wants his audience to perform some action, say *a*; and he might intend this intention of his to be wholly overt, to be clearly recognized by the audience. Then, provided certain other conditions on utterer's intention are fulfilled, the utterer may be said, in the relevant sense, to mean something by his utterance: specifically, to mean that *p*, in the declarative mode, in the first case and to mean, in the imperative mode, that the audience is to perform action *a* in the second case. Grice, for one, has given us reason to think that, with sufficient care, and far greater refinement than I have indicated, it is possible to expound such a concept of communication-intention or, as he calls it, utterer's meaning, which is proof against objection and which does not presuppose the notion of linguistic meaning.

Now a word about how the analysis of linguistic meaning in terms of utterer's meaning is supposed to proceed. Here again I shall not go into details. The details would be very complex. But the fundamental idea is comparatively simple. We are accustomed, and reasonably, to think of linguistic meaning in terms of rules and conventions, semantic and syntactic. And when we consider the enormous elaboration of these rules and conventions – their capacity, as the modern linguists stress, to generate an infinite number of sentences in a given language – we may feel infinitely removed from the sort of primitive communication situation which we naturally think of when trying to understand the notion of utterer's meaning in terms which clearly do not presuppose linguistic meaning. But rules or conventions govern human practices and purposive human activities. So we should ask what purposive activities are governed by *these* conventions. What are *these* rules rules for doing? And the very simple thought I spoke of which underlies the suggested type of analysis is that these rules are, precisely, rules for communicating, rules by the observance of which the utterer may achieve his purpose, fulfil his communication-intention; and that this is their *essential* character. That is, it is not just a fortunate fact that these rules allow of use for this purpose; rather, the very nature of the rules concerned can be understood only if they are seen as rules whereby this purpose can be achieved.

This simple thought may seem too simple; and in several ways.

For it is clear that we can, and do, communicate very complicated things by the use of language; and if we are to think of language as, fundamentally, a system of rules for facilitating the achievement of our communication-intentions, and if the analysis is not to be circular, must we not credit ourselves with extremely complicated communication-intentions (or at least desires) independently of having at our disposal the linguistic means of fulfilling those desires? And is not this absurd? I think this is absurd. But the programme of analysis does not require it. All that the analysis requires is that we can explain the notion of conventions of communication in terms of the notion of pre-conventional communication at a rather basic level. Given that we can do this, then there is more than one way in which we can start pulling ourselves up by our own linguistic boot-straps. And it looks as if we can explain the notion of conventions of communication in terms of the notion of pre-conventional communication at a rather basic level.

We can, for example, tell ourselves a story of the analytic-genetic variety. Suppose an utterer achieves a pre-conventional communication success with a given audience by means of an utterance, say x. He has a complex intention, *vis-à-vis* the audience of the sort which counts as a communication-intention and succeeds in fulfilling that intention by uttering x. Let us suppose that the primary intention was such that the utterer *meant* that p by uttering x; and, since, by hypothesis, he achieved a communication-success, he was so *understood* by his audience. Now if the same communication-problem presents itself later to the same utterer in relation to the same audience, the fact, known to both of them, that the utterer meant that p by uttering x before, gives the utterer a reason for uttering x again and the audience a reason for interpreting the utterance in the same way as before. (The reason which each has is the knowledge that the other has the knowledge which he has.) So it is easy to see how the utterance of x could become established as between this utterer and this audience as a means of meaning that p. Because it has worked, it becomes established; and then it works *because* it is established. And it is easy to see how this story could be told so as to involve not just a group of two, but a wider group. So we can have a movement from an utterer pre-conventionally meaning that p by an utterance of x to the utterance-type x conventionally meaning that *p* within a group and thence back to utterer-members of the group meaning that *p* by a token of the type, but now *in accordance with the conventions.*

Now of course this explanation of conventional meaning in terms of utterer's meaning is not enough by itself. For it only covers the case, or only obviously covers the case, of utterance-types without structure – i.e. of utterance-types of which the meaning is not systematically derived from the meanings of their parts. But it is characteristic of linguistic utterance-types to have structure. The meaning of a sentence is a syntactic function of the meanings of its parts and their arrangement. But there is no reason in principle why a pre-conventional utterance should not have a certain complexity – a kind of complexity which allowed an utterer, having achieved one communication-success, to achieve another by repeating one part of the utterance while varying the other part, what he means on the second occasion having something in common with, and something which differentiates it from, what he meant on the first occasion. And if he does thus achieve a second success, the way is open for a rudimentary *system* of utterance-types to become established, i.e. to become conventional within a group.

A system of conventions can be modified to meet needs which we can scarcely imagine existing before the system existed. And its modification and enrichment may in turn create the possibility of thoughts such as we cannot understand what it would be for one to have, without supposing such modification and enrichment to have taken place. In this way we can picture a kind of alternating development. Primitive communication-intentions and successes give rise to the emergence of a limited conventional meaning-system, which makes possible its own enrichment and development which in turn makes possible the enlargement of thought and of communication-needs to a point at which there is once more pressure on the existing resources of language which is in turn responsive to such pressure. . . . And of course there is an element of mystery in this; but so there is in human intellectual and social creativity anyway.

All the foregoing is by way of the roughest possible sketch of some salient features of a communication-intention theory of meaning and of a hint as to how it might meet the obvious objection that certain communication-intentions presuppose the existence of language. It has all been said before, and with far greater refinement. But it will serve, I hope, as a sufficient basis for the confrontation of views that I wish to arrange.

Now, then, for the at least apparently opposed view, which I have so far characterized only in its negative aspect. Of course the holders of this view share some ground with their opponents. Both agree that the meanings of the sentences of a language are largely determined by the semantic and syntactic rules or conventions of that language. Both agree that the members of any group or community of people who share knowledge of a language – who have a common linguistic competence – have at their disposal a more or less powerful instrument or means of communicating, and thereby of modifying each other's beliefs or attitudes or influencing each other's actions. Both agree that these means are regularly used in a quite conventional way, that what people intend to communicate by what they say is regularly related to the conventional meanings of the sentences they utter. Where they differ is as to the relations between the meaning-determining rules of the language, on the one hand, and the function of communication, on the other: one party insists, and the other (apparently) refuses to allow, that the general nature of those rules can be understood only by reference to this function.

The refusal naturally prompts a question, viz. What *is* the general character of those rules which must in some sense have been mastered by anyone who speaks and understands a given language? The rejected answer grounds their general character in the social function of communicating, for example, beliefs or wishes or instructions. If this answer is rejected, another must be offered. So we ask again: What is the general character of these meaning–determining rules?

It seems to me that there is only one type of answer that has ever been seriously advanced or developed, or needs to be seriously considered, as providing a possible alternative to the thesis of the communication-theorist. This is an answer which rests on the notion of truth-conditions. The thought that the sense of a sentence is determined by its truth-conditions is to be found in Frege and in the early Wittgenstein, and we find it again in many subsequent writers. I take, as an example, a recent article by Professor Davidson. Davidson is rightly concerned with the point that an adequate account of the meaning-rules for a language L will show how the meanings of sentences depend on the meanings of words in L; and a theory of meaning for L will do this, he says, if it contains a recursive definition of truth-in-L. The 'obvious connection', he says, between such a definition of truth and the concept of meaning is this: 'the definition works by giving the necessary and sufficient conditions for the truth of every sentence, and *to give truth-conditions is a way of giving the meaning of a sentence*. To know the semantic concept of truth for a language is to know what it is for a sentence – any sentence – to be true, and *this amounts, in one good sense we can give to the phrase, to understanding the language*.'[1]

Davidson, in the article I quote from, has a limited concern. But the concern finds its place inside a more general idea; and the general idea, plainly enough, is that the syntactic and semantic rules together determine the meanings of all the sentences of a language and do this by means, precisely, of determining their truth-conditions.

Now if we are to get at the root of the matter, to isolate the crucial issue, it seems to me important to set aside, at least initially, one class of objections to the adequacy of such a conception of meaning. I say one class of objections; but it is a class which admits of subdivisions. Thus it may be pointed out that there are some kinds of sentences – e.g. imperatives, optatives, and interrogatives – to which the notion of truth-conditions seems inappropriate, in that the conventional utterance of such sentences does not result in the saying of anything true or false. Or again it may be pointed out that even sentences to which the notion of truth-conditions does seem appropriate may contain expressions which certainly make a difference to their conventional meaning, but not the sort of difference which can be explained in terms of their truth-conditions. Compare the sentence 'Fortunately, Socrates is dead' with the sentence 'Unfortunately, Socrates is dead'. Compare a sentence of the form 'p and q' with the corresponding sentence of the form 'p but q'. It is clear that the meanings of the members of each pair of sentences differ; it is far from clear that their truth-conditions differ. And there are not just one or two expressions which give rise to this problem, but many such expressions.

Obviously both a comprehensive general theory of meaning

[1] 'Truth and Meaning' (*Synthese*, 1967, p. 310). My italics.

and a comprehensive semantic theory for a particular language must be equipped to deal with these points. Yet they may reasonably be regarded as peripheral points. For it is a truth implicitly acknowledged by communication-theorists themselves[1] that in almost all the things we should count as sentences there is a substantial central core of meaning which is explicable either in terms of truth-conditions or in terms of some related notion quite simply derivable from that of a truth-condition, for example the notion, as we might call it, of a compliance-condition in the case of an imperative sentence or a fulfilment-condition in the case of an optative. If we suppose, therefore, that an account can be given of the notion of a truth-condition itself, an account which is indeed independent of reference to communication-intention, then we may reasonably think that the greater part of the task of a general theory of meaning has been accomplished without such reference. And by the same token, on the same supposition, we may think that the greater part of the particular theory of meaning of a particular language L can also be given, free of any such, even implicit, reference; for it can be given by systematically setting out the syntactic and semantical rules which determine truth-conditions for sentences of L.

Of course, as already admitted, something will have to be added to complete our general theory and to complete our particular theories. Thus for a particular theory an account will have to be added of the transformations that yield sentences with compliance-conditions or fulfilment-conditions out of sentences with truth-conditions; and the general theory will have to say what sort of thing, semantically speaking, such a derived sentence in general is. But this, though yielding a large harvest in sentences, is in itself a relatively small addition to either particular or general theory. Again, other additions will be necessary in connection with the other objections I mentioned. But, heartened by his hypothesized success into confidence, the theorist may reckon on

[1] This acknowledgement is probably implicit, though not very clearly so, in Austin's concept of *locutionary meaning* (see *How to do things with Words* Oxford, 1962); it is certainly implicit in Grice's distinction between what speakers *actually say*, in a favoured sense of 'say', and what they imply (see 'Utterer's Meaning, Sentence-Meaning and Word-Meaning', in *Foundations of Language*, 1968); and again in Searle's distinction between the *proposition* put forward and the illocutionary mode in which it is put forward (see *Speech Acts*, Cambridge, 1969).

dealing with some of these additions without essential reference to communication-intention; and, heartened by his hypothesized success into generosity, he may be happy to concede rights in some small outlying portion of the *de facto* territory of theoretical semantics to the theorist of communication-intention, instead of confining the latter entirely to some less appetizing territory called theoretical pragmatics.

I hope it is now clear what the central issue is. It consists in nothing other than the simple-seeming question whether the notion of truth-conditions can itself be explained or understood without reference to the function of communication. One minor clarification is called for before I turn to examine the question directly. I have freely used the phrase 'the truth-conditions of sentences' and I have spoken of these truth-conditions as determined by the semantical and syntactical rules of the language to which the sentences belong. In such a context we naturally understand the word 'sentence' in the sense of a 'type-sentence'. (By a sentence in the sense of a type I mean the sense in which there is just one English sentence, say, 'I am feeling shivery', or just one English sentence, say, 'She had her sixteenth birthday yesterday', which one and the same sentence may be uttered on countless different occasions by different people and with different references or applications.) But for many type-sentences, such as those just mentioned, the question whether they, the *sentences*, are true or false is one that has no natural application: it is not the invariant type-sentences themselves that are naturally said to be true or false, but rather the systematically varying things that people say, the propositions they express, when they utter those sentences on different particular occasions. But if the notion of truth-*values* is in general inappropriate to type-sentences, how can the notion of truth-*conditions* be appropriate? For presumably the truth-conditions of something are the conditions under which it is true.

The difficulty, however, is quite easily resolved. All that needs to be said is that the statement of truth-conditions for many type-sentences – perhaps most that are actually uttered in ordinary conversation – has to be, and can be, relativized in a systematic way to contextual conditions of utterance. A general statement of truth-conditions for such a sentence will then be, not a statement of conditions under which that sentence is a truth, but a general statement of a type of conditions under which different particular utterances of it will issue in different particular truths. And there are other more or less equivalent, though rather less natural, ways of resolving the difficulty.

So now, at last, to the central issue. For the theorists of formal semantics, as I have called them, the whole weight, or most of the weight, both of a general theory of meaning and of particular semantic theories, falls on the notion of truth-conditions and hence on the notion of truth. We agree to let it rest there. But we still cannot be satisfied that we have an adequate general understanding of the notion of meaning unless we are satisfied that we have an adequate general understanding of the notion of truth.

There is one manoeuvre here that would completely block all hope of achieving adequate understanding; and, if I am not mistaken, it is a manoeuvre which has a certain appeal for some theorists of formal semantics. This is to react to a demand for a general explication of the notion of truth by referring us back to a Tarski-like conception of truth-in-a-given-language, *L*, a conception which is elucidated precisely by a recursive statement of the rules which determine the truth-conditions for sentences of *L*. This amounts to a refusal to face the general philosophical question altogether. Having agreed to the general point that the meanings of the sentences of a language are determined, or largely determined, by rules which determine truth-conditions, we then raise the general question what sort of thing truth-conditions are, or what truth-conditions are conditions *of*; and we are told that the concept of truth for a given language is defined by the rules which determine the truth-conditions for sentences of that language.

Evidently we cannot be satisfied with this. So we return to our general question about truth. And immediately we feel some embarrassment. For we have come to think there is very little to say about truth *in general*. But let us see what we can do with this very little. Here is one way of saying something uncontroversial and fairly general about truth. One who makes a statement or assertion makes a true statement if and only if things are as, in making that statement, he states them to be. Or again: one who expresses a supposition expresses a true supposition if and only if things are as, in expressing that supposition, he expressly supposes them to be. Now let us interweave with such innocuous remarks as these the agreed thoughts about meaning and truth-conditions. Then we have, first: the meaning of a sentence is determined by those rules which determine how things are stated to be by one who, in uttering the sentence, makes a statement; or, how things are expressly supposed to be by one who, in uttering the sentence, expresses a supposition. And then, remembering that the rules are relativized to contextual conditions, we can paraphrase as follows: the meaning of a sentence is determined by the rules which determine *what* statement is made by one who, in uttering the sentence in given conditions, makes a statement; or, which determine *what* supposition is expressed by one who, in uttering the sentence in given conditions, expresses a supposition; and so on.

Thus we are led, by way of the notion of truth, back to the notion of the *content* of such speech acts as stating, expressly supposing and so on. And here the theorist of communication-intention sees his chance. There is no hope, he says, of elucidating the notion of the content of such speech acts without paying some attention to the notions of those speech acts themselves. Now of all the speech acts in which something true or false may, in one mode or another, be put forward, it is reasonable to regard that of statement or assertion as having an especially central position. (Hot for certainties, we value speculation primarily because we value information.) And we cannot, the theorist maintains, elucidate the notion of stating or asserting except in terms of audience-directed intention. For the fundamental case of stating or asserting, in terms of which all variants must be understood, is that of uttering a sentence with a certain intention – an intention wholly overt in the sense required by the analysis of utterer's meaning – which can be incompletely described as that of letting an audience know, or getting it to think, that the speaker has a certain belief; as a result of which there may, or may not, be activated or produced in the audience that same belief. The rules determining the conventional meaning of the sentence join with the contextual conditions of its utterance to determine what the belief in question *is* in such a primary and fundamental case. And in determining what the belief in question is in such a case, the rules determine what statement is made in such a case. To determine the former *is* to determine the latter. But this is precisely what we wanted. For when we set out from the agreed point that the rules which determine truth-conditions thereby determine meaning, the conclusion to which we were led was precisely that those rules determined what statement was made by one who, in uttering the sentence, made a statement. So the agreed point, so far from being an alternative to a communication theory of meaning, leads us straight in to such a theory of meaning.

The conclusion may seem a little too swift. So let us see if there is any way of avoiding it. The general condition of avoiding it is clear. It is that we should be able to give an account of the notion of truth-conditions which involves no essential reference to communicative speech acts. The alternative of refusing to give any account at all – of just resting on the notion of truth-conditions – is, as I have already indicated, simply not open to us if we are concerned with the philosophical elucidation of the notion of meaning: it would simply leave us with the concepts of meaning and truth each pointing blankly and unhelpfully at the other. Neither would it be helpful, though it might at this point be tempting, to retreat from the notion of truth-conditions to the less specific notion of correlation in general; to say, simply, that the rules which determine the meanings of sentences do so by correlating the sentences, envisaged as uttered in certain contextual conditions, with certain possible states of affairs. One reason why this will not do is that the notion of correlation in general is simply too unspecific. There are many kinds of behaviour (including verbal behaviour) – and many more kinds could be imagined – which are correlated by rule with possible states of affairs without its being the case that such correlation confers upon them the kind of relation to those possible states of affairs that we are concerned with.

Another reason why it will not do is the following. Consider the sentence 'I am tired'. The rules which determine its meaning are indeed such as to correlate the sentence, envisaged as uttered by a particular speaker at a particular time, with the possible state of affairs of the speaker's being tired at that time. But this feature is not peculiar to that sentence or to the members of the class of sentences which have the same meaning as it. For consider the sentence 'I am not tired'. The rules which determine its meaning are also such as to correlate the sentence, envisaged as uttered by a certain speaker at a certain time, with the possible state of affairs of that speaker's being tired at that time. Of course the kinds of correlation are different. They are respectively such that one who uttered the first sentence would normally be understood as affirming, and one who uttered the second sentence would normally be understood as denying, that the state of affairs in question obtained; or again they are such that one who utters the first sentence when the state of affairs in question obtains has made a true statement and one who utters the second sentence in these circumstances has made a false statement. But to invoke these differences would be precisely to give up the idea of employing only the unspecific notion of correlation in general. It is not worth labouring the point further. But it will readily be seen not only that sentences different, and even opposed, in meaning are correlated, in one way or another, with the same possible state of affairs, but also that one and the same unambiguous sentence is correlated, in one way or another, with very many different and in some cases mutually incompatible states of affairs. The sentence 'I am tired' is correlated with the possible state of affairs of the speaker's being at the point of total exhaustion and also with the state of affairs of his being as fresh as a daisy. The sentence 'I am over 40' is correlated with any possible state of affairs whatever regarding the speaker's age; the sentence 'Swans are white' with any state of affairs whatever regarding the colour of swans.

The quite unspecific notion of correlation, then, is useless for the purpose in hand. It is necessary to find some way of specifying a particular correlation in each case, viz. the correlation of the sentence with the possible state of affairs the obtaining of which would be necessary and sufficient for something *true* to have been said in the uttering of the sentence under whatever contextual conditions are envisaged. So we are back once more with the notion of truth-conditions and with the question, whether we can give an account of this notion which involves no essential reference to communicative speech acts, i.e. to communication-intention.

I can at this point see only one resource open, or apparently open, to the theorist of meaning who still holds that the notion of communication-intention has no essential place in the analysis of the concept of meaning. If he is not to swallow his opponent's hook, he must take some leaves out of his book. He sees now that he cannot stop with the idea of truth. That idea leads straight to the idea of *what is said*, the content of what is said, when utterances are made; and that in turn to the question of what is being *done* when utterances are made. But may not the theorist go some way along this path without going as far along it as his opponent? Might it not be possible to *delete* the reference to communication-intention while *preserving* a reference to, say, belief-expression? And will not this, incidentally, be more realistic in so far as we often voice our thoughts to ourselves, with no communicative intention?

The manoeuvre proposed merits a fuller description. It goes as follows. First, follow the communication-theorist in responding to the challenge for an elucidation of the notion of truth-conditions by invoking the notion of, e.g. and centrally, statement or assertion (accepting the uncontroversial point that one makes a true statement or assertion when things are as, in making that assertion, one asserts them to be). Second, follow the communication-theorist again in responding to the challenge for an elucidation of the notion of asserting by making a connection with the notion of belief (conceding that to make an assertion is, in the primary case, to give expression to a belief; to make a true assertion is to give expression to a correct belief; and a belief is correct when things are as one who holds that belief, in so far as he holds that belief, believes them to be). But third, part company with the communication-theorist over the nature of this connection between assertion and belief; deny, that is, that the analysis of the notion of asserting involves essential reference to an intention, for example, to get an audience to think that the maker of the assertion holds the belief; deny that the analysis of the notion of asserting involves *any* kind of reference to audience-directed intention; maintain, on the contrary, that it is perfectly satisfactory to accept as fundamental here the notion of simply voicing or expressing a belief. Then conclude that the meaning-determining rules for a sentence of the language are the rules which determine *what* belief is conventionally articulated by one who, in given contextual conditions, utters the sentence. As before, determining what this belief is, is the same thing as determining what assertion is made. So all the merits of the opponent's theory are preserved while the reference to communication is extruded.

Of course, more must be said by this theorist, as by his opponent. For sentences which can be used to express beliefs need not always be so used. But the point is one to be made on both sides. So we may neglect it for the present.

Now will this do? I do not think it will. But in order to see that
it will not, we may have to struggle hard against a certain illusion.
For the notion of expressing a belief may seem to us perfectly
straightforward; and hence the notion of expressing a belief in
accordance with certain conventions may seem equally straightforward. Yet, in so far as the notion of expressing a belief is
the notion we need, it may borrow all its force and apparent
straightforwardness from precisely the communication-situation
which it was supposed to free the analysis of meaning from
depending on. We may be tempted to argue as follows. Often we
express beliefs with an audience-directed intention; we intend that
our audience should take us to have the belief we express and
perhaps that that belief should be activated or produced in the
audience as well. But then what could be plainer than this: that
what we can do with an audience-directed intention we can also
do without any such intention? That is to say, the audience-
directed intention, when it is present, is something added on to
the activity of expressing a belief and in no way essential to it – *or*
to the concept of it.

Now what a mixture of truth and falsity, of platitude and
illusion, we have here! Suppose we reconsider for a moment that
analysis of utterer's meaning which was roughly sketched at the
beginning. The utterer produces something – his utterance x –
with a complex audience-directed intention, involving, say, getting
the audience to think that he has a certain belief. We cannot detach
or extract from the analysis an element which corresponds to his
expressing a belief with no such intention – though we could
indeed produce the following description and imagine a case for
it: he acts *as if* he had such an intention though as a matter of fact
he has not. But here the description depends on the description
of the case in which he has such an intention.

What I am suggesting is that we may be tempted, here as elsewhere, by a kind of bogus arithmetic of concepts. Given the concept of Audience Directed Belief Expression (ADBE), we can
indeed think of Belief Expression (BE) without Audience Direction (AD), and find cases of this. But it does not follow that the
concept of ADBE is a kind of logical compound of the two
simpler concepts of AD and BE and hence that BE is conceptually
independent of ADBE.

Of course these remarks do not show that there is no such thing

N

as an independent concept of belief-expression which will meet the needs of the anti-communication-theorist. They are only remarks directed against a too simple argument to the effect that there is such a concept.

This much is clear. If there is such an essentially independent concept of belief-expression which is to meet the needs of the analysis of the notion of meaning, we cannot just stop with the phrase 'expressing a belief'. We must be able to give some *account* of this concept, to tell ourselves some intelligible story about it. We can sometimes reasonably talk of a man's actions or his behaviour as expressing a belief when, for example, we see those actions as directed towards an end or goal which it is plausible to ascribe to him in so far as it is also plausible to ascribe to him that belief. But this reflection by itself does not get us very far. For one thing, on the present programme, we are debarred from making reference to the end or goal of communication an essential part of our story. For another, the sort of behaviour we are to be concerned with must be, or be capable of being, formalized or conventionalized in such a way that it can be regarded as subjected to, or performed in observance of, rules; and of rules, moreover, which regulate the behaviour precisely in its aspect as expression of belief. It will not do to say simply: we might suppose a man to find *some* satisfaction (unspecified) or *some* point (unspecified) in performing certain formalized (perhaps vocal) actions on some occasions, these actions being systematically related to his having certain beliefs. For suppose a man had a practice of vocalizing in a certain way whenever he saw the sun rise and in another, partly similar, partly different, way whenever he saw it set. Then this practice would be regularly related to certain beliefs, i.e. that the sun was rising or that it was setting. But this description gives us no reason at all for saying that when the man indulged in this practice he was *expressing the belief* that the sun was rising or setting, in accordance with a rule for doing so. We really have not enough of a description to know *what* to say. As far as we could tell, we might say, he just seems to have this ritual of *saluting* the rising or the setting sun in this way. What need of his it satisfies we don't know.

Let us suppose, however – for the sake of the argument – that we can elaborate some relevant conception of expressing a belief which presupposes nothing which, on the present programme, we are debarred from presupposing; and that we draw on this concept of expressing a belief in order to give an account, or analysis, on the lines indicated, of the notion of linguistic meaning. Then an interesting consequence ensues. That is, it will appear as a quite contingent truth about language that the rules or conventions which determine the meanings of the sentences of a language are public or social rules or conventions. This will be, as it were, a natural fact, a fact of nature, in no way essential to the concept of a language, and calling for a natural explanation which must not be allowed to touch or modify that concept. There must be nothing in the *concept* to rule out the idea that every individual might have his own language which only he understands. But then one might ask: Why should each individual observe his own rules? or any rules? Why shouldn't he express any belief he likes in any way he happens to fancy when he happens to have the urge to express it? There is one answer at least which the theorist is debarred from giving to this question, if only in the interests of his own programme. He cannot say: Well, a man might wish to *record* his beliefs so that he could refer to the records later, and then he would find it convenient to have rules to interpret his own records. The theorist is debarred from giving this answer because it introduces, though in an attenuated form, the concept of communication-intention: the earlier man communicates with his later self.

There might be one way of stilling the doubts which arise so rapidly along this path. That would be to offer possible natural explanations of the supposed natural fact that language is public, that linguistic rules are more or less socially common rules; explanations which successfully avoided any suggestion that the connection of public rules with communication was anything but incidental and contingent. How might such an explanation go? We might say that it was an agreed point that the possession of a language enlarges the mind, that there are beliefs one could not express without a language to express them in, thoughts one could not entertain without a rule-governed system of expressions for articulating them. And it is a fact about human beings that they simply would not acquire mastery of such a system unless they were exposed, as children, to conditioning or training by adult members of a community. Without concerning ourselves about the remote origins of language, then, we may suppose the adult members of a community to wish their successors to have this mind-enlarging instrument at their disposal – and evidently the whole procedure of training will be simplified if they all teach the same, the common language. We may reasonably suppose that the learners, to begin with, do not quite appreciate what they will ultimately be doing with language; that it is for them, to begin with, a matter of learning to do the right thing rather than learning to say the true thing, i.e. a matter of responding vocally to situations in a way which will earn them reward or avoid punishment rather than a matter of *expressing their beliefs*. But later they come to realize that they have mastered a system which enables them to perform this (still unexplained) activity whenever they wish to; and *then* they are speaking a language.

Of course it must be admitted that in the process they are liable also to acquire the *secondary* skill of communicating their beliefs. But this is simply something added on, an extra and conceptually uncovenanted benefit, quite incidental to the description of what it is to have mastered the meaning-rules of the language. If, indeed, you pointedly direct utterances, of which the essential function is belief-expression, to another member of the community, he will be apt to take it that you hold whatever beliefs are in question and indeed that you intend him to take this to be so; and this fact may give rise, indeed, it must be admitted, does give rise, to a whole cluster of social consequences; and opens up all sorts of possibilities of kinds of linguistic communication other than that which is based on belief-expression. This is why, as already acknowledged, we may have ultimately to allow some essential reference to communication-intention into outlying portions of our semantic theory. But this risk is incurred only when we go beyond the central core of meaning, determined by the rules which determine truth-conditions. As far as the central core is concerned, the function of communication remains secondary, derivative, conceptually inessential.

I hope it is clear that any such story is going to be too perverse and arbitrary to satisfy the requirements of an acceptable theory. If this is the way the game has to be played, then the communication-theorist must be allowed to have won it.

But must the game, finally, be played in this way? I think, finally, it must. It is indeed a generally harmless and salutary thing to say that to know the meaning of a sentence is to know under what conditions one who utters it says something true. But if we wish for a philosophical elucidation of the concept of meaning, then the dictum represents, not the end, but the beginning, of our task. It simply narrows, and relocates, our problem, forcing us to inquire what is contained in the little phrase '. . . says something true'. Of course there are many ways in which one can say something which is in fact true, give expression, if you like, to a true proposition, without thereby expressing belief in it, without asserting that proposition: for example when the words in question form certain sorts of subordinate or co-ordinate clauses, and when one is quoting or play-acting and so on. But when we come to try to explain in general what it is to say something true, to express a true proposition, reference to belief or to assertion (and thereby to belief) is inescapable. Thus we may harmlessly venture: Someone says something true if things are as he says they are. But this 'says' already has the force of 'asserts'. Or, to eschew the 'says' which equals 'asserts', we may harmlessly venture: Someone propounds, in some mode or other, a true proposition if things are as anyone who believed what he propounds would thereby believe them to be. And here the reference to belief is explicit.

Reference, direct or indirect, to belief-expression is inseparable from the analysis of saying something true (or false). And, as I have tried to show, it is unrealistic to the point of unintelligibility – or, at least, of extreme perversity – to try to free the notion of the linguistic expression of belief from all essential connection with the concept of communication-intention.

Earlier I hinted that the habit of some philosophers of speaking as if 'true' were a predicate of type-sentences was only a minor aberration, which could readily enough be accommodated to the facts. And so it can. But it is not a simple matter of pedantry to insist on correcting the aberration. For if we are not careful, it is liable to lead us totally wrong. It is liable, when we inquire into the nature of meaning, to make us forget what sentences are *for*. We connect meaning with truth and truth, too simply, with sentences; and sentences belong to language. But, as theorists, we know nothing of human *language* unless we understand human *speech*.

10. *Truth*

Mr Austin offers us a purified version of the correspondence theory of truth.[1] On the one hand he disclaims these manticists' error of supposing that 'true' is a predicate of sentences; on the other, the error of supposing that the relation of correspondence is other than purely conventional, the error which models the word on the world or the world on the word. His own theory is, roughly, that to say that a statement is true is to say that a certain speech-episode is related in a certain conventional way to something in the world exclusive of itself. But neither Mr Austin's account of the two terms of the truth-conferring relation, nor his account of the relation itself, seems to me satisfactory. The correspondence theory requires, not purification, but elimination.

I. STATEMENTS. It is, of course, indisputable that we use various substantival expressions as grammatical subjects of 'true'. These are, commonly, noun-phrases like 'What he said' or 'His statement'; or pronouns or noun-phrases, with a 'that'-clause in apposition, for example, 'It . . . that *p*' and 'The statement that *p*'. Austin proposes that we should use 'statement' to do general duty for such expressions as these. I have no objection. This will enable us to say, in a philosophically non-committal way, that, in using 'true', we are talking about statements. By 'saying this in a non-committal way', I mean saying it in a way which does not commit us to any view about the nature of statements so talked about; which does not commit us, for example, to the view that statements so talked about are historic events.

The words 'assertion' and 'statement' have a parallel and convenient duplicity of sense. 'My statement' may be either what I say or my saying it. My saying something is certainly an episode. What I say is not. It is the latter, not the former, we declare to be true. (Speaking the truth is not a manner of speaking: it is saying something true.) When we say 'His statement was received with thunderous applause' or 'His vehement assertion was followed by a startled silence', we are certainly referring to, characterizing, a historic event, and placing it in the context of others. If I say that

[1] In *Proceedings of The Aristotelian Society, Supplementary Volume,* 1950.

the same statement was first whispered by John and then bellowed by Peter, uttered first in French and repeated in English, I am plainly still making historical remarks about utterance-occasions; but the word 'statement' has detached itself from reference to any particular speech-episode. The episodes I am talking about are the whisperings, bellowings, utterings, and repetitions. The statement is not something that figures in all these episodes. Nor, when I say that the statement is true, as opposed to saying that it was, in these various ways, made, am I talking indirectly about these episodes or any episodes at all. (Saying of a statement that it is true is not related to saying of a speech-episode that it was true as saying of a statement that it was whispered is related to saying of a speech-episode that it was a whisper.) It is futile to ask what thing or event I *am* talking about (over and above the subject-matter of the statement) in declaring a statement to be true; for there is no such thing or event. The word 'statement' and the phrase 'What he said', like the conjunction 'that' followed by a noun clause, are convenient, grammatically substantival, devices, which we employ, on certain occasions, for certain purposes, notably (but not only) the occasions on which we use the word 'true'. What these occasions are I shall try later to elucidate. To suppose that, whenever we use a singular substantive, we are, or ought to be, using it to refer to something, is an ancient, but no longer a respectable, error.

More plausible than the thesis that in declaring a statement to be true I am talking about a speech-episode is the thesis that in order for me to declare a statement true, there must have occurred, within my knowledge, at least one episode which was a making of that statement. This is largely, but (as Austin sees) not entirely, correct. The occasion of my declaring a statement to be true may be not that someone has made the statement, but that I am envisaging the possibility of someone's making it. For instance, in discussing the merits of the Welfare State, I might say: 'It is true that the general health of the community has improved (that p), but this is due only to the advance in medical science.' It is not necessary that anyone should have said that p, in order for this to be a perfectly proper observation. In making it, I am not talking *about* an actual or possible speech-episode. I am myself asserting that p, in a certain way, with a certain purpose. I am anticipatorily conceding, in order to neutralize, a possible objection. I forestall someone's making the statement that *p* by making it myself, with additions. It is of prime importance to distinguish the fact that the use of 'true' always glances backwards or forwards to the actual or envisaged making of a statement by someone, from the theory that it is used to characterize such (actual or possible) episodes.

It is not easy to explain the non-episodic and non-committal sense of 'statement' in which 'statement' = 'what is said to be true or false'. But, at the risk of being tedious, I shall pursue the subject. For if Austin is right in the suggestion that it is basically of speech-episodes that we predicate 'true', it should be possible to 'reduce' assertions in which we say of a statement in the non-episodic sense that it is true to assertions in which we are predicating truth of episodes. Austin points out that the same sentence may be used to make different statements. He would no doubt agree that different sentences may be used to make the same statement. I am not thinking only of different languages or synonymous expressions in the same language; but also of such occasions as that on which you say of Jones 'He is ill', I say *to* Jones 'You are ill', and Jones says 'I am ill'. Using, not only different sentences, but sentences with different meanings, we all make 'the same statement'; and this is the sense of 'statement' we need to discuss, since it is, prima facie, of statements in this sense that we say that they are true or false (e.g. 'What they all said, viz. that Jones was ill, was quite true'). We could say: People make the same statement when the words they use in the situations in which they use them are such that they must (logically) either all be making a true statement or all be making a false statement. But this is to use 'true' in the elucidation of 'same statement'. Or we could say, of the present case: Jones, you, and I all make the same statement because, using the words we used in the situation in which we used them, we were all applying the same description to the same person at a certain moment in his history; anyone applying that description to that person (etc.), would be making that statement. Mr Austin might then wish to analyse (A) 'The statement that Jones was ill is true' in some such way as the following: 'If anyone has uttered, or were to utter, words such that in the situation in which they are uttered, he is applying to a person the same description as I apply to that person when I now utter the words "Jones was ill", then the resulting speech-episode was, or would be, true.' It seems plain, however, that nothing but the desire to find a metaphysically irreproachable first term for the correspondence relation could induce anyone to accept this analysis of (A) as an elaborate general hypothetical. It would be a plausible suggestion only if the grammatical subjects of 'true' were *commonly* expressions referring to particular, uniquely dateable, speech-episodes. But the simple and obvious fact is that the expressions occurring as such grammatical subjects ('What they said', 'It . . . that *p*', and so on) never do, in these contexts, stand for such episodes.[1] *What they said* has no date, though their several sayings of it are dateable. *The statement that p* is not an event, though it had to be made for the first time and made within my knowledge if I am to talk of its truth or falsity. If I endorse Plato's view, wrongly attributing it to Lord Russell ('Russell's view that *p* is quite true'), and am corrected, I have not discovered that I was talking of an event separated by centuries from the one I imagined I was talking of. (Corrected, I may say: 'Well it's true, whoever said it.') My *implied* historical judgement is false; that is all.

II. FACTS. What of the second term of the correspondence relation? For this Mr Austin uses the following words or phrases: 'thing', 'event', 'situation', 'state of affairs', 'feature', and 'fact'. All these are words which should be handled with care. I think that through failing to discriminate sufficiently between them, Mr Austin (1) encourages the assimilation of facts to things, or (what is approximately the same thing) of stating to referring; (2) misrepresents the use of 'true'; and (3) obscures another and more fundamental problem.

In Section 3 of his paper, Mr Austin says, or suggests, that all stating involves both referring ('demonstration') and characterizing ('description'). It is questionable whether all statements do involve both,[2] though it is certain that some do. The following sentences, for example, could all be used to make such statements, i.e. statements in the making of which both the referring and describing functions are performed, the performance of the two

[1] And the cases where such phrases might most plausibly be exhibited as having an episode-referring role are precisely those which yield most readily to another treatment, viz. those in which one speaker corroborates, confirms, or grants what another has just said (see Section IV below).

[2] See Section V below. The thesis that all statements involve both demonstration and description is, roughly, the thesis that all statements are, or involve, subject-predicate statements (not excluding relational statements).

functions being approximately (though not exclusively) assignable to different parts of the sentences as uttered:

> The cat has the mange.
> That parrot talks a lot.
> Her escort was a man of medium build, clean-shaven, well-dressed, and with a North Country accent.

In using such sentences to make statements, we refer to a thing or person (object) in order to go on to characterize it (we demonstrate in order to describe). *A reference* can be correct or incorrect. A *description* can fit, or fail to fit, the thing or person to which it is applied.[1] When we refer correctly, there certainly is a conventionally established relation between the words, so used, and the thing to which we refer. When we describe correctly, there certainly is a conventionally established relation between the words we use in describing and the type of thing or person we describe. These relations, as Mr Austin emphasizes, are different. An expression used referringly has a different logical role from an expression used describingly. They are differently related to the object. And *stating* is different from referring, and different from describing; for it is (in such cases) both these at once. Statement (*some* statement) is reference-cum-description. To avoid cumbersome phrasing, I shall speak henceforward of *parts* of statements (the referring part and the describing part); though parts of statements are no more to be equated with parts of sentences (or parts of speech-episodes) than statements are to be equated with sentences (or speech-episodes).

That (person, thing, etc.) to which the referring part of the statement refers, and which the describing part of the statement fits or fails to fit, is that which the statement is *about*. It is evident that there is nothing else in the world for the statement itself to be related to either in some further way of its own or in either of the different ways in which these different parts of the statement are related to what the statement is about. And it is evident that the demand that there should be such a relatum is logically absurd: a logically fundamental type-mistake. But the demand for something in the world *which makes the statement true* (Mr Austin's phrase), or *to which the statement corresponds when it is true*, is just this demand.

---

[1] Cf. the phrase 'He is described as. . . .' What fills the gap is not a sentence (expression which could normally be used to make a statement), but a phrase which could occur as a part of an expression so used.

And the answering theory that to say that a statement is true is to say that a speech-episode is conventionally related in a certain way to such a relatum reproduces the type-error embodied in this demand. For while we certainly say that a statement corresponds to (fits, is borne out by, agrees with) the facts, as a variant on saying that it is true, we *never* say that a statement corresponds to the thing, person, etc., it is about. What 'makes the statement' that the cat has mange 'true', is not the cat, but the *condition* of the cat, i.e. the fact that the cat has mange. The only plausible candidate for the position of what (in the world) makes the statement true is the fact it states; but the fact it states is not something in the world.[1] It is not an object; not even (as some have supposed) a complex object consisting of one or more particular elements (constituents, parts) and a universal element (constituent, part). I can (perhaps) hand you, or draw a circle round, or time with a stopwatch the things or incidents that are referred to when a statement is made. Statements are about such objects; but they state facts. Mr Austin seems to ignore the complete difference of type between, for example, 'fact' and 'thing'; to talk as if 'fact' were just a very general word (with, unfortunately, some misleading features) for 'event', 'thing', etc., instead of being (as it is) both wholly different from these, and yet the only possible candidate for the desired non-linguistic correlate of 'statement'. Roughly: the thing, person, etc., referred to is the material correlate of the referring part of the statement; the quality or property the referent is said to 'possess' is the *pseudo*material correlate of its describing part; and the fact to which the statement 'corresponds' is the *pseudo*material correlate of the statement as a whole.

These points are, of course, reflected in the behaviour of the word 'fact' in ordinary language; behaviour which Mr Austin notes, but by which he is insufficiently warned. 'Fact', like 'true', 'states', and 'statement' is wedded to 'that'-clauses; and there is nothing unholy about this union. Facts are known, stated, learned,

---

[1] This is not, of course, to deny that there is that in the world which a statement of this kind is about (true or false *of*), which is *referred to* and *described* and which the description fits (if the statement is true) or fails to fit (if it is false). This truism is an inadequate introduction to the task of elucidating, not our use of 'true', but a certain general way of using language, a certain type of discourse, viz. the fact-stating type of discourse. What confuses the issue about the use of the word 'true' is precisely its entanglement with this much more fundamental and difficult problem. [See (ii) of this section.]

forgotten, overlooked, commented on, communicated, or noticed. (Each of these verbs may be followed by a 'that'-clause or a 'the fact that'-clause.) Facts are what statements (when true) state; they are not what statements are about. They are not, like things or happenings on the face of the globe, witnessed or heard or seen, broken or overturned, interrupted or prolonged, kicked, destroyed, mended or noisy. Mr Austin notes the expression 'fact that', warns us that it may tempt us to identify facts with true statements and explains its existence by saying that for certain purposes in ordinary life we neglect, or take as irrelevant, the distinction between saying something true and the thing or episode of which we are talking. It would indeed be wrong – but not for Mr Austin's reasons – to identify 'fact' and 'true statement'; for these expressions have different roles in our language, as can be seen by the experiment of trying to interchange them in context. Nevertheless, their roles – or those of related expressions – overlap. There is no nuance, except of style, between 'That's true' and 'That's a fact'; nor between 'Is it true that . . . ?' and 'Is it a fact that . . . ?'[1] But Mr Austin's reasons for objecting to the identification seem mistaken, as does his explanation of the usage which (he says) tempts us to make it. Because he thinks of a statement as something in the world (a speech-episode) and a fact as something else in the world (what the statement either 'corresponds to' or 'is about'), he conceives the distinction as of overriding importance in philosophy, though (surprisingly) sometimes negligible for ordinary purposes. But I can conceive of no occasion on which I could possibly be held to be 'neglecting or taking as irrelevant' the distinction between, say, my wife's bearing me twins (at midnight) and my saying (ten minutes later) that my wife had borne me twins. On Mr Austin's thesis, however, my announcing 'The fact is that my wife has borne me twins' would be just such an occasion.

Elsewhere in his paper, Mr Austin expresses the fact that there is no theoretical limit to what could truly be said about things in

---

[1] I think in general the difference between them is that while the use of 'true', as already acknowledged, glances backwards or forwards at an actual or envisaged making of a statement, the use of 'fact' does not generally do this though it may do it sometimes. It certainly does not do it in, for example, the phrase 'The fact is that . . .' which serves rather to prepare us for the unexpected and unwelcome.

the world, while there are very definite practical limits to what human beings actually can and do say about them, by the remark that statements 'always fit the facts more or less loosely, in different ways for different purposes'. But what could fit more perfectly the fact that it is raining than the statement that it is raining? Of course, statements and facts fit. They were made for each other. If you prise the statements off the world you prise the facts off it too; but the world would be none the poorer. (You don't also prise off the world what the statements are about – for this you would need a different kind of lever.)

A symptom of Mr Austin's uneasiness about facts is his preference for the expressions 'situation' and 'state of affairs'; expressions of which the character and function are a little less transparent than those of 'fact'. They are more plausible candidates for inclusion in the world. For while it is true that situations and states of affairs are not seen or heard (any more than facts are), but are rather *summed up* or *taken in at a glance* (phrases which stress the connection with statement and 'that'-clause respectively), it is also true that there is a sense of 'about' in which we do talk about, do describe, situations and states of affairs. We say, for example, 'The international situation is serious' or 'This state of affairs lasted from the death of the King till the dissolution of Parliament'. In the same sense of 'about', we talk about facts; as when we say 'I am alarmed by the fact that kitchen expenditure has risen by 50 per cent in the last year'. But whereas 'fact' in such usages is linked with a 'that'-clause (or connected no less obviously with 'statement', as when we 'take down the facts' or hand someone the facts on a sheet of paper), 'situation' and 'state of affairs' stand by themselves, states of affairs are said to have a beginning and an end, and so on. Nevertheless, situations and states of affairs so talked of are (like facts so talked of), abstractions that a logician, if not a grammarian, should be able to see through. Being alarmed by a fact is not like being frightened by a shadow. It is being alarmed because. . . . One of the most economical and pervasive devices of language is the use of substantival expressions to abbreviate, summarize, and connect. Having made a series of descriptive statements, I can comprehensively connect with these the remainder of my discourse by the use of such expressions as 'this situation' or 'this state of affairs'; just as, having produced what I regard as a set of reasons for a certain conclusion I allow

myself to draw breath by saying 'Since *these things* are so, then . . .',
instead of prefacing the entire story by the conjunction. A
situation or state of affairs is, roughly, a set of facts, not a set of
things.

A point which it is important to notice in view of Mr Austin's
use of these expressions (in Sections 3a and 3b of his paper) is that
when we *do* 'talk about' situations (as opposed to things and
persons) the situation we talk about is not, as he seems to think it
is, correctly identified with the fact we state (with 'what makes the
statement true'). If a situation is the 'subject' of our statement, then
what 'makes the statement true' is not the situation, but the fact
that the situation has the character it is asserted to have. I think
much of the persuasiveness of the phrase 'talking about situations'
derives from that use of the word on which I have just commented. But if a situation is treated as the 'subject' of a statement,
then it will not serve as the non-linguistic term, for which
Mr Austin is seeking, of the 'relation of correspondence'; and if
it is treated as the non-linguistic term of this relation, it will not
serve as the subject of the statement.

Someone might now say: 'No doubt "situation", "state of
affairs", "facts" are related in this way to "that"-clauses and
assertive sentences; can serve, in certain ways and for certain purposes, as indefinite stand-ins for specific expressions of these
various types. So also is "thing" related to some nouns; "event"
to some verbs, nouns, and sentences; "quality" to some adjectives; "relation" to some nouns, verbs, and adjectives. Why
manifest this prejudice in favour of things and events as alone
being parts of the world or its history? Why not situations and
facts as well?' The answer to this (implicit in what has gone
before) is twofold.

(i) The first part of the answer[1] is that the whole charm of talking of situations, states of affairs, or facts as included in, or parts
of, the world, consists in thinking of them as things, and groups
of things; that the temptation to talk of situations, etc., in the
idiom appropriate to talking of things and events is, once this
first step is taken, overwhelming. Mr Austin does not withstand

[1] Which could be more shortly expressed by saying that if we read 'world'
(a sadly corrupted word) as 'heavens and earth', talk of facts, situations, and
states of affairs, as 'included in' or 'parts of' the world is, obviously,
metaphorical. The world is the totality of things, not of facts.

it. He significantly slips in the word 'feature' (noses and hills are *features*, of faces and landscapes) as a substitute for 'facts'. He says that the reason why photographs and maps are not 'true' in the way that statements are true is that the relation of a map or a photograph to what it is a map or a photograph of is not wholly (in the first case) and not at all (in the second) a conventional relation. But this is not the only, or the fundamental, reason. (The relation between the Prime Minister of England and the phrase 'the Prime Minister of England' *is* conventional; but it doesn't make sense to say that someone uttering the phrase out of context is saying something true or false.) The (for present purposes) fundamental reason is that 'being a map of' or 'being a photograph of' *are* relations, of which the non-photographic, non-cartographical, relata are, say, personal or geographical *entities*. The trouble with correspondence theories of truth is not primarily the tendency to substitute non-conventional relations for what is really a wholly conventional relation. It is the misrepresentation of 'correspondence between statement and fact' *as a relation, of any kind, between events or things or groups of things* that is the trouble. Correspondence theorists think of a statement as 'describing that which makes it true' (fact, situation, state of affairs) in the way a descriptive predicate may be used to describe, or a referring expression to refer to, a thing.[1]

---

[1] Suppose the pieces set on a chessboard, a game in progress. And suppose someone gives, in words, an exhaustive statement of the position of the pieces. Mr Austin's objection (or one of his objections) to earlier correspondence theories is that they would represent the relation between the description and the board with the pieces on it as like, say, the relation between a newspaper diagram of a chess problem and a board with the pieces correspondingly arranged. He says, rather, that the relation is a purely conventional one. My objection goes further. It is that there is no thing or event called 'a statement' (though there is the making of the statement) and there is no thing or event called 'a fact' or 'situation' (though there is the chessboard with the pieces on it) which stand to one another in any, even a purely conventional, relation as the newspaper diagram stands to the board-and-pieces. The facts (situation, state of affairs) cannot, like the chessboard-and-pieces, have coffee spilled on them or be upset by a careless hand. It is because Mr Austin needs such events and things for his theory that he takes the making of the statement as the statement, and that which the statement is about as the fact which it states.

Events can be dated and things can be located. But the facts which statements (when true) state can be neither dated nor located. (Nor can the statements, though the making of them can be.) Are they included in the world?

(ii) The second objection to Mr Austin's treatment of facts, situations, states of affairs, as 'parts of the world' which we declare to stand in a certain relation to a statement when we declare that statement true, goes deeper than the preceding one but is, in a sense, its point. Mr Austin rightly says or implies (Section 3) that for some of the purposes for which we use language, there must be conventions correlating the words of our language with what is to be found in the world. Not all the linguistic purposes for which this necessity holds, however, are identical. Orders, as well as information, are conventionally communicated. Suppose 'orange' always meant what we mean by 'Bring me an orange' and 'that orange' always meant what we mean by 'Bring me that orange', and, in general, our language contained only sentences in some such way imperative. There would be no less need for a conventional correlation between the word and the world. Nor would there be any less to be found in the world. But these pseudo-entities which *make statements true* would not figure among the non-linguistic correlates. They would no more be found (they never were found, and never did figure among the non-linguistic correlates). The point is that the word 'fact' (and the 'set-of-facts' words like 'situation' and 'state of affairs') have, like the words 'statement' and 'true' themselves, a certain type of word-world-relating discourse (the informative) *built in* to them. The occurrence in ordinary discourse of the words 'fact', 'statement', 'true' signalizes the occurrence of this type of discourse; just as the occurrence of the words 'order', 'obeyed' signalizes the occurrence of another kind of conventional communication (the imperative). If our task were to elucidate the nature of the first type of discourse, it would be futile to attempt to do it in terms of the words 'fact', 'statement', 'true', for these words contain the problem, not its solution. It would, for the same reason, be equally futile to attempt to elucidate any one of these words (in so far as the elucidation of *that* word would be the elucidation of *this* problem) in terms of the others. And it is, indeed, very strange that people have so often proceeded by saying 'Well, we're pretty clear what a statement is, aren't we? Now let us settle *the further question*, viz. what it is for a statement to be true.' This is like 'Well, we're clear about what a command is: now what is it for a command to be obeyed?' As if one could divorce statements and commands from the point of making or giving them!

Suppose we had in our language the word 'execution' meaning 'action which is the carrying out of a command'. And suppose someone asked the philosophical question: What is *obedience*? What is it for a command to be *obeyed*? A philosopher might produce the answer: 'Obedience is a conventional relation between a command and an execution. A command is obeyed when it corresponds to an execution.'

This is the Correspondence Theory of Obedience. It has, perhaps, a little less value as an attempt to elucidate the nature of one type of communication than the Correspondence Theory of Truth has as an attempt to elucidate that of another. In both cases, the words occurring in the solution incorporate the problem. And, of course, this intimate relation between 'statement' and 'fact' (which is understood when it is seen that they both incorporate this problem) explains why it is that when we seek to explain *truth* on the model of naming or classifying or any other kind of conventional or non-conventional relation between one thing and another, we always find ourselves landed with 'fact', 'situation', 'state of affairs' as the non-linguistic terms of the relation.

But why should the problem of Truth (the problem about our use of 'true') be seen as this problem of elucidating the fact-stating type of discourse? The answer is that it shouldn't be; but that the Correspondence Theory can only be fully seen through when it is seen as a barren attempt on this second problem. Of course, a philosopher concerned with the second problem, concerned to elucidate a certain general type of discourse, must stand back from language and talk about the different ways in which utterances are related to the world (though he must get beyond 'correspondence of statement and fact' if his talk is to be fruitful). But – to recur to something I said earlier – the occurrence *in ordinary discourse* of the words 'true', 'fact', etc., signalizes, without commenting on, the occurrence of a certain way of using language. When we use these words in ordinary life, we are talking within, and not about, a certain frame of discourse; we are precisely not talking about the way in which utterances are, or may be, conventionally related to the world. We are talking about persons and things, but in a way in which we could not talk about them if conditions of certain kinds were not fulfilled. The problem about the use of 'true' is to see how this word fits into that frame of discourse. The surest

o

route to the wrong answer is to confuse this problem with the question: What type of discourse is this?[1]

III. CONVENTIONAL CORRESPONDENCE. It will be clear from the previous paragraph what I think wrong with Mr Austin's account of the relation itself, as opposed to its terms. In Section 4 of his paper he says that, when we declare a statement to be true, the relation between the statement and the world which our declaration 'asserts to obtain' is 'a purely conventional relation' and 'one which we could alter at will'. This remark reveals the fundamental confusion of which Mr Austin is guilty between:

>   (*a*) the semantic conditions which must be satisfied for the statement that a certain statement is true to be itself true; and
>   (*b*) what is asserted when a certain statement is stated to be true.

Suppose A makes a statement, and B declares A's statement to be true. Then for B's statement to be true, it is, *of course*, necessary that the words used by A in making the statement should stand in a certain conventional (semantical) relationship with the world; and that the 'linguistic rules' underlying this relationship should be rules 'observed' by both A and B. It should be remarked that these conditions (with the exception of the condition about B's observance of linguistic rules) are equally necessary conditions of A's having made a true statement in using the words he used. *It is no more and no less absurd to suggest that B, in making his statement, asserts that these semantic conditions are fulfilled than it is to suggest that A, in making his statement, asserts that these semantic conditions are fulfilled* (i.e. that we can never use words without mentioning them). *If* Mr Austin is right in suggesting that to say that a statement is true is to say that 'the historic state of affairs to which it (i.e. for Mr Austin, the episode of making it) is correlated by the demonstrative conventions (the one it "refers to") is of a type with which the sentence used in making the statement is correlated by the descriptive conventions', *then* (and this is shown quite clearly by his saying that the relation we assert to obtain is a

---

[1] A parallel mistake would be to think that in our ordinary use (as opposed to a philosopher's use) of the word 'quality', we were talking about people's uses of words; on the ground (correct in itself) that this word would have no use but for the occurrence of a certain general way of using words.

'purely conventional one' which 'could be altered at will') in declaring a statement to be true, we are either:

(*a*) talking about the meanings of the words used by the speaker whose making of the statement is the occasion for our use of 'true' (i.e. profiting by the occasion to give semantic rules); or

(*b*) saying that the speaker has used correctly the words he did use.

It is *patently* false that we are doing either of these things. Certainly, we use the word 'true' when the semantic conditions described by Austin[1] are fulfilled; but we do not, in using the word, *state* that they are fulfilled. (And this, incidentally, is the answer to the question with which Mr Austin concludes his paper.) The damage is done (the two problems distinguished at the end of the previous section confused) by asking the question: *When* do we use the word 'true'? instead of the question: *How* do we use the word 'true'?

Someone says: 'It's true that French Governments rarely last more than a few months, but the electoral system is responsible for that.' Is the fact he states in the first part of his sentence alterable by changing the conventions of language? It is not.

---

[1] In what, owing to his use of the words 'statement', 'fact', 'situation', etc., is a misleading form. The quoted account of the conditions of truthful statement is more nearly appropriate as an account of the conditions of correct descriptive reference. Suppose, in a room with a bird in a cage, I say 'That parrot is very talkative'. Then my use of the referring expression ('That parrot') with which my sentence begins is correct when the token-object (bird) with which my token-expression (event) is correlated by the conventions of demonstration is of a kind with which the type-expression is correlated by the conventions of description. Here we do have an event and a thing and a (type-mediated) conventional relation between them. If someone corrects me, saying 'That's not a parrot; it's a cockatoo', he may be correcting either a linguistic or a factual error on my part. (The question of which he is doing is the question of whether I would have stuck to my story on a closer examination of the bird.) Only in the former case is he declaring a certain semantic condition to be unfulfilled. In the latter case, he is talking about the bird. He asserts that it is a cockatoo and not a parrot. This he could have done whether I had spoken or not. He also *corrects* me, which he could not have done if I had not spoken.

IV. USES OF 'THAT'-CLAUSES; AND OF 'STATEMENT', 'TRUE', 'FACT', 'EXAGGERATED', ETC. (*a*) There are many ways of making an assertion about a thing, X, besides the bare use of the sentence-pattern 'X is Y'. Many of these involve the use of 'that'-clauses. For example:

How often shall I have to tell you
Today I learned
It is surprising
The fact is
I have just been reminded of the fact $\Big\}$ that X is Y.
It is indisputable
It is true
It is established beyond question

These are all ways of asserting, in very different context and circumstances, that X is Y.[1] Some of them involve autobiographical assertions as well; others do not. In the grammatical sense already conceded, all of them are 'about' facts or statements. In no other sense is any of them about either, though some of them carry *implications* about the *making* of statements.

(*b*) There are many different circumstances in which the simple sentence-pattern 'X is Y' may be used to do things which are not merely stating (though they all involve stating) that X is Y. In uttering words of this simple pattern we may be encouraging, reproving, or warning, someone; reminding someone; answering, or replying to, someone; denying what someone has said; confirming, granting, corroborating, agreeing with, admitting what someone has said. Which of these, if any, we are doing depends on the circumstances in which, using this simple sentence-pattern, we assert that X is Y.

(*c*) In many of the cases in which we are doing something besides merely stating that X is Y, we have available, for use in suitable contexts, certain abbreviatory devices which enable us to state that X is Y (to make our denial, answer, admission, or whatnot) *without* using the sentence-pattern 'X is Y'. Thus, if someone asks us 'Is X Y?', we may state (in the way of reply) that X is Y by saying 'Yes'. If someone says 'X is Y', we may state (in the

---

[1] One might prefer to say that in some of these cases one was asserting only *by implication* that X is Y; though it seems to me more probable that in all these cases we should say, of the speaker, not 'What he said implied that X is Y', but 'He *said* that X was Y'.

way of denial) that X is not Y, by saying 'It is not' or by saying 'That's not true'; or we may state (in the way of corroboration, agreement, granting, etc.) that X is Y by saying 'It is indeed' or 'That is true'. In all these cases (of reply, denial, and agreement) the context of our utterance, as well as the words we use, must be taken into account if it is to be clear what we are asserting, viz. that X is (or is not) Y. It seems to me plain that in these cases 'true' and 'not true' (we rarely use 'false') are functioning as abbreviatory statement-devices of the same general kind as the others quoted. And it seems also plain that the *only* difference between these devices which might tempt us, while saying of some ('Yes', 'It is indeed', 'It is not') that, in using them, we were talking about X, to say of others ('That's true', 'That's not true') that, in using them, we were talking about something quite different, viz. the utterance which was the occasion for our use of these devices, is their difference in grammatical structure, i.e. the fact that 'true' occurs as a grammatical predicate.[1] (It is obviously not a predicate of X.) If Mr Austin's thesis, that in using the word 'true' we make an assertion about a statement, were no more than the thesis that the word 'true' occurs as a grammatical predicate, with, as grammatical subjects, such words and phrases as 'That', 'What he said', 'His statement', etc., then, of course, it would be indisputable. It is plain, however, that he means more than this, and I have already produced my objections to the more that he means.

(*d*) It will be clear that, in common with Mr Austin, I reject the thesis that the phrase 'is true' is logically superfluous, together with the thesis that to say that a proposition is true is *just* to assert it and to say that it is false is *just* to assert its contradictory. 'True' and 'not true' have jobs of their own to do, *some*, but by no means all, of which I have characterized above. In using them, we are not *just* asserting that X is Y or that X is not Y. We are asserting this in a way in which we could not assert it unless certain conditions were fulfilled; we may also be granting, denying, confirming, etc. It will be clear also that the rejection of these two theses does not

---

[1] Compare also the English habit of making a statement followed by an interrogative appeal for agreement in such forms as 'isn't it?', 'doesn't he?', etc., with the corresponding German and Italian idioms, 'Nicht wahr?', 'non è vero?' There is surely no significant difference between the phrases which do not employ the word for 'true' and those which do: they all appeal for agreement in the same way.

206 Logico-Linguistic Papers

entail acceptance of Mr Austin's thesis that in using 'true' we are making an assertion about a statement. Nor does it entail the rejection of the thesis which Mr Austin (in Section 4 of his paper) couples with these two, viz. the thesis that to say that an assertion is true is not to make any further *assertion* at all. This thesis holds for many uses, but requires modification for others.

(*e*) The occasions for using 'true' mentioned so far in this section are evidently not the only occasions of its use. There is, for example, the generally concessive employment of 'It is true that *p* . . .', which it is difficult to see how Mr Austin could accommodate. All these occasions have, however, a certain contextual immediacy which is obviously absent when we utter such sentences as 'What John said yesterday is quite true' and 'What La Rochefoucauld said about friendship is true'. Here the context of our utterance does not identify for us the statement we are talking about (in the philosophically non-committal sense in which we *are* 'talking about statements' when we use the word 'true'), and so we use a descriptive phrase to do the job. But the descriptive phrase does not identify an event; though the statement we make carries the implication (in some sense of 'implication') that there occurred an event which was John's making yesterday (or Rochefoucauld's making sometime) the statement that *p* (i.e. the statement we declare to be true). We are certainly not telling our audience that the event occurred, for example, that John made the statement that *p*, for (i) we do not state, either by way of quotation or otherwise, what it was that John said yesterday, and (ii) our utterance achieves its main purpose (that of making, by way of confirmation or endorsement, the statement that *p*) only if our audience already knows that John yesterday made the statement that *p*. The abbreviatory function of 'true' in cases such as these becomes clearer if we compare them with what we say in the case where (i) we want to assert that *p*; (ii) we want to indicate (or display our knowledge that) an event occurred which was John's making yesterday the statement that *p*; (iii) we believe our audience ignorant or forgetful of the fact that John said yesterday that *p*. We then use the formula 'As John said yesterday, *p*' or 'It is true, as John said yesterday, that *p*', or 'What John said yesterday, namely that *p*, is true'. (Of course the words represented by the letter *p*, which we use, may be – sometimes, if we are to make the same statement, must be – different from the words which John used.) Sometimes, to embarrass, or test, our audience, we use, in cases where the third of these conditions is fulfilled, the formula appropriate to its non-fulfilment, viz. 'What John said yesterday is true'.

(*f*) In criticism of my view of truth put forward in *Analysis*,[1] and presumably in support of his own thesis that 'true' is used to assert that a certain relation obtains between a speech-episode and something in the world exclusive of that episode, Mr Austin makes, in Section 7 of his paper, the following point. He says: 'Mr Strawson seems to confine himself to the case when I say "Your statement is true" or something similar – but what of the case when you state that S and I say nothing, but *look and see* that your statement is true?' The point of the objection is, I suppose, that since I *say* nothing, I cannot be making any performatory use of 'true'; yet I can see *that* your statement is true. The example, however, seems to have a force precisely contrary to what Mr Austin intended. Of course, 'true' has a different role in 'X sees that Y's statement is true' from its role in 'Y's statement is true'. What is this role? Austin says in my hearing 'There is a cat on the mat' and I look and see a cat on the mat. Someone (Z) reports: 'Strawson saw that Austin's statement was true'. What is he reporting? He is reporting that I have seen a cat on the mat; but he is reporting this in a way in which he could not report it except in certain circumstances, viz. in the circumstances of Austin's having said in my hearing that there was a cat on the mat. Z's remark also carries the implication that Austin made a statement, but cannot be regarded as *reporting* this by implication since it fulfils its main purpose only if the audience already knows that Austin made a statement and what statement he made; and the implication (which *can* be regarded as an implied report) that I heard and understood what Austin said.[2] The man who looks and sees that the statement that there is a cat on the mat is true, sees no more and no less than the man who looks and sees that there is a cat on the mat, or the man who looks and sees that there is *indeed* a cat on the mat. But the *settings* of the first and third cases may be different from that of the second.

[1] Vol. IX, No. 6 (1949).

[2] If *I* report: 'I see that Austin's statement is true', this is simply a first-hand corroborative report that there is a cat on the mat, made in a way in which it could not be made except in these circumstances.

This example has value, however. It emphasizes the importance of the concept of the 'occasion' on which we may make use of the assertive device which is the subject of this symposium (the word 'true'); and minimizes (what I was inclined to over-emphasize) the performatory character of our uses of it.

(*g*) Mr Austin stresses the differences between negation and falsity; rightly, in so far as to do so is to stress the difference (of occasion and context) between asserting that X is not Y and denying the assertion that X is Y. He also exaggerates the difference; for, if I have taken the point of his example, he suggests that there are cases in which 'X is not Y' is inappropriate to a situation in which, if anyone stated that X was Y, it would be correct to say that the statement that X was Y was false. These are cases where the question of whether X is or is not Y does not arise (where the conditions of its arising are not fulfilled). They are equally, it seems to me, cases when the question of the truth or falsity of the statement that X is Y does not arise.

(*h*) A qualification of my general thesis, that in using 'true' and 'untrue' we are not talking about a speech-episode, is required to allow for those cases where our interest is not primarily in what the speaker asserts, but in the speaker's asserting it, in, say, the fact of his having *told the truth* rather than in the fact which he reported in doing so. (We may, of course, be interested in both; or our interest in a man's evident truthfulness on one occasion may be due to our concern with the degree of his reliability on others.)

But this case calls for no special analysis and presents no handle to any theorist of truth; for to use 'true' in this way is simply to characterize a certain *event* as *the making*, by someone, of a true statement. The problem of analysis remains.

(*i*) Mr Austin says that we shall find it easier to be clear about 'true' if we consider other adjectives 'in the same class', such as 'exaggerated', 'vague', 'rough', 'misleading', 'general', 'too concise'. I do not think these words *are* in quite the same class as 'true' and 'false'. In any language in which statements can be made at all, it must be possible to make true and false statements. But statements can suffer from the further defects Mr Austin mentions only when language has attained a certain richness. Imagine one of Mr Austin's rudimentary languages with 'single words' for 'complex situations' of totally different kinds. One could make true or false statements; but not statements which were exaggerated, over-concise, too general, or rather rough. And even given a language as rich as you please, whereas all statements made in it could be true or false, not all statements could be exaggerated. When can we say that the statement that p is exaggerated? *One* of the conditions is this: that, if the sentence S_1 is used to make the statement that p, there should be some sentence S_2 (which could be used to make the statement that q) such that S_1 and S_2 are related somewhat as 'There were 200 people there' is related to 'There were 100 people there'. (To the remark 'We got married yesterday', you cannot, except as a joke, reply: 'You are exaggerating'.)

Mr Austin's belief, then, that the word 'exaggerated' stands for a relation between a statement and something in the world exclusive of the statement, would at least be an over-simplification, even if it were not objectionable in other ways. But it is objectionable in other ways. The difficulties about statement and fact recur; and the difficulties about the relation. Mr Austin would not want to say that the relation between an exaggerated statement and the world was like that between a glove and a hand too small for it. He would say that the relation was a conventional one. But the fact that the statement that p is exaggerated is not in any sense a conventional fact. (It is, perhaps, the fact that there were 1,200 people there and not 2,000.) If a man says: 'There were at least 2,000 people there', you may reply (A) 'No, there were not so many (far more)', or you may reply (B) 'That's an exaggeration (understatement)'. (A) and (B) say the same thing. Look at the situation more closely. In saying (A), you are not merely asserting that there were fewer than 2,000 people there: you are also correcting the first speaker, and correcting him in a certain general way, which you could not have done if he had not spoken as he did, though you could merely have asserted that there were fewer than 2,000 there without his having spoken. Notice also that what is being asserted by the use of (A) – that there were fewer than 2,000 there – cannot be understood without taking into account the original remark which was the occasion for (A). (A) has both contextually assertive and performatory features. (B) has the same features, and does the same job as (A), but more concisely and with greater contextual reliance.

Not all the words taken by Austin as likely to help us to be clear about 'true' are in the same class as one another. 'Exaggerated' is, of those he mentions, the one most relevant to his thesis; but has been seen to yield to my treatment. Being 'over-concise' and 'too general' are not ways of being 'not quite true'. These obviously relate to the specific purposes of specific makings of statements; to the unsatisfied wishes of specific audiences. No alteration in things in the world, nor any magical replaying of the course of events, could bring statements so condemned into line, in the way that an 'exaggerated assessment' of the height of a building could be brought into line by inorganic growth. Whether the statement (that p) is true or false is a matter of the way things are (of whether p); whether a statement is exaggerated (if the question arises – which depends on the type of statement and the possibilities of the language) is a matter of the way things are (e.g. of whether or not there were fewer than 2,000 there). But whether a statement is over-concise[1] or too general depends on what the hearer wants to know. The world does not demand to be described with one degree of detail rather than another.

V. THE SCOPE OF 'STATEMENT', 'TRUE', 'FALSE', AND 'FACT'. Commands and questions obviously do not claim to be statements of fact: they are not true or false. In Section 6 of his paper, Mr Austin reminds us that there are many expressions neither interrogative nor imperative in form which we use for other purposes than that of reportage or forecast. From our employment of these expressions he recommends that we withhold (suspects that we do, in practice, largely withhold) the appellation 'stating facts', the words 'true' and 'false'. Philosophers, even in the sphere of language, are not legislators; but I have no wish to challenge the restriction, in some philosophical contexts, of the words 'statement', 'true', 'false', to what I have myself earlier called the 'fact-stating' type of discourse.

What troubles me more is Mr Austin's own incipient analysis of this type of discourse. It seems to me such as to force him to carry the restriction further than he wishes or intends. And here

---

[1] 'Concise' is perhaps less often used of what a man says than of the way he says it (e.g. 'concisely put', 'concisely expressed', 'a concise formulation'). A may take 500 words to say what B says in 200. Then I shall say that B's formulation was more concise than A's, meaning simply that he used fewer words.

there are two points which, though connected, need to be distinguished. First, there are difficulties besetting the relational theory of truth as such; second, there is the persistence of these difficulties in a different form when this 'theory of truth' is revealed as, rather, an incipient analysis of the statement-making use of language.

First then, facts of the cat-on-the-mat-type are the favoured species for adherents of Mr Austin's type of view. For here we have one thing (one chunk of reality) sitting on another: we can (if we are prepared to commit the errors commented on in Section II above) regard the two together as forming a single chunk, if we like, and call it a fact or state of affairs. The view may then seem relatively plausible that to say that the statement (made by me to you) that the cat is on the mat is true is to say that the three-dimensional state of affairs with which the episode of my making the statement is correlated by the demonstrative conventions is of a type with which the sentence I use is correlated by the descriptive conventions. Other species of fact, however, have long been known to present more difficulty: the fact that the cat is not on the mat, for example, or the fact that there are white cats, or that cats persecute mice, or that if you give my cat an egg it will smash it and eat the contents. Consider the simplest of these cases, that involving negation. With what type of state-of-affairs (chunk of reality) is the sentence 'The cat is not on the mat' correlated by conventions of description? With a mat *simpliciter*? With a dog on a mat? With a cat up a tree? The amendment of Mr Austin's view to which one might be tempted for negative statements (i.e. 'S is true' = 'The state of affairs to which S is correlated by the demonstrative conventions is *not* of a type with which *the affirmative form of* S is correlated by the descriptive conventions') destroys the simplicity of the story by creating the need for a different sense of 'true' when we discuss negative statements. And worse is to follow. Not all statements employ conventions of demonstration. Existential statements don't, nor do statements of (even relatively) unrestricted generality. Are we to deny that these are statements, or create a further sense of 'true'? And what has become of the non-linguistic correlate, the chunk of reality? Is this, in the case of existential or general statements, the entire world? Or, in the case of negatively existential statements, an ubiquitous non-presence?

As objections to a correspondence theory of truth, these are familiar points; though to advance them as such is to concede too much to the theory. What makes them of interest is their power to reveal how such a theory, in addition to its intrinsic defects, embodies too narrow a conception of the fact-stating use of language. Mr Austin's description of the conditions under which a statement is true, regarded as an analysis of the fact-stating use, applies only to affirmative subject-predicate statements, i.e. to statements in making which we refer to some one or more localized thing or group of things, event or set of events, and characterize it or them in some positive way (identify the object or objects and affix the label). It does not apply to negative, general, and existential statements nor, straightforwardly, to hypothetical and disjunctive statements. I agree that any language capable of the fact-stating use must have some devices for performing the function to which Mr Austin exclusively directs his attention, and that other types of statements of fact can be understood only in relation to this type. But the other types *are* other types. For example, the word 'not' can usefully be regarded as a kind of crystallizing-out of something *implicit* in all use of descriptive language (since no predicate would have any descriptive force if it were compatible with everything). But from this it does not follow that negation (i.e. the *explicit* exclusion of some characteristic) is a kind of affirmation, that negative statements are properly discussed in the language appropriate to affirmative statements. Or take the case of existential statements. Here one needs to distinguish two kinds of demonstration or reference. There is, first, the kind whereby we enable our hearer to identify the thing or person or event or set of these which we then go on to characterize in some way. There is, second, the kind by which we simply indicate a locality. The first ('*Tabby* has the mange') answers the question 'Who (which one, what) are you talking about?' The second ('*There's* a cat') the question 'Where?' It is plain that no part of an existential statement performs the first function; though Austin's account of reference-cum-description is appropriate to reference of this kind rather than to that of the other. It is clear also that a good many existential statements do not answer the question 'Where?' though they may license the inquiry. The difference between various types of statements, and their mutual relations, is a matter for careful description. Nothing is gained by lumping them all together under a description appropriate only to one, even though it be the basic, type.

VI. CONCLUSION. My central objection to Mr Austin's thesis is this. He describes the conditions which must obtain if we are correctly to declare a statement true. His detailed description of these conditions is, with reservations, correct as far as it goes, though in several respects too narrow. The central mistake is to suppose that in using the word 'true' we are asserting such conditions to obtain. That this is a mistake is shown by the detailed examination of the behaviour of such words as 'statement', 'fact', etc., and of 'true' itself, and by the examination of various different types of statement. This also reveals some of the ways in which 'true' actually functions as an assertive device. What supremely confuses the issue is the failure to distinguish between the task of elucidating the nature of a certain type of communication (the empirically informative) from the problem of the actual functioning of the word 'true' within the framework of that type of communication.

11. *A Problem about Truth*

I

The point on which Mr Warnock principally insists in his paper[1] is that someone who says that a certain statement is true thereby makes a statement about a statement. The point is not one that I shall dispute; and since it will be convenient to have a name for it, I shall refer to it as the undisputed thesis. The importance of the undisputed thesis appears to Mr Warnock to lie in the bearing it has on attempts to answer, or on criticisms of attempts to answer, certain philosophically debated questions. These questions, as alluded to by Mr Warnock at various points in his paper, can be distinguished (or, perhaps, grouped) as follows:

(1) What is done (or what speech-act is standardly performed) by one who says that a statement is true?

(2) What is meant (or what is asserted) by a statement (or by someone who states) that a statement is true?

(3) What is the meaning of the word 'true' (or of the phrase 'is true' or of the phrase 'That's true')?

About (1) I shall say no more. In accepting the undisputed thesis I am clearly committed to agreeing that at least part of what anyone does who says that a statement is true is to make a statement about a statement. With the *differences* between (2) and (3) we need not be much concerned. For Mr Warnock makes it very clear that he is mainly interested in such interpretations of (2) as would bind acceptable answers to (2) very closely to acceptable answers to (3). (He is not, for example, primarily concerned about what one who says that a statement is true may 'have in mind' in doing so.) I shall follow him in this.

A main part of Mr Warnock's purpose, then, is to insist that no answer to the questions at (2) and (3), and no criticism of any such answer, is acceptable if that answer or criticism is incompatible with the undisputed thesis. The undisputed thesis imposes, as it

[1] 'A Problem about Truth', by G. J. Warnock, in *Truth*, ed. by George Pitcher (Prentice-Hall, Englewood Cliffs, 1964).

were, an adequacy condition which must be satisfied by any acceptable view on these matters. This adequacy condition I shall accept.

Now Mr Warnock certainly does not regard acceptance of this condition as counting decisively in favour of any one philosophical view about the correct answers to questions at (2) and (3). But I think it is true that he does regard acceptance of this condition as *removing an obstacle* to acceptance of such a view as Austin appeared to espouse[1] about the correct answers to these questions and also as *constituting an obstacle* to acceptance of any view of a certain apparently strongly contrasting type which I can indicate by saying that views of this type are often associated (rightly or wrongly) with the name of Ramsey and (happily or unhappily) with some such description as 'the "assertive redundancy" thesis about the meaning of "true"'. It is at this point that I shall differ from Mr Warnock. I shall argue that acceptance of the undisputed thesis does not favour an Austin-type as opposed to a Ramsey-type view. I shall also suggest that, in so far as they might be regarded as competitors, Mr Warnock is himself committed to preferring a Ramsey-like to an Austinian view. Finally – for there is something absurd about the continuation of this appearance of vast disagreement – I shall suggest that we do not really here have conflicting views on one and the same question, but views which, where they overlap, agree and, where they differ, do not overlap. If the areas of difference do not overlap, they are, however, adjacent; and the *Theory of Truth* is perhaps a title ample and generous enough to accommodate beneath it a number of discussions in different, though adjacent, areas.

II

Before we consider exactly what restrictions on philosophical analysis are imposed by the undisputed thesis, it is worth remarking that the thesis is capable of being generalized in two different directions and is indeed perhaps already implicitly generalized by Mr Warnock in one of them. The thesis as we have it is that someone who states that a certain statement is true thereby *makes a statement* about a statement. Mr Warnock would presumably be equally willing to insist on the parallel thesis that someone who

[1] See above, pp. 190 ff.

asks whether a certain statement is true thereby *asks a question* about a statement; that one who expresses a doubt as to whether a certain statement is true thereby *expresses a doubt* about a statement; that one who advances the hypothesis that a certain statement is true thereby *advances a hypothesis* about a statement; and so on. Perhaps the generalization of the thesis in this direction can be expressed as follows: one who says anything at all by uttering a sentence which is or contains a clause within which 'is true' is predicated of a statement is thereby talking about (saying something about) a statement. This allows for the clause in question being a main assertoric or interrogative clause; or one of two disjoined clauses; or a conditional clause; or any other kind of co-ordinate or subordinate clause. A slightly modified way of expressing the generalization would be this: anyone who says anything such that, in the course of his saying it, the phrase 'is true' is predicated, assertorically or conditionally or in any other way, of a statement is thereby talking about (saying something about) a statement. Or, more shortly: in any predication of 'is true' of a statement, something is said, though not necessarily asserted, about a statement. Mr Warnock does not, even implicitly, generalize the undisputed thesis in this direction; but it seems almost certain that he would be willing to do so.

Now let us consider the other possible direction of generalization. Here the issues involved are a little more complicated and Mr Warnock's intentions are not perhaps wholly clear. We have first to ask a question about Mr Warnock's use of the word 'statement' in the phrase 'says that a statement is true' and in the phrase 'says something about a statement'.

Consider the following cases (which may be thought of as quite unrelated to each other):

(1) Person A states, or asserts, that *p*
(2) Person B conjectures that *q*
(3) It becomes clear, without C's actually saying so, that person C holds on a certain matter the view that *r*.

In each case a comment involving the predication of 'is true' is made by some person other than A, B, or C respectively. For simplicity's sake we will allow the comments to take the form of assertions in each case. The comments are:

(1) A's statement is true
(2) B's conjecture is true
(3) The view which C holds on this matter is true.

It seems quite clear that Mr Warnock would hold, and would be right in holding, that the person who makes comment (1) is making a statement about a statement (viz. the statement that *p*). What is not quite so clear is whether he would also hold that each of the persons who make comments (2) and (3) is likewise making a statement about a statement (about the statement that *q* and about the statement that *r* respectively).

There are some indications in Mr Warnock's paper, though they are not decisive indications, that he *would* hold this. For instance, he remarks, in effect, in one place[1] that it is not necessary, for the statement that *p* to be said to be true, that anyone should actually have *stated* that *p*; and he *seems* in another place[2] to treat '*x* is the kind of thing that can be true (or untrue)' as equivalent to '*x* is a statement'. Let us assume, first, that he really intends this equivalence and that he is using the word 'statement' unequivocally throughout. It will be well to distinguish this use of the word; and I shall do so by always writing the word, when so used, with an initial capital letter and by generally following it, when so used, with the word 'proposition' in parentheses; for the word 'proposition' has often been used by philosophers to stand quite generally for the kind of thing which can be true or untrue (the kind of thing of which 'is true' can properly be predicated) even though their explanations of this use of it have usually been confused or mistaken and have sometimes been encumbered with regrettable accretions of theory.

Now from the assumption just made about Mr Warnock's intentions and practice, two important consequences seem to follow regarding the undisputed thesis. The first is that it is already fully generalized in the second direction I am considering. Since any significant predication of 'is true' is a predication of it of a Statement (proposition), we can simplify our previous and, as it seemed, only partially generalized reformulation of the undisputed thesis by dropping from it what is now a redundant phrase. Instead of writing 'In any predication of "is true" *of a statement*, something is said (though not necessarily asserted) about a

[1] Op. cit., p. 56.
[2] Op. cit., p. 64.

P

statement', we can write: 'In any predication of "is true", some-thing is said (though not necessarily asserted) about a Statement (proposition).'

The second consequence of this assumption regarding Mr Warnock's intentions is perhaps a little less obvious and a little less definite. It seems likely, however, that if we do make this assumption, the conditions imposed upon philosophical analysis by acceptance of the undisputed thesis will be rather less exacting than if we make the contrary assumption. To explore this possi-bility we will now consider the consequences of making the contrary assumption. That is, we will consider the consequences of interpreting the phrase 'makes a statement about a statement' in such a way that the person who makes comment (1) above certainly *is* making a statement about a statement whereas the persons who make comments (2) and (3) are not, or need not be, making statements about statements, though they certainly *are* making statements about, respectively, a conjecture and a view. If the phrase is interpreted in this way – and it must be admitted to be a natural way of interpreting it – then the interpretation of the undisputed thesis is correspondingly affected. It cannot be regarded as a thesis already generalized in the direction we are now considering. It can be regarded, however, as a member of a *set* of theses such that other members of the set can be obtained from this member by substituing such words as 'conjecture', 'view', 'suggestion', etc. for the word 'statement' in the formula we already have, i.e. in the formula, 'In any predication of "is true" of a statement, something is said, though not necessarily asserted, about a statement.'

Why do I say that on this interpretation the undisputed thesis is likely to impose more exacting conditions than on the interpreta-tion we considered first? It will impose more exacting conditions *if* it is insisted that the *differences* between different members of the set of theses just referred to must be reflected in any adequate analyses of different cases of predication of 'is true'. Thus suppose we have a case in which 'is true' is predicated of a conjecture and a case in which 'is true' is predicated of a statement. Then it might be held that no analysis of these predications is adequate unless the analysis reflects the fact that in one case something is said about a conjecture (rather than about, for example, a statement) and in the other case something is said about a statement (rather than about, for example, a conjecture). Since either of these facts entails the fact that something is said about a Statement (proposition), while the entailment does not hold conversely, this requirement is, at least formally, more stringent than the requirement that the analysis shall reflect the fact that something is said about a Statement (proposition).

I have spoken as if we (and Mr Warnock) were obliged to choose between two interpretations of the undisputed thesis at this point. But of course this is not so; for there is no obligation to use the phrase 'saying something about a statement' unequivocally. It is open to Mr Warnock to claim to have advanced both versions of the undisputed thesis, and it is further open to him to embrace all the members of the set of theses of which the potentially more exacting version of the undisputed thesis is a member. That is to say, Mr Warnock can hold both:

(1) the thesis that in all predications of 'is true', something is said about a Statement (proposition), and
(2) all members of the set of theses to which belongs the thesis that in all predications of 'is true' in which 'is true' is predicated of a statement, something is said about a statement.

Indeed, though it would be possible for someone to *advance* the thesis referred to at (1) without actually *advancing* any of the theses referred to at (2) (and conversely), it would, I think, be very difficult with any plausibility to *accept* the thesis referred to at (1) while *rejecting* the theses referred to at (2) (and conversely). So I shall assume that Mr Warnock is willing to embrace both versions of the undisputed thesis, that is, that he is willing to embrace both (1) the thesis that in *all* predications of 'is true' something is said about a Statement (proposition) and (2) the thesis that in all predications of 'is true' in which 'is true' is predicated of a statement, something is said about a statement. This leaves me still uncertain whether he *also* wishes to insist on the more exacting requirement, which, as we've seen, can be derived from thesis (2), regarding any philosophical analysis of predications of 'is true' in which 'is true' is predicated of a statement. I shall, however, make things as difficult as possible for myself by assuming that he does intend to insist on the more exacting requirement which can be derived from thesis (2); and I shall accept this requirement, too, as imposing adequacy conditions on philosophical analysis or explication of predications of 'is true' in which 'is true' is predicated of a statement.

Before we proceed, perhaps one more word is called for about the relations between 'saying something about a Statement (proposition)' and 'saying something about a statement'. Anyone who says something about a statement (= what is stated by someone) or about a conjecture (= what is conjectured by someone) or about a belief (= what is believed by someone) *thereby* says something about a Statement (proposition). The relation this way is clear enough. But, further, any Statement (proposition) is a potential, if not an actual, statement; a potential, if not an actual, conjecture; a potential, if not an actual, belief. And we *may* use the phrase 'the belief that *p*' without implying that anyone ever believed or will believe that *p* (and without implying the contrary) and we *may* use the phrase 'the statement that *p*' without implying that anyone ever stated or will state that *p* (and without implying the contrary); and yet we may not *quite* intend in so using these phrases to use them altogether in the neutral sense of 'the Statement (proposition) that *p*'. And then we may be inclined to say that anyone who says something about the Statement (proposition) that *p thereby* says something about the belief that *p*, about the conjecture that *p*, about the statement that *p*, about the judgement that *p*, and so on. But if we wish to keep in the field the potentially more exacting version of the undisputed thesis, we must distinguish between the sense of the phrase 'says something about the statement that *p*' in which one who says something about the Statement (proposition) that *p thereby* says something about the statement that *p* and the sense of that phrase in which it does not follow, from the fact that someone says something about the Statement (proposition) that *p*, that he says anything about a statement, for he might have been saying something, not about a statement (something *stated* by someone) but about a conjecture (something *conjectured* by somebody). This, I repeat, is a condition we must observe if we wish to keep in the field the potentially more exacting version of the undisputed thesis. But we shall find in practice that there is no greater difficulty in complying with the formally more exacting than with the formally less exacting requirements of the undisputed thesis. Any difficulties that arise in practice arise with equal force in connection with both versions of the thesis.

III

In any predication of 'is true', in which 'is true' is predicated of a statement, something is said about that statement. It is agreed that any acceptable account of predications of 'is true' must be compatible with this thesis. If we assume that philosophical explication of predications of 'is true' is to proceed by the old and honourable method of paraphrase or analysis,[1] then the above requirement may be expressed as follows: no analysis or paraphrase of any predication of 'is true' in which 'is true' is predicated of a statement is acceptable unless in the analysis or paraphrase of that predication something is said about that statement.

But now what about 'about'? Suppose our analysandum is 'A's statement is true'. How are we to interpret the requirement that any acceptable analysis for this analysandum must be *about* A's statement? We might say that the analysis must be about A's statement in the same sense as that in which the analysandum is about it. But this too poses problems of interpretation. Is it, for example, supposed to exclude any sense of 'about' in which the analysandum might be said to be about A? Clearly the analysandum contains just one predicative phrase, viz. 'is true'; and clearly the unique subject of predication of this unique predicative phrase is A's statement. But equally clearly Mr Warnock cannot intend the requirement about 'about' to be taken so strictly that any analysis or paraphrase is disqualified unless it too contains just one predicative phrase of which A's statement is the unique subject of predication. For this interpretation would disqualify the type of analysis he views with favour, the type suggested by Austin.

Suppose we say, rather, that for any analysis to be about some item, it is necessary and sufficient that that item should be the subject of predication of *some* predicative phrase occurring essentially in the analysis. Then we shall indeed be able to say that the Austinian analysis is about (1) the words uttered by A in making his statement and that it is about (2) those words *as* uttered by him on the occasion of his making that statement. But we shall not be able to say that the analysis is about A's statement. Neither (1) nor (2) is to be identified with the statement (= what is stated) which

[1] Not all philosophical elucidation by paraphrase would be allowed the name of 'analysis' by purists.

is the subject of predication of 'is true' in the analysandum.[1] Reference to the statement comes essentially into the analysis only by way of *specifying* the items (1) and (2). All this is somewhat obscured in Austin's original drafting of his form of analysis; but that drafting incorporates what is either, as Mr Warnock suggests, a slip or at least a different use of the word 'statement' from that in which every statement is a Statement, i.e. from that in which 'statement' = 'what is stated and may be said to be true or untrue'.

It is worth taking a little space to make these points clearer. I begin by reproducing, with the omission of two parentheses, Mr Warnock's redrafting of the Austinian analysans for the case where the analysandum is 'The statement that S is true'. It runs: 'The words uttered in making the statement that S are correlated by demonstrative conventions with a "historic" situation or state of affairs which is of the "type" with which the sentence used in making that statement is correlated by descriptive conventions.'

Mr Warnock's redrafting is not unexceptionable. It does not seem at first that there could be any difference between *the words uttered* in making the statement that S and *the sentence used* in making that statement. Why the change in style? Mr Warnock has not made quite explicit the difference he wishes to convey. It can, I think, be made explicit by the following reformulation: 'The words uttered in making the statement that S are, as uttered in making *that* statement, correlated by demonstrative conventions with a "historic" situation or state of affairs which is of the "type" with which the words uttered, as uttered in making *any* statement, are correlated by descriptive conventions.' Alternatively, using 'the sentence used' instead of 'the words uttered', we could have: 'The sentence used in making the statement that S is, as used in making *that* statement, correlated by demonstrative conventions with a "historic" situation or state of affairs with which the sentence used, as used in making *any* statement, is correlated by descriptive conventions.' The phrase 'as uttered in making *any*

---

[1] Mr Warnock clearly recognizes that any identification of either (1) or (2) with a statement (or with a Statement) would be incorrect. For an admirably clear account of distinctions which must be drawn between a statement (= what is stated and may be said to be true or untrue) and other things with which a statement (= what is stated, etc.) is liable to be confused, see R. Cartwright, 'Propositions', in *Analytical Philosophy*, R. J. Butler, ed. (Basil Blackwell & Mott, Ltd., 1962).

statement' (or 'as used in making *any* statement') is put in for the sake of underlining the difference intended, but could (and hereafter will) simply be omitted. As for the point which Mr Warnock intends to convey by the parenthetical phrases which I left out in reproducing his draft, this could, I think, be more happily conveyed by prefacing the above reformulation with the words, 'If on any occasion the statement that S is actually made, then. . . .'

The analysans as we now have it has an unsatisfactorily betwixt-and-between character which makes it a little difficult to measure directly against the requirements of either version of the undisputed thesis. However we can easily obtain from it both a more general form and a less general form of analysis. Let us take as our analysanda:

(*a*) the Statement (proposition) that *p* is true
(*b*) A's statement (what A stated) is true.

In (*a*) something is said about a proposition with nothing implied about its having actually been stated or otherwise formulated (outside [*a*]) on any occasion. In (*b*) something is said about a statement actually made (about something actually stated) by person A on a certain occasion. In formulating the Austinian analysans for each of these analysanda I shall take the opportunity to do a little recasting in order to make the logical structure of the analysans a little clearer.[1]

The analysans for (*a*) is:

There exists a 'historic' situation or state of affairs of a certain 'type' such that, if the proposition that *p* is actually formulated on any occasion, then (i) the words used in formulating it are, *as* so used, correlated by demonstrative conventions with that situation and (ii) those words are correlated by descriptive conventions with that type.

The analysans for (*b*) is:

There exists a 'historic' situation or state of affairs of a certain 'type' such that (i) the words uttered by A are, *as* uttered by him on the occasion of making his statement, correlated by demonstrative conventions with that situation and (ii) those words are correlated by descriptive conventions with that type.

We may take the analysans for (*b*) as the one to measure against

[1] I do not mean perfectly clear, but clear enough for present purposes.

the requirements of the more formally exacting version of the undisputed thesis. Obviously it would be extravagant so to interpret those requirements that we had to declare that the analysans was *not* about A's statement. For A's statement is certainly *referred* to in the analysans although it is not a subject of predication there. It looks as though we had better allow that in a paraphrase of a predication of 'is true' of a statement, something is said about that statement if that statement is referred to in the paraphrase, even though it is not a subject of predication there.

Now the words 'is referred to', though sometimes given a stricter meaning in philosophy, have naturally a rather indefinite meaning. So though it is clear that we have relaxed the requirements about 'about', it is not clear how far we have relaxed them. However, if Mr Warnock is right, it should be possible to set a reasonable limit to this relaxation which differentiates sharply between the results of an Austinian type of analysis or paraphrase of such a predication as (*b*) and the results of a Ramsey-like or 'assertive redundancy' type of analysis or paraphrase of such a predication. The former method should yield, while the latter method fails to yield, an analysis or paraphrase for (*b*) in which something is said about A's statement, in which A's statement is referred to.

It might seem at first as if this result was very easily achieved. If invited to give a swift summary of a Ramsey-like treatment of predications of 'is true', one might at first respond with something like the following receipt. To obtain the sense of any predication of 'is true': substitute for the clause in which 'is true' is predicated an appropriate formulation of the proposition itself of which 'is true' is predicated. If we simply follow this receipt where we can – it is, of course, one of the standard objections to the receipt that we cannot always follow it – we shall certainly not (in general) obtain a form of words which can be said, on even the most liberal interpretation of 'about', to be about the proposition of which 'is true' was predicated. For few propositions are about themselves. More specifically, if we follow the receipt in a case, like (*b*), in which 'is true' is predicated of a statement, we shall certainly not (in general) obtain a form of words which can be said, on even the most liberal interpretation of 'about', to be about the statement of which 'is true' is predicated. For few statements are about themselves.

However, it would be a great mistake to conclude at once, and merely from the citing of this receipt, that Mr Warnock is right. The Ramsey-like receipt is but a clue to a general method of elucidating the predication of 'is true', a method which has far greater flexibility than the mere citing of the receipt suggests. Thus it would be altogether too blind a following of the receipt to suggest that the sense of the following predication of 'is true':

(*c*) A's statement, that X is eligible, is true

is given simply by the words:

X is eligible.

For we may say, entirely in the spirit of the Ramsey-like method, that it is given, rather, by the words:

As A stated, X is eligible.

Is not one who says this saying something about A's statement? Does he not refer to A's statement?

Now here it might be objected, but only in desperation, that whereas in an Austinian analysans A's statement would be an object of definite substantival reference (for the analysans would contain some such substantival expression as 'A's statement'), in the suggested Ramsey-like explicans A's statement is *not* an object of definite substantival reference (for the explicans contains no such expression). Here, it might be said, is where we are to draw the line in relaxing the requirements for 'about'. But this objection could be made only in desperation. For the stipulation about 'about' is both arbitrary and ineffective.

First, let me illustrate its arbitrariness by means of an analogous example. Someone might hold that no explication of predications of 'preceded', in cases where 'preceded' is predicated of events, is adequate unless the offered explicans, like the explicandum, is a form of words in uttering which one would be saying something about events. Suppose the explicandum is:

The coronation of the Emperor preceded the signing of the treaty.

If we adopted an analogously restrictive requirement for 'about', we should have to reject as an explicans:

The Emperor was crowned before the treaty was signed

on the ground that it was not about events. But it would certainly be quite contrary to normal usage to deny that the explicans was about just the same events as the explicandum; and I might add, though it is not relevant to our present concerns, that if this stipulation about 'about' were *generally* joined to the kind of requirement about explication which we are considering, then the scope of acceptable philosophical analysis would be regrettably restricted.

The stipulation is not only arbitrary, it is ineffective. For it is quite possible to frame somewhat inelegant variants on 'As A stated, X is eligible' which *would* contain substantival expressions of the kind stipulated: e.g. 'X is eligible, which is *what A stated*', 'X is eligible – as per *A's statement*', 'As *A's statement* has it, X is eligible', etc.

The next probable line of objection is a familiar one in discussions of the Ramsey-like treatment of predications of 'is true'. It runs as follows. Perhaps this treatment appears to work for cases in which, as in (*c*), the predication of 'is true' itself contains a formulation of the proposition of which 'is true' is predicated. But what of cases, like (*b*), which contain no such formulation? What, in particular, of cases in which the person who predicates 'is true' *could* not formulate, because he does not know the content of, the propositions of which he is nevertheless able to predicate, and is perhaps prepared assertorically to predicate, 'is true'?

We must answer that such cases introduce no new difficulty of principle for a Ramsey-like treatment. For Mr Warnock's own example, 'That's true', we may offer 'It is as you say (state)'. For (*b*), 'A's statement is true', we may offer 'It is as A states' or 'It is as A says it is' or 'Things are as A says they are'. Clearly ignorance, on the part of one who predicates 'is true', of the content of the propositions of which 'is true' is predicated makes no difference to the availability of such paraphrases as these. Consider:

(*d*) I don't know what the Pope is going to say, but I do know that what the Pope says is always true

(*e*) I don't know exactly what you're thinking, but, knowing you, I'm sure that what you're thinking isn't true.

For the relevant clause of (*d*) we have

... things are always as the Pope says they are

and for the relevant clause of (*e*) we have

. . . things are not as you think they are.

In general, whenever the proposition (statement or conjecture or thought) of which 'is true' is predicated is referred to, but not formulated, in the clause in which 'is true' is predicated, it will always be possible to comply with the requirements of the undisputed thesis by reproducing the substance of this reference in a clause introduced by 'as' or by some other conjunction.[1]

A curious minor point is here worth noting. Consider the case in which (1) 'is true' is predicated in a clause of the form 'it is true that *p*' and in which (2) the proposition that *p* is not therein presented as an actual statement or conjecture or thought, i.e. as one that has actually been stated by someone or as a conjecture that someone has actually made or as what someone is (for certain) actually thinking. In this case, because of condition (2), the requirements of the undisputed thesis in its more exacting form might appear to be non-applicable; and Mr Warnock might (*might*) insist instead on the requirements of the undisputed thesis in its more general and less exacting form (i.e. he might insist that something is said, in the predication and in any satisfactory analysis of the predication, about a Statement [proposition]). The Austinian-style analysans for (*a*), i.e. for 'The Statement (proposition) that *p* is true', is then available for any Austinian who wishes to offer it: i.e. the analysans which begins 'There exists a "historic" situation or state of affairs such that, if the proposition that *p* is actually formulated on any occasion, then the words used in formulating it . . . etc.' But how can the requirements of the undisputed thesis be met, in this case, on a Ramsey-like treatment? We have seen that Ramsey-like explication is not limited to blindly following that receipt which would, in this case, instruct us simply to dock the whole clause of its 'it is true that'. But what, in this case, are we to replace it by?

The answer follows from the reflection that any speaker who prefaces his formulation of the proposition that *p* by the phrase 'it is true that' under conditions such as those mentioned at (2) will normally be envisaging the proposition that *p* as something

---

[1] Thus for 'What he said about the house is true' we might have 'The house is as he said it was' or (unnaturally, but not unintelligibly) 'There is something which he said the house was and which it is'. For 'What he said about the time the last train leaves is true' we have 'The last train does leave when he said'.

which *might* be, say, urged or objected (though by hypothesis it has not been) by some participant in the discussion. To put the point more generally. When a proposition, instead of being *merely* formulated in a clause, is also made the subject of predication of 'is true' in that clause, this is essentially because the proposition is being thought of as actually or possibly figuring in one of the many guises in which propositions may figure (e.g. as what someone states, supposes, conjectures, thinks, objects, etc.) – in addition, of course, to its so figuring in the currently framed clause. It is not, in such a case as we are considering, that there is no answer to the question in which of these guises the proposition is thought of as figuring. It is simply that a description which fits the whole class of cases gives us only a part, and only a negative part, of the answer for each one. Thus we have been told, for example, that the proposition is *not* thought of as one which has been actually stated. But in any actual case there must be a better answer than this; and the application of the Ramsey-like treatment in any actual case is straightforward enough once the answer is known. Thus suppose our example is 'It is true that the house is an old one'. Then appropriate knowledge will enable us to paraphrase it in such a way as to meet the requirements of the undisputed thesis by some such clause as 'The house is, as you may urge (or object), an old one'. For in saying this one is referring to *what may be urged or objected* (viz. that the house is an old one) as well as to the house. If the general point I have made about adding the phrase 'it is true that' to a formulated proposition is borne in mind, it will appear as mere bluster to insist that there must be an *invariant* form of paraphrase for 'It is true that *p*'. We can, however, supply the *general* form, of which any particular case will be an instance, viz. 'As may be urged/objected/stated/thought/ assumed/ . . . etc., *p*'.

I call this minor point a curious one because it has usually been supposed that the phrase 'it is true that *p*' supplies the easiest of all cases for a Ramsey-like treatment; whereas we see that, in view of the requirements of the undisputed thesis, it in fact presents a certain prima facie difficulty absent from other cases.

My conclusion, in this section, is that the requirements of the undisputed thesis do not favour an Austinian account of the sense of predications of 'is true' rather than a Ramsey-like account. If this were all that could be established from the considerations before us, those considerations would, of course, give us no grounds for deciding between the two accounts. But this is by no means all.

IV

What are the resemblances, and what are the differences, between the Austinian style of paraphrase and the Ramsey-like style of paraphrase of predications of 'is true'? Consider the resemblances. First, paraphrases in both styles have this in common: that something is said both about how things are in the world[1] and, if the predication of 'is true' is of a statement, about a statement. Second – and this is extremely important – the very thing which is said explicitly in the Ramsey-like style of paraphrase about how things are in the world and about a statement is also said implicitly in the Austinian style of paraphrase. For in both styles of paraphrase it is said that things in the world are as they are stated to be by one who makes the statement. Of course, a paraphrase in the Austinian style says more than this; but it says at least this. Now since there is nothing in the Ramsey-like paraphrase except what it has in common with the Austinian paraphrase, and since both paraphrases are equally successful in dispensing with the expression 'is true', it seems natural to conclude that it is in virtue of what they have in common that both paraphrases achieve this success. As far as the sense of 'is true' is concerned, then, it seems that the Austinian additions add nothing to the Ramsey-like account.

Then how are we to understand the Austinian additions? Well, we may say that while a Ramsey and an Austin give a common answer to one question, Austin goes on to give a further answer to another. Roughly, they are at one on what it is for a (made) statement to be *true*; but Austin additionally offers a (partial) account of what it is for a (true) statement to be *made*. This is only a mnemonic. The reason for including in it the qualification 'partial' is that what Austin additionally offers is not an account of *all* the necessary conditions of a *statement's being made* but an account of *some* of the necessary conditions of a *proposition's being formulated* (expressed in words). But, of course, any necessary

---

[1] In the Austinian style the relevant phrase is: 'There exists a "historic" situation of a certain type such that. . . .' In the general form of the Ramsey-like style it is, for example, 'Things are as. . . .'

condition of formulating a proposition is also a necessary condition of making a statement.

To see this more clearly, let us consider a little more closely the differences between the styles of paraphrase. About the resemblances we are already clear. In the Austinian style, as in the Ramsey-like style, something is said about how things are in the world and, if the predication is of a statement, about a statement. The essential difference is that in the Austinian style something is also explicitly said, whereas in the Ramsey-like style nothing at all is explicitly said, about *words* and *semantic conventions*. A root-and-branch Austinian must maintain that these references to words and conventions are essential to explaining what is said about a statement (or, more generally, about a Statement) in any predication of 'is true' of that statement (or Statement); and he must maintain this in the face of the 'proof' just offered to the contrary. On the other hand, anyone who offers that 'proof' is under some obligation to give an alternative account of these explicit references to words and conventions. If they are not essential to elucidating the sense of 'is true', what are they doing in the picture at all? They do not seem altogether out of place there.

Well, reference to words and conventions *is* clearly essential to elucidating what it is for a proposition to be *formulated* in any mode, assertive or other. And the Austinian formula of analysis can be simply incorporated in any such elucidatory design, as follows: a necessary (though not sufficient)[1] condition of A's formulating the proposition that p (and hence of A's making the statement that p) is that A utters words such that, if and only if p, then there is a historic situation of a certain type such that both (i) those words, as then uttered by A, are correlated by demonstrative conventions with that situation and (ii) those words are correlated by descriptive conventions with that type.

Obviously this form of (partial) analysis could be intended to apply only to empirical propositions, and scarcely seems wide enough to accommodate all of them (it could scarcely be held, for example, to cover scientific laws). Equally obviously, it offers no account of the differences between the various modes in which propositions may be formulated – assertoric, conditional, or

---

[1] Calling it sufficient would amount, *inter alia*, to treating all logically equivalent propositions as identical.

other; and this may well be a merit, as clearly separating separable questions. But it is not my business now to comment on this form of analysis.[1] The point is to show that what Austin offers is not really a rival to a Ramsey-like account of the meaning of 'is true', but a further essay in analysis in an adjacent field.

Now it is interesting to notice that Mr Warnock, in spite of his professed sympathies, seems, at least at one point in his paper,[2] to be really of just this opinion. He criticizes Austin for what he calls the 'not very important slip' of maintaining that what is asserted in the assertion that a statement is true is the holding of certain 'purely conventional' relations between words and world. He says that Austin's *real* view (and presumably his own) is that 'all that is "purely conventional" is that to utter the sentence "S" is to make the statement that S'; and adds: 'whether or not the statement so made *is true* is of course not a matter of convention but of fact'. By this he presumably means, not a matter of fact about conventions (unless the statement happens to be about conventions). What, then, is it a matter of fact about? Presumably a matter of fact about what the statement is about. So presumably to *say* that the statement is true is to say something about *this* matter, and also, as we have seen, about the statement – to say, in fact, that matters are as stated – and *not* to say *anything* about conventions. But, of course, if we wish, as philosophers, to go on from saying what a statement's *being true* is a matter of to saying what *making* a statement is a matter of, then we *shall* have to say

[1] It must *not* be supposed that I think it (except in the respect mentioned) free from objection. This is by no means so. See the following paper in this volume.

[2] See op. cit. footnote, p. 67, from which my quotations come.
In this same footnote Mr Warnock offers to correct another 'slip' of Austin's. He says that on Austin's view, as properly understood, the fact that a particular statement relates or refers to a particular 'historic' *situation* is a matter, neither of convention nor of fact, but of logic, i.e. it is a matter of the identity of the statement, of *what* statement it is. But problems arise about specifying, for a particular statement, the particular 'historic' *situation* which it is a matter of the statement's identity that it refers to. It cannot be the situation which the statement states to obtain. For this would mean that every statement was true, that it was impossible to make a false statement. Thus, if our statement is the statement that John is eligible, the situation in question cannot be the situation of John's being eligible. But, *so long as we stick to the word 'situation'*, it will not be easy to find a plausible substitute to mention as the historic item which it is a matter of the statement's identity that it refers to. Many questions arise here; but I cannot now pursue them.

something about conventions; though we shall have to mention more kinds of convention than Austin mentions, and perhaps to speak of other things as well, if we are to distinguish *asserting* a proposition from other modes of formulating it.

V

In the above I have not been at pains to distinguish (1) what a statement's (or Statement's) *being true* is a matter of, (2) what is meant (or what is stated) by a statement (or by someone who states) that a certain statement (or Statement) *is true*, and (3) what the meaning (the sense) of the phrase '*is true*' is; but have taken it that the answer to any one of these questions carries directly with it the answer to the others. In this I have followed Mr Warnock. I have tried to show that he is mistaken in suggesting that what I have called a Ramsey-like account of 'is true' is ruled out by the requirements of the undisputed thesis; to show that this account is an essential element in the theory Mr Warnock views with cautious favour; and to indicate what further questions *this* theory may be regarded as an attempt to answer. But I have not the slightest wish to dogmatize about what is properly included under the title of *A Theory of Truth*; nor, once my point is conceded, to be ultimately restrictive about the meaning of 'the meaning of "is true".' If someone wishes to contend that we do not *really*, or do not *fully*, know the *meaning* of 'is true' unless we know what types of conventional relation obtain between words and things when something true is stated or otherwise expressed in words, then the contention seems to me by no means extravagant. Again, if it is maintained, as it has been, that the *real* problem of truth is the problem of the nature of belief or of judgement; or, yet again, that we do not *really* understand our phrase unless we know under what conditions we are *justified* in taking something to be true (and hence, in one sense, justified in asserting it); then these contentions too might be received, at least, with sympathy. Nor is it a waste of time or irrelevant to our topic to supplement the common element in the Ramsey-like and Austinian accounts with some discussion of the actual utility of our phrase in common talk. Under the general title *Truth* all these matters have, by one philosopher or another, been discussed; and since the Ramsey-like account of the word 'true' is rather thin fare, it would seem somewhat of a pity that so notable a title should be reserved for so unexciting a thesis. Better, perhaps, let the theory of truth become, as it has shown so pronounced a historical tendency to become, part of some other theory: that of knowledge; or of mind; or of meaning.

12. Truth: A Reconsideration of Austin's Views

I. A statement is said to be true when the historic state of affairs to which it is correlated by the demonstrative conventions (the one to which it 'refers') is of a type with which the sentence used in making it is correlated by the descriptive coventions.

Thus Austin in 1950.[1] Mr Warnock has recently[2] pointed out that this formulation incorporates what, on Austin's own view, is an error in drafting. What is said to be true (the statement) must be distinguished not only from the words (the sentence) used in making it but also from those words *as uttered on the (or any) particular occasion of making the statement*. It is the words uttered, *as uttered on the particular occasion*, which are correlated by demonstrative conventions with a particular historic state of affairs; and that they are so correlated is, according to Warnock, precisely what results in their utterance on that occasion issuing in a making of that statement. Part of what Warnock has in mind, in declaring this correction to be in accordance with Austin's own views, is clearly an earlier remark of Austin's to the effect that two distinct utterances of the same sentence are utterances of the same statement only if the utterances are made with reference to the same state of affairs.[3] To quote Warnock: 'On his own [Austin's] view, that a particular *statement* relates to a particular "historic" situation is a matter not of convention, nor in this case of fact, but of logic: for he implies earlier that a statement is identified, in part, by reference to the situation to which it relates. What "demonstrative conventions" in part determine is not how statements are related to the world, but what statement is made by the utterance of certain words on a particular occasion.'[4]

Let us begin, then, by amending Austin's dictum to meet

[1] J. L. Austin, *Philosophical Papers* (Oxford, 1961), p. 90.
[2] *Truth*, ed. by George Pitcher (Englewood Cliffs, 1964), p. 67, footnote.
[3] Op. cit., p. 88.
[4] Loc. cit.

Warnock's point. I shall adopt a form of amendment proposed by Warnock himself. It runs as follows:

II. A statement is said to be true when the historic state of affairs to which the words used in making it are, as *then* used, correlated by demonstrative conventions is of a type with which those words are, *standardly*, correlated by descriptive conventions.

The substitution of the phrase 'with which those words are, standardly, correlated' for 'with which the sentence used in making it is correlated' is not intended to, and I think does not, make any significant difference to the sense of the draft.

Warnock has also suggested[1] that in my own contribution to the 1950 symposium I adopted an incorrectly restrictive interpretation of what Austin meant by 'reference' and that some of my criticisms of Austin's thesis are thereby invalidated. Roughly, I took 'reference' to mean reference to particular objects or events made by means of definitely identifying substantival expressions occurring in the sentence uttered, whereas Austin was thinking of the reference of the utterance as a whole to a total historic situation or state of affairs. For this reason, Warnock maintains, my contention that Austin's analysis would apply, at best, only to a limited class of statements – viz. affirmative categorical statements containing definitely identifying substantival expressions – is unfounded. I think there is some substance in Warnock's criticism, enough substance at least to call for a re-examination of Austin's dictum. Such a re-examination I propose to undertake in this paper. I shall not repeat those of my original criticisms of the Austinian dictum which bore, not on its truth, but on its acceptability as an analysis of the meaning of 'is true'. I shall address myself instead to the prior question whether the dictum in fact embodies a clear statement of a truth at all. I shall argue that it does not.

There is one further preliminary amendment I shall make to the Austinian formula, an amendment for which I think it can clearly be claimed, as for Warnock's, that it is in accordance with Austin's intentions. The word 'statement' is allowed in philosophical usage a very wide range of application indeed, a range of application far

---

[1] Cf. *Knowledge and Experience*, ed. by C. D. Rollins (Pittsburgh, 1964), pp. 15–16.

wider, it is clear, than Austin intended his own use of the word to have.[1] I want to discuss the acceptability of Austin's thesis with reference to a class of statements at least no wider than that which he intended his thesis to apply to. To make this clear I shall qualify the word 'statement' as it appears in the Austinian formula with the word 'historical'. The class of historical statements is to be understood as including statements about the present and the future as well as statements about the past. The class can be roughly characterized by saying that, in the making of a historical statement, some historical situation is stated to obtain. Of course the notion of a historical situation is to be understood very broadly indeed. Statements of totally unrestricted generality may be allowed to fall outside the class of historical statements, but all other statements which can be empirically confirmed or falsified fall within it.

That there exists a large and important class of statements of this kind seems an uncontroversial point. Two other relevant points seem equally uncontroversial: (1) that in the making of such statements it is normally the case that semantical conventions of at least two kinds, which may reasonably be called descriptive and demonstrative, are exploited or made use of; and (2) that a historical statement is true – or without qualification true – if and only if the particular historical situation which, in the making of it, is stated to obtain does actually obtain. The Austinian formula is, of course, related to these uncontroversial points; but it is far from being merely a summary of them. It is, rather, an attempt to bring together the notions of a historical statement, of a historical situation, of demonstrative and descriptive conventions and of truth in a single elucidatory philosophical generalization. That it fails in this aim, that it is, indeed, an example of an over-hasty theoretical generalization such as Austin often properly criticized in other connections, is what I have to show.

Incorporating our second amendment, and trimmed of a few words, the generalization now runs as follows:

III. A historical statement is true when the historic situation with which the words used in making it are, as then used, correlated by demonstrative conventions is of a type with which those words are standardly correlated by descriptive conventions.

[1] Cf. op. cit., p. 99.

My difficulties with this formula – difficulties which in fact interpenetrate each other – may be roughly sorted out by saying that they are concerned, first, with the use made of the distinction between demonstrative and descriptive conventions; secondly, with the use made of the notion of a particular historical situation or state of affairs; and, thirdly, with the notion of conventional correlation.

First, then, as to demonstrative and descriptive conventions. Austin appears to suggest that, at least as far as concerns those conventions which are relevant to the truth or falsity of statements, we have here a dichotomous division of the conventions employed or invoked in making statements. That characterization of each type of convention which is implicit in the generalization itself is explicitly laid down in the sentences immediately preceding Austin's version of it: descriptive conventions are said to correlate the words (= sentences) with the *types* of situation, thing, event, etc. to be found in the world, demonstrative conventions to correlate the words (= statements) with the *historical* situations, etc., to be found in the world. We have noted already that this characterization must be amended in its second part: for 'words (= statements)' we must substitute 'words as uttered on particular occasions of making statements'.

Let us consider some words (= sentences), in abstraction from utterances of them on any particular occasion.

> At least one guest will drink no wine at dinner.
> This guest is drinking no wine at dinner.
> That guest drank no wine at dinner.

All these sentences have, as we should ordinarily say, different meanings. Are we to regard them as each correlated by descriptive conventions with a different type of situation? or as all correlated with the same type? or some two of them as correlated with one type and the third with another? I think it safe to assume that Austin would give the second of these answers: he would hold that all three sentences are correlated by descriptive conventions with one and the same general type of situation, the type, viz. of which all cases of *a guest's drinking no wine at dinner* are instances. Similarly he would hold, I think, that all the members of the trio of sentences obtained by deleting the word 'no' from the original three were also correlated with one and the same general type of

Q

situation, but a different type of situation from the first, viz. the type of which all cases of *a guest's drinking wine at dinner* are instances; and similarly, *mutatis mutandis,* for the trio of sentences obtained by substituting the word 'water' for the word 'wine' or for the trio of sentences obtained by substituting the word 'woman' for the word 'guest', etc. If I am right in this, it seems that we may conclude that descriptive conventions include at least those conventions which differentiate the meanings of such words as 'guest', 'wine', 'water', 'drink', etc. – a result which will surely not be found in any way surprising or unacceptable. We shall also be entitled to conclude that descriptive conventions include those which determine the force of the word 'no' as a quantifying adjective, and also some conventions (which we need not pause to try to specify) relating to the syntactic structure of sentences. The first of these last two results may strike us as a little more surprising, but not unacceptable, granted that what is aimed at is a dichotomous division between descriptive and demonstrative conventions. Finally, the results in general may seem at first glance to promise reasonably well for the other side of the dichotomy: the conventions relating to the different tenses of verbs, for example, do not seem, on this view, to be destined for the descriptive side of the dichotomy and seem therefore to be available, as we should expect, to go on the other side.

A difficulty, hardly insuperable, arises when we turn to sentences including proper names. Consider, for example, the two sentences 'Alexander died young' and 'Napoleon died young'. Are we to say that they are both correlated with the same general type of situation or with different types? If different, how are the two types to be specified? If the same, are they both correlated with the same general type of situation as (1) 'a (or this) great commander died young' or as (2) 'a (or this) man died young' or as (3) 'someone dies young'? – a trio of which presumably no one member is correlated in the required sense with just the same general type of situation as any other. To these questions it might be replied that if there is no clearly correct answer to them, the answer can be made a matter of decision. Let us accept this reply.

We are to take it, then, that we know, with respect to any unambiguous sentence which we understand and which is capable of being used to make a historical statement, just what general type of situation that sentence is conventionally correlated with;

and that descriptive conventions are just those conventions our grasp of which enables us to know this. Now what about demonstrative conventions? If the division of types of convention is really a dichotomous division, we shall at any rate be able to give a residual characterization of demonstrative conventions as all those conventions relevant to the truth or falsity of statements which are not descriptive conventions. But now we must ask how well Austin's positive characterization of demonstrative conventions fits this residue of non-descriptive conventions. The positive characterization, you will remember, is this: demonstrative conventions correlate particular utterances of sentences (or: correlate words as uttered on particular occasions) with particular historical situations, etc., to be found in the world. But this characterization is surely too ample for any residue of conventions that remains when descriptive conventions have been subtracted; for it embraces descriptive conventions too. It would be most unplausible to maintain that none of the latter has any part to play in correlating sentences as uttered with particular historical items to be found in the world – whether these are called 'situations' or anything else. It would be most unplausible, for example, to maintain that the conventional meanings of the words 'guest', 'wine', 'drinks', 'dinner', while clearly involved in determining the correlation of the sentence 'That guest drank wine at dinner' with a general type of situation, would not be at all involved in determining the reference of any particular utterance of the sentence. If I say 'This inkwell has no ink in it', the meaning of the word 'inkwell' bears certainly on the correlation of my sentence with a general type of situation, the type of which all inkless inkwells are instances; but it bears no less certainly on the reference of my particular utterance of the sentence to a particular historical item, to this particular (perhaps inkless) inkwell.

The situation is really more serious than this suggests. I have spoken as if Austin's characterization of descriptive conventions really did leave a residue of other conventions and as if his mistake were simply to assign exclusively to the latter a role which they in fact share with the former. But on Austin's characterization of descriptive conventions, the whole notion of a residue of non-descriptive conventions also drawn on in making any historical statement is a questionable notion. Consider, for example, the sentences 'At least one guest drank wine', 'No guest drank wine', and 'This guest drank wine'. The first and the third are correlated with one general type of situation, the second with another; but the fact that this is so is no less a consequence of the conventions governing the use of the word 'this' than it is of the conventions governing the use of the word 'no'. It is, though a true, yet a lame rejoinder to say that one might get the correlations right with a less than complete knowledge of these conventions.

Let me make it quite clear what I am, and what I am not, denying. First, I am not denying that in the making of any historical statement two sorts of things are done, that two functions, complementarily necessary to the making of such a statement, are performed, functions which might roughly but not unreasonably be characterized as

(1) the specification of a general type of situation.

(2) the attachment of this specification to the world (to 'the particular').

If anyone wishes to call these two functions respectively the *descriptive function*, and the *demonstrative function*, let him do so. There is not necessarily any harm in it.

Secondly, I am not denying that there are useful and workable distinctions between different kinds of linguistic convention, or that 'descriptive' may be a good working title for one group of linguistic conventions and 'demonstrative' for another. Thus the conventions governing the use of expressions of which the use is essentially token-reflexive are not inaptly called demonstrative, while the conventions which fix the meanings of very many common nouns and adjectives are not inaptly called descriptive. It seems indeed unlikely that if one were concerned to classify the types of linguistic convention relevant to the truth or falsity of statements, one would, or should, be content with only two types. (One would not, for example, and surely should not, normally wish to assimilate the conventions governing the use of logical particles like 'not' and 'all' either to the conventions governing the use of words like 'inkwell' or to the conventions governing the use of words like 'here', 'now', and 'I'.) But I am not here concerned to insist on this point. Let us agree that we can distinguish types of linguistic convention and among them can distinguish descriptive and demonstrative conventions.

What I am denying, then, is not the duality of *function* which

Austin notes as present in the making of historical statements nor the distinguishability of types of linguistic convention involved in the making of such statements. What I am denying is the existence of any duality of conventions correlated in the way that Austin's formula requires with this duality of function. The dichotomy between (1) conventions which correlate sentences with general types of states of affairs, and (2) conventions which correlate utterances of sentences with particular historical states of affairs is a false dichotomy, one to which nothing answers; and in so far as the Austinian formula rests on this dichotomy, that formula is defective.[1]

Now I want to pass on to another deficiency which is, I think, closely connected with this one. But, though connected, I think they are distinguishable. To show they are distinguishable it will be sufficient to amend the Austin-Warnock formula in such a way as to remove the first defect, and then go on to draw attention to the second. An amendment which would do the job runs as follows:

IV. A historical statement is true when the particular historical situation with which the words used in making it are, as then used, correlated by semantical convention is of the general type with which those words are standardly correlated by semantical convention.

This amendment allows, obviously, for any degree of overlap you please, up to identity, between the semantical conventions involved in correlating utterances with situations and those involved in correlating sentences with types of situation. So it certainly removes the ground of my first objection.

The second deficiency is revealed if one asks how exactly the particular historical situation in question in any case is to be specified. The Austin-Warnock view is that one does not know exactly what statement is being made in any case unless one knows what particular historical situation is being referred to. So presumably it must be possible in principle in every case to specify this situation. Now one might think at first that there was no particular difficulty about that. For suppose our statement is: 'This inkwell has no ink in it'. Then one might think that the

[1] In the first sentence of footnote 3 on p. 90, Austin appears to register some awareness of this fact. But he does not amend the formula.

particular historical situation in question is simply the situation of this particular inkwell's being inkless at the time at which the statement is made. And this is obviously a generalizable style of answer. But this style of answer won't do at all. For we are trying to specify the particular historical situation which it is a matter of the statement's *identity* that it refers to, and we must be able to do this in such a way as not to settle in advance the question of the statement's truth-value and, moreover, settle it in favour of the statement's truth. If the historical situation which it is a matter of the statement's identity that it refers to was specifiable only in a way which had the consequence that the statement was true, then every statement (or every historical statement) would be true; which is absurd. So we must think again.

Suppose we have two statements made respectively by the use of the sentences 'The cat is on the mat' and 'The cat is eating the mat', and made, let's say, at the same moment and with reference to the same cat and mat. Evidently the general *types* of situation with which the two *sentences* are correlated by semantical conventions are different general types of situation; which is not to say, of course, that one and the same particular situation might not exemplify both general types. But what about the particular *situations* which the two *statements* respectively refer to (which it is a matter of their identity that they refer to)? Are they, too, numerically different? Or are they numerically the same? Does the difference between our two statements consist partly in their referring to different historical situations? or does it consist solely in their respectively assigning one and the same historical situation to different general types?

Suppose, first, that the situations referred to are different. Then how are we to specify these situations so as to bring out their difference? One way which might suggest itself is the following. The situation in question in the case of 'The cat is on the mat' is the situation of this particular cat's either-being-or-not-being on this particular mat at this particular moment; whereas the situation in question in the case of 'The cat is eating the mat' is the situation of this particular cat's either-being-or-not-being at this particular moment engaged in eating this particular mat. It seems unlikely, however, that Austin would wish to pass off either of *these* phrases as a genuine specification of a distinct historical item to be found in the world, viz. a situation which could, without prejudice to its identity, be of one of two incompatible types. Not that these forms of words are unintelligible. Each might perhaps be taken to refer to a *question* (i.e. in the first case, the question which of two possible situations, viz. the situation of that cat's being on that mat at that time or the situation of that cat's not being on that mat at that time, actually obtains) or to a *truism* (i.e. that either one situation obtains or the other does). But it seems quite clear that this way of interpreting the notion of a historical situation as it figures in Austin's dictum has nothing to be said for it in itself and does not correspond to Austin's or Warnock's intentions. If the relevant notion were intended to be understood in this easily generalized, though very unattractive, way, it would have been odd to remain silent on the point.

Is there any other way of saving the first answer to our question, i.e. of continuing to maintain that our two statements refer to different particular historical situations? I think there is no satisfactory way. One might indeed try to maintain this answer without going quite so far as the suggestion just considered. One might try saying, for example, that the situation referred to by the first statement was the situation of the cat's *having some merely spatial relation or other* to the mat; and, perhaps, that the situation referred to by the second statement was the situation of the cat's *doing something or other* to the mat. But the second suggestion obviously won't do; for the second statement might be *made*, and made, therefore, with reference to the relevant situation, whatever that may be, without its being the case that the cat was in fact doing anything at all to the mat. This objection does not apply to the first of these two suggestions; for cat and mat must have some relative spatial positions. Nevertheless this suggestion seems almost as unattractive as the one previously considered, and for much the same reason. The form of words offered (i.e. 'the situation of the cat's having some merely spatial relation or other to the mat') seems scarcely intelligible unless taken as alluding either to the question *what* situation actually obtains or obtained with regard to the relative spatial positions of the cat and the mat at the time the statement was made (cf. such phrases as 'the whereabouts of the cat (in relation to the mat)') or to the truism that *some* situation of this kind must obtain.

Let us consider, therefore, whether it might not be more satisfactory to adopt the alternative type of answer to my question and say that the situation referred to by the statement made in the words 'The cat is on the mat' was numerically the same situation as that referred to by the statement made in the words 'The cat is eating the mat', given that the two statements are made at the same moment and with reference to the same cat and mat. The situation in question might be said to be just *the* situation with respect to that cat and that mat at that moment; and this situation is to be regarded as one and the same historical item, whatever range of general *types* of situation it may in fact exemplify or fail to exemplify. Now let us ask what is the general principle underlying this alternative reply. The principle seems to be that the situation referred to in any statement is to be regarded as identified or defined by what I hope it is not too unclear to call the sum or combination of all the identifying or definite references to particular times or stretches of time, to particular places, occasions, objects, etc., which are made in making the statement, by whatever means these references may be made (e.g. whether by the tense of the verb, by demonstrative adverbs, by substantival expressions or otherwise).

If we adopt this principle for the identification of situations, however, it is easy to see that we obtain results which are strikingly contrary to what we should ordinarily understand by the words 'the same situation'. To take first an example not at all relatively unfavourable to the principle: we should have to say that the two statements 'Jack dined with Jill one day last month' and 'Jack played tennis with Jill one day last month', provided that they were made within the same month and with reference to the same two people, both referred to one and the same situation; and we should also have to say that two statements made in those words and with reference to the same people, but made within different months, referred to two different situations. Moreover, we should have to say these things even if the two statements made within the same month were separated by weeks and were verified by engagements separated by weeks, whereas the two statements made in different months were made on successive days and were verified by engagements kept on successive days. I do not say that it would always be wrong so to use 'same' and 'different' with 'situation', only that it would be wrong so to use them always; and that the reasons which would make it sometimes right are quite out of line with the principle which would make it always right.

More examples. We should have to say that the state of affairs referred to by the statement, made in the U.K. now, 'There was a general election last year' was *identical* with the state of affairs referred to by the statement, made anywhere now, 'There was a dry summer in the U.K. last year'. We should have to say that the statement 'There have been wars before now' referred to the same situation as the statement 'Men have loved women before now'. And so on. One might not object to straining the notion of a *situation* or *state of affairs* in this way, if some theoretical clarification were to be gained thereby; but the effect in this case is not clarifying, but confusing. For the expressions 'situation' and 'state of affairs' have, in the present connection, much more natural employments, which are bound to obscure from us the strained sense in which they are (one is forced to presume) being employed in the Austinian formula.

Evidently these difficulties about the word 'situation' (or the phrase 'state of affairs') arise from trying to preserve for the word the logical place reserved for it in the amended Austinian formula, i.e. trying to ensure that the situation in question in every case is understood as an actual historical item that can be definitely identified without pre-judging the issue of the truth or falsity of the statement. So perhaps we should inquire whether we could not escape from these difficulties by giving up this attempt. Now we can certainly escape from the difficulties and yet preserve the word 'situation' if we are prepared to go far enough. For example, we can return to the uncontroversial point I made earlier and say that a historical statement is true if there obtains or exists the particular historical situation which, in the making of the statement, is stated to obtain. The word 'situation' here gives no trouble at all, or at least comparatively little. We need, indeed, to know just what situation is stated to obtain in order to know what statement is made. But we do not need to know that this situation actually obtains, and we do not have to rack our brains for a way of specifying what situation it is, while leaving open the question whether it is or is not of a certain general type. If there does exist such a situation, it will simply be the situation which, in the making of the statement, is stated to obtain, for example, the situation of that particular cat's being at that particular time on that particular mat.

However, it will be correctly felt that this new formulation is less an amendment to the Austinian formula than an abandonment of it. It radically departs from the structure of the original formula by abandoning altogether the notion of an identified existing situation which it is a matter of the statement's identity that it refers to and with respect to which the question arises whether it is or isn't of a certain general type; and at the same time it drops all explicit allusion to conventional (semantical) relations between words and things. We cannot reverse the first change, for that was essential to getting out of the difficulties about 'situation' and 'state of affairs'. But might we not at least take a step back towards Austin by reversing the second?

One way of doing this would seem *not* to meet the case, i.e. not to be at all what is desired by a defender of Austin; and that would be just to *add* to the formula.

> A historical statement is true if there obtains the historical state of affairs which, in the making of the statement, is stated to obtain

the following observation, viz.

> It is (at least partly) in virtue of semantical conventions that the utterance of the words uttered constitutes the making of the statement made.

This simple conjunction of points does not seem at all to be what was originally aimed at in the Austinian formula. So perhaps we should, instead, try redrafting as follows:

> V. A historical statement is true when there exists or obtains a particular historical situation of a certain general type such that the words used in making the statement are, as then used, correlated by semantical conventions with just that particular situation and are, standardly, correlated by semantical conventions with just that type of situation.

But now we bump up against difficulties arising from the vagueness of the notion of correlation by semantical conventions. It seems necessary, if the draft is to be acceptable, that the *kind* of correlation by semantical conventions that is in question should be more fully specified. Let us grant that we could properly say that the words 'The cat is not in the room', uttered on some occasion, would, as uttered on that occasion, be correlated by semantical conventions with the situation of the cat's *not* being in the room, if *that* situation obtained; and that the words are, standardly, correlated by semantical conventions with the general type of situation of which that situation, if it obtained, would be an instance. Must we not add that we could, with equal propriety, say that the words as uttered would be correlated by semantical conventions with the situation of the cat's *being* in the room, if *that* situation obtained; and that the words are, standardly, correlated by semantical conventions with the general type of situation of which that situation, if it obtained, would be an instance? It can hardly be maintained that it is any less a matter of semantical convention that the utterance of certain words constitutes a *denial* that a certain type of situation obtains in a particular case than it is that their utterance constitutes an *assertion* that the complementary type of situation obtains in that case.

It seems that it should be a simple matter so to amend the generalization as to meet this last objection without any sacrifice of generality. And so it is; but not, I think, without any sacrifice of appeal. Two formulations suggest themselves to me, and I doubt if there could be any others which did not incorporate the crucial feature of one or the other of them. They run:

> VIa. A historical statement is true if there exists or obtains a particular historical situation with which the words used in making it are, as then used, so correlated by semantical conventions that the statement is true.

> VIb. A historical statement is true if there exists or obtains a particular historical situation with which the words used in making it are, as then used, so correlated by semantical conventions as to constitute a statement to the effect that that situation obtains.

The first of these formulations will scarcely appeal if the formula is intended to be in any way analytical of the concept of truth. What of the second? The second formulation is misleading or deceptive in just that respect in which it is reminiscent of the original Austinian form. For it blurs the point that *the semantical conventions play exactly the same role* in determining, or helping to determine, *what* the statement is a statement-to-the-effect-that, *whether the statement is true or false*. We can cure this deficiency. But if we do, we are back where we were, at the point at which we seemed to have abandoned the Austinian form altogether. That is, the semantical conventions (help to) determine what the statement is a statement to the effect that, what situation is stated to obtain in the making of the statement; whereas the statement's being true, if it is, is another matter altogether, viz. a matter of that situation's obtaining.

I conclude that Austin's formula, in spite of its amendment by Warnock, is really unsatisfactory in all of its distinctive features. I would agree that my 1950 reading of it was inaccurate, but I do not think it could be said to have been ungenerously restrictive. For that reading at least allowed the formula some application; but when carefully read it seems doubtful whether it has any. If we ask ourselves what went wrong, what the sources of confusion were, I think we must reply that they were multiple. But it is perhaps worth emphasizing two in particular, which Warnock's defence has forced into prominence. The first is to be found in what Warnock sees as an unimportant 'slip', calling for a minor amendment, viz. Austin's tendency to identify what is, truly or falsely, stated, when a statement is made, with the words uttered, as uttered in making it. In the text of his article the same word 'statement' is used for both. Statements, in the first sense, are undoubtedly true (or false); statements, in the second sense, are undoubtedly correlated by semantical conventions with items and types of item in the world. If the linguistic term of such correlations is mistakenly supposed to be identical with the subject of the problematic predicate, the bearer of the problematic property, it becomes easier to suppose also that the sense of that predicate is to be analysed in terms of those correlations. What Warnock sees as a minor slip indicates in fact, I think, an important source of error.

The second source of error which I shall mention is indicated by that same misreading of mine which Warnock takes as the starting-point of his second defence of Austin. If we abstract from that aspect of Austin's theory which relates to conventional (semantical) correlations between words and the world, we see that its general form is that of a theory to the effect that a statement is true if some particular historical item, to which the statement refers in an identifying fashion, is of some general type or kind specified in the statement. And it is of course quite correct, and one of the truisms of logic, to say that, given a statement in the making of which a particular item is specified or identified and is affirmed to be (or have been) an instance of some general property or type or kind, then the statement is true if and only if that particular item is (or was) an instance of that general property or type or kind. This truism lends itself easily to illustration with the help of statements such as might be made by the use of such sentences as 'Julius Caesar was bald' or 'The cat is a female' – statements with respect to which we find it easy to specify what particular item it is that is identifyingly referred to, and what general type or property that item is said to be (or to have been) an instance of. What makes the general form of Austin's account initially attractive is, I suspect, just the fact that it is reminiscent of this easily understood and illustrated truism. Of course the truism, so long as it remains such, is of limited application; it does not cover the whole range of historical statements; and what Austin aimed at was a generalization which would cover the whole range. But it was a fatal mistake to suppose that the *form* of the limited truism could be preserved in such a generalization. The reassuring-sounding expressions, 'situation' and 'state of affairs', introduced to provide the machinery for the form-preserving generalization, turned out to be traps in which the theory was hopelessly caught.

Index

Anscombe, G. E. M., 96
Aristotle, 27
Austin, J. L., 82, 149–69, 172, 178, 190–213, 215–33, 234–49
Ayer, Sir Alfred, 28, 30

Cartwright, R., 222
Chomsky, N., 130–48, 172

Davidson, D., 176–7
Dummett, M., 82

Frege, G., 120, 172, 176

Geach, P. T., 96
Grice, H. P., 155–68, 172–3, 178

Hart, H. L. A., 158

Katz, J. J., 141, 147

Leibniz, 20

Locke, 22

McGuinness, B., 162
Moore, G. E., 13

Price, H. H., 40

Quine, W. V., 53–74, 75, 82, 88, 116–29, 143

Ramsey, F., 28–32, 58, 215–33
Russell, Lord, 2–27, 51, 62–3, 82
Ryle, G., 170–1

Searle, J., 178
Stout, G. F., 34

Tarski, A., 180

Warnock, G. J., 214–33, 234–49
Wittgenstein, L., 172, 176